What the reviewers said …

"Canadian history with a bang."

— *Vancouver Sun*

"There's none of the boring Canadian penchant here for dwelling on institutional heroes."

— *Globe and Mail*

"*Bandits and Privateers* is fun but also instructive — a good way to discover that we "nice Canadians" aren't really that nice all the time."

— *Montreal Gazette*

"It introduces us to bad guys we never knew we had.".

— *Vancouver Sun*

"A fun look at Canadian history. … Horwood and Butts introduce us to a group of characters unlikely to find their way into most Canadian history books."

— *Thompson News Wire*

"Do you think Canadian history is dull? … This book could figuratively shoot holes in that idea."

— *Toronto Star*

Presenting Goodread Biographies

The Goodread Biographies imprint was established in 1983 to reprint the best of Candian biography, autobiography, diaries, memoirs and letters in paperback format.

Books in this series are chosen from the hardcover list of all of Canada's publishing houses. By selecting a wide range of interesting books that have been well received in the bookstores and well reviewed in the press, we aim to give readers inexpensive and easy access to titles they missed in hardcover.

You'll probably find other books in the Goodread Biographies series that you will enjoy. Check the back pages of this book for details on other titles in the series. You'll find our books on the paperback shelves of your local bookstore. If you have difficulty obtaining any of our titles, get in touch with us and we'll give you the name of a bookstore near you which stocks our complete list.

BANDITS & PRIVATEERS

Canada in the Age of Gunpowder

Harold Horwood
Ed Butts

1988
Goodread Biographies

Published in hardcover in 1987 by Doubleday of Canada

First published in paperback in 1988
by Goodread Biographies

Canadian Cataloguing in Publication Data

Horwood, Harold, 1923-
Bandits and privateers
(Goodread Biographies)
ISBN 0-88780-157-9

1. Outlaws -- Canada -- History. 2. Privateering -- Canada --
History. I. Butts, Edward, 1951-. II. title. III. Title: Bandits and privateers.

HV6453.C2H67 1988 364.1'64'0971 C88-098593-3

Goodread Biographies is the paperback imprint of

Formac Publishing Company Limited
5359 Inglis Street
Halifax, Nova Scotia
B3H 1J4

Printed and bound in Canada

Contents

For Pat and Teddy

Acknowledgements

The authors would like to thank the following:
Public Archives and National Library of Canada
Public Archives of Ontario
Public Archives of British Columbia
The Glenbow Institute of Alberta
The Metropolitan Toronto Police Museum
The New Brunswick Museum
Mississauga Central Library
Pinkerton Detective Agency
The St. Albans Free Library, St. Albans Vermont
The Metropolitan Library of Toronto
Bettman Newsphotos, New York
Department of the Navy, Naval Historical Centre, Washington D.C.
Library of Congress, Washington D.C.

Introduction

THIS BOOK, a sequel to *Pirates and Outlaws of Canada*, continues our history of violence in Canada during the centuries before World War II. We are again exploring banditry on both land and sea, but this time our sea stories focus on privateers, seafarers who go to war in private ships, licensed by their government. A pirate is someone with no such authority, who usually preys on the ships of all nations, even his own. In rare instances this distinction disappears. Francis Drake, the arch-pirate El Draco of Spanish history, plundered the Spanish colonies of the New World with a privateering commission issued by the great Queen Elizabeth of England and was rewarded with a knighthood. Sometimes the distinction was so fine that a privateer might stray into piracy almost by accident. This seems to be what happened to Captain William Kidd, who began life as a respectable naval officer, commanded the most splendid privateer of his time, with a commission from Great Britain to police the Indian Ocean, but ended his life on the gallows as a pirate in 1701. Though the distinction should have been simple, it wasn't always so, and it was sometimes a question of what you could get away with. If you succeeded, all might be forgiven. If you failed, you might be hanged, drawn and quartered, or broken on the wheel.

Privateers—licensed pirates—were a major force in early Canada. Even before the Cartier voyages, when the records are scanty indeed, there is enough to show that privateers helped to determine which nations should benefit from the all-important New World fisheries and the less important, but growing, trade in furs. Jacques Cartier himself, who explored the Gulf of St. Lawrence in 1534 with a commission from the King of France, is believed by historians to have been a privateer—perhaps even a pirate—before becoming a respectable explorer. Privateering was also vital in Britain's wars against New France. It prevented the infant United States from being crushed by British regulars and enriched the maritime colonies in the Napoleonic Wars. Finally, it saved Canada from conquest in the War of 1812.

The first great privateering voyage to what is now Canada was fitted out by Jean Ango of Havre de Grâce, the most powerful sea lord of his time, sailing under letters of marque—documents authorizing retaliation against foreign powers—from the King of France. In 1520, a mere twenty-three years after the first Cabot voyage, Ango sent a squadron to Newfoundland commanded by two brothers named Parmentier. Already there was a thriving Newfoundland fishery with Spanish, Portuguese, Basque, French, and English ships making annual voyages. The Parmentier brothers captured and looted the ships of all nations except the French. They also sacked and burned whatever fishing premises they could find ashore. They named the port of Havre de Grâce in Conception Bay after the port their patron had founded in France. Anglicized, later, to Harbour Grace, it became a pirate stronghold in the seventeenth century and a great fishing and trading centre in the nineteenth. Eventually it was the second-largest centre of population, after St. John's. Ango continued to send armed ships to the Newfoundland fishery for some twenty years, acting as escorts for French fishing ships and with a licence to plunder the ships of other nations. His privateering expeditions had the effect of making France the ascendant power in the New World fisheries for almost half a century, until the English began to take control in the 1570s.

Privateers were commissioned to capture enemy property and interfere with enemy commerce, not to destroy human life. Their aim was to capture ships with as little damage as possible, for the sale of such ships, with their cargoes, was the privateersman's sole hope of reward. They preferred to attack unarmed or lightly armed merchantmen, presenting them, when possible, with overwhelming odds, if not in guns, then at least in manpower. In this way they could usually secure a surrender without bloodshed.

Privateering was, therefore, a far less dangerous trade than service in the navy and was a favourite refuge from naval conscription: by enlisting on a privateer you might hope to escape the navy with its hardships, harsh discipline, and high risk. Though the privateers were just as overcrowded as any man-of-war, there was little danger of being hanged or flogged to death and only slight danger of being killed in action. Even the famous slugging matches, when broadsides were exchanged almost rail-to-rail and masts went crashing over the side, often resulted in few casualties: a man or two killed, one or two wounded was typical. Casualties in these battles generally depended on how the ships fired their guns. Raking decks with grape-shot, designed to kill the crew, was not a favoured tactic; between honourable opponents it was a contemptible way to fight. You didn't aim at the water-line, trying to sink your enemy either. You aimed at the rigging, hoping to disable the ship and force her to surrender in a condition fit for repair—and eventual resale.

We have to thank the new science of marine archaeology for our knowledge of what the raiders of the early sixteenth century were like. Wrecks of some of the ships that sailed as pirates and privateers in the earliest days of New World settlement have been recovered, and it is obvious that even in those days ships were being built specifically for the job of privateering. Looking more like the Viking ships of earlier centuries, they bore little resemblance to either the merchant ships or the warships of their time. In the sixteenth century the warship was a real monster, beautifully portrayed in detailed paintings of the time, with as many as seven decks piled one above another, projecting far over bow and stern and appropriately called "castles." They were floating forts, and they were almost as top-heavy as they looked. They rarely ventured far from land and would certainly not have attempted a transatlantic voyage. Merchant ships were built like barges, with round bows and round sterns, as much beam as possible, and could travel at a speed, with a good following wind, of perhaps five or six knots.

The privateer was something quite different from either of these. Though she might run between one hundred and two hundred tons, she had a narrow racing hull and pointed bow and stern, with light timbering. She was rigged with lateen sails that could be spread wing-and-wing in a following wind or close-hauled for sailing much closer to a head wind than any merchant ship or warship. She was armed with a couple of long bow-chasers to make her effective at a distance and with rows of swivel guns along each side for close-in fighting. She was built for action, an ideal ship for piracy as well as the somewhat more reputable profession of privateering.

Piracy was a grave problem to the colonies that eventually became Canada, and issuing letters of marque and reprisal was one way to deal with it. Privateering against pirates was an ancient institution, even then. The first Vice-Admiralty Court outside the realm of England was set up at Trinity in Newfoundland in 1615, to deal with piracy in the New World. In 1620 the Duke of Buckingham, Lord Admiral of England, issued a commission to John Mason, governor of the Cupids colony in Newfoundland, and to Captain William Bushell, to "take up and press such ships with mariners, soldiers, gunners, munitions of war, stores, etc. as may be necessary for the purpose of suppressing pirates and Sea Rovers." They were commissioned specifically to set forth in "the good ship *Peter and Andrew* of London of 320 tons burthen" for Newfoundland with such men and ordnance as they needed for the purpose of taking pirates and their ships. Their pay was to be possession of one half the value of the pirate ships they captured.

From this commission it is obvious that privateering companies were authorized to use press-gangs to recruit their crews. But such high-handedness was never popular in the colonies, and by the late years of the eighteenth century privateering captains, or other agents of companies in the business, were relying exclusively on volunteers. These men signed contracts of service, guaranteeing each one a share of the loot. Under the terms of one such contract a cabin boy walked off with an incredible fortune of more than £1,000, a sum that he would have been lucky to earn after fifty years of honest toil.

In our first book we dealt with pirates and outlaws, the distinction, so far as it exists, being mostly a question of transportation. The pirate had a ship of some sort. The distinction in this book may seem broader, for the privateer was often a rich merchant and at least in later times was supposed to respect international rules of warfare. But to the privateer's victim he was often a pirate and sometimes a criminal just as vicious as Blackbeard or any other freebooter of the Spanish Main. Some of the privateers we will meet in this book played by the rules. Others raped women, looted private homes, murdered defenceless farmers, and took the scalps of Indian children.

In the second section of this book we describe the exploits of another class of gunmen who operated outside all laws except, in some cases, the laws of their outlaw employers. They ranged from well-organized gangs supported by powerful financial interests to lone tricksters carrying on their trade in the shadow of the gallows. Some of them seem to have been born criminals. Others were clearly driven to an outlaw life by injustice and desperation. But in every case they lived by the law of the gun in the age of gunpowder, which may roughly be said to have extended from the days of the first settlers on Canada's eastern shores down to the eve of World War II, when you still might wonder, seeing a man with a violin case on a downtown street, whether he sported a fiddle or a machine gun.

We tend to romanticize and civilize our past. In fact, the age of gunpowder was not a comfortable age in which to live, whether you were in Bytown, terrorized by the Shiners; in the east end of Toronto, with the Brook's Bush Gang for neighbours; or in coastal Nova Scotia, with shiploads of drunken thugs out to rob you, burn your house, or if you were an Indian, ship you off as a slave to the West Indian sugar plantations.

Part 1
Gentlemen Adventurers

Chapter 1
David Kirke and the
Band of Brothers

FEW OF THE GREAT ADVENTURERS of early Canada led such flamboyant lives as the Kirkes. Five brothers who sailed as captains of a privateering fleet, they enjoyed careers that even Francis Drake or Walter Raleigh might have envied. Three of them were knighted by the King of England. One became governor of Quebec; another, governor of Newfoundland. They cornered the Canadian fur trade, made and lost fortunes, counted the crowned heads of Europe among their friends and enemies, and, when their other enterprises had reached the lowest ebb, they founded a fishing colony at Ferryland.

The Kirke brothers were born at Dieppe, on the French side of the English Channel. The name is spelled "Kirq" in French documents of the seventeenth century. But the channel ports had been disputed territory for hundreds of years, and the Kirkes may always have regarded themselves as subjects of the English king. In any case, England was the country they served, and all their commercial ties were with London. David Kirke, the eldest, was the unquestioned leader of the clan. Serving with him were his brothers Lewis, Thomas, John, and James, all soldiers of fortune in an age when it was still possible to own a private navy and to conquer and rule a country on behalf of a corporation of merchants. That, among many other things, is just what they did.

Sometime around 1625 the Kirkes hatched a bold plan to capture the Canadian fur trade, which was then mainly in the hands of a French monopoly centred in Quebec and Acadia (New Brunswick and Nova Scotia). A series of monopolies had been granted by the King of France, though never enforced with complete success. The Kirkes' chance came in 1627, when, after a relatively long peace, Britain and France were at war over the question of the rights of French Protestants. David Kirke and his brothers secured letters of marque from King Charles I of England, authorizing them to annoy the King's enemies, and they formed a company to outfit and provision a squadron for an attack on New France. One of their backers was the young Duke of Hamilton, who was in line to succeed to the throne of Scotland after Charles's own family, and was a trusted councillor of the King's.

Six years earlier Charles's father, James I, had made a grant to another Scottish nobleman, Sir William Alexander, giving him title to what are now the provinces of Nova Scotia and New Brunswick. The territory was then occupied by the French, and James was not at war with France, but following the policy of his predecessor Elizabeth I, he always took the attitude that you could have peace in Europe while privateering and piracy continued with official blessing in the New World.

So when the five Kirkes, in five strongly armed ships, set out to seize the fur trade from the French, the first place they steered for was New Scotland, as the English had begun to call it. Besides their privateering crews, they carried a few Scottish colonists who had their own ideas about fur trading and a willingness to set up and defend forts in Sir William Alexander's domain, once the Kirkes had made it safe for occupation. The arrival of a Scottish governor (Alexander's son) and a Scottish colony was made easy by the fact that Acadia was undefended and the few French peasants who lived there were content to accept any government that would allow them to get on with their own lives.

The ships in which David Kirke and his brothers sailed from England in 1628 were an improvement over the floating castles that the Spaniards had used in their futile attempt to invade England forty years earlier—handier, more seaworthy, lower in the water—but still clumsy and slow compared with the ships that were to come later in the "golden age of sail." All five ships seem to have been large and well armed: three-masted, carrying at least one full course of guns on each side, perhaps ten to twenty to a broadside. Apart from this, their great strength consisted in the fact that each was fitted out for warfare, with crews of eighty men or more, compared with the twenty to thirty sailors manning the merchant ships of the time.

The mainmast, carrying three courses of square sails, was stepped somewhat aft of amidships; the foremast, next in importance, with either two or three courses, was near the bow. The third mast, at the stern, carried a lateen sail as well as a square sail. This helped the ship to steer and run a little closer to the wind than a ship with all square sails. Headsails—jibs rigged to the bowsprit—helped the ship to manoeuvre, but in even the best ships of the time the bowsprit might also be made to carry a spritsail topsail—a square sail on a kind of miniature mast projecting upward from the tip of the bowsprit. This awkward-looking rig could be used to help tack the ship, to bring the bow around in a hurry. In addition to their sails the two principal masts would also carry fighting tops—railed platforms high above the deck, from which a seaman could hurl pots of burning pitch or canisters filled with gunpowder and scrap iron onto the enemy deck. There was also galleries built around the stern—railed walkways that could be manned by pikemen and musketmen to help fend off boarders.

The ship's wheel for steering had not yet been invented. Instead the rudder was controlled by a whipstaff, a long lever connected to the tiller, so that moving the whipstaff one way moved the tiller the other. In heavy weather the ship was kept on course by ropes rigged to the rudder and run through pulleys, with three or four men on either side to haul or slack away as ordered by the sailing master. With the help of sails trimmed for steering, it was not as awkward as it sounds, but the wheel, when it finally forced itself upon the attention of ship designers, provided a great mechanical advantage, allowing one man to do the work of two or three, controlling even a large ship in heavy weather.

David Kirke, a seaman ahead of his time, may have fought his ships "in line of battle" when the occasion arose. In this manoeuvre the ships of a squadron sailed a single course, close together, allowing them to concentrate their fire on a target. It was a simple, effective tactic invented by the pirate squadrons of the early seventeenth century to multiply the effect of a broadside by the

number of ships firing. But such is the conservatism of the professional military mind that the navies of Europe did not adopt
it until 1650 or later (probably under the influence of Sir Henry
Mainwarring, who was privateersman, pirate, and admiral, in
turn.*)

Kirke had the advantage of a strong personality, unquestioned
leadership, and the full loyalty of the four captains, his brothers, all of whom were members of the privateering corporation
and seeking their family fortune together. A pirate at heart, a
born commander, with five well-found fighting machines in his
squadron, Kirke also had great fortune that first year in North
America.

He sailed first to the southern tip of Nova Scotia, where he
captured and burnt a number of small French trading posts,
among them Miscou and Chebouge, just south of the inlet where
the town of Yarmouth now stands. Having ''annoyed'' the
enemy in Acadia most effectively, the Kirkes circled back through
the Strait of Canso and headed up the St. Lawrence to Tadoussac,
the post at the mouth of the Saguenay River which had been a
centre of the fur trade long before Quebec was founded and
continued as a centre of fur trading, walrus hunting, and whale
hunting long afterwards. Despite its importance Tadoussac was
not heavily fortified. The French fur monopolies had never
managed to get more than a few dozen colonists to go out to
Canada at any one time, and on the St. Lawrence they had
concentrated all their efforts at Quebec. Tadoussac, which received furs coming down from the region of Hudson Bay, was a
way station, occupied by a few middlemen in the fur trade, most
of them Basque fishing captains. The Kirkes took it over almost
without firing a shot and transferred a year's supply of furs to
their holds. A nice beginning. Even better was to follow.

This was the point where luck played straight into David
Kirke's hands. He had expected three or four supply ships to
call at Tadoussac on their way upriver to Quebec. They always
stopped there to take on local pilots before continuing to the

---

*For a full discussion of Mainwarring's career see the authors' *Pirates and
Outlaws of Canada*, Doubleday Canada, 1984.

French capital, where Samuel de Champlain held sway, collecting furs from canoe routes running into the heart of the continent. But instead of three or four ships, no fewer than eighteen French vessels sailed into the trap. It was the year of the great colonizing fleet fitted out by the Company of the Hundred Associates of New France, intended to launch Canada on a new era of farming as well as fur trading. The ships were armed merchantmen, and the colonists included a few soliders sent to reinforce Champlain's precarious hold on the St. Lawrence, always threatened as it was by the powerful Indian confederacy of the Iroquois. But the French ships were not fitted out for naval warfare; they had expected, at the worst, to have to deal with a lone pirate or two, and the Kirke brothers rounded them up like sheep. One ship escaped upriver in the fog, but the other seventeen were taken into Tadoussac as prizes and later shepherded home to England in triumph. This coup not only paid all the expenses of the expedition several times over but left Champlain's colony at Quebec in a state bordering on starvation. It survived the winter on roots and berries and what food it could get from neighbouring Montagnais hunters.

Among the shiploads of prisoners that David Kirke took home with him that year for eventual repatriation to France was Claude La Tour, a colonist and fur trader who had been among the early settlers at Port Royal and whose son Charles owned trading posts at Cape Sable and LaHave on Nova Scotia's Atlantic shore. Somehow, Kirke seems to have missed those small forts. By the time they reached England, Kirke had persuaded La Tour to refuse patriation and to enter the service of the King of England. New France, he assured La Tour, was finished. Henceforth North America would be an English continent.

Charles I was especially grateful to Kirke's company, because the Crown's share of the loot helped to rescue his treasury from bankruptcy. The King gave Kirke a knighthood and received him at court. La Tour too must have been received by the King, because he not only entered the services of Sir William Alexander's colonizing company but also married one of the ladies-in-waiting to the Queen. Alexander was already secretary for Scotland and lieutenant governor of Nova Scotia. A year or so later he would become the Viscount Stirling and eventually Earl of Donovan. He made a large grant of land to La Tour on the Atlantic coast of Nova Scotia, including the trading posts at Cape Sable and LaHave, occupied by La Tour's son, and created him a knight-baronet of New Scotland.

In the spring of 1629 Sir David Kirke took his privateering fleet back to Canada, landed Alexander's colonists at several posts, most of them, including Sir Claude La Tour and his wife, at Port Royal, then sailed off to complete his conquest of New France. Except for small-time farmers raising grain and pasturing sheep and cattle around the shores of the Annapolis Basin, the French had abandoned Port Royal. The fort had long since been destroyed. So the Scottish settlers built a new fort at a place now called Granville Beach, where it remained in various states of disrepair for the next two hundred years under the name of the Scotch Fort, though the Scots remained there for only three years.

While this was going on, La Tour headed off to his own domain on the Atlantic coast to enlist his son Charles in the service of England. Much to his astonishment Charles refused. The elder La Tour then brought a party of armed men to Cape Sable and tried to take the post by force, but Charles defended his little fort at gunpoint and drove his father back to Port Royal. So Claude La Tour never did occupy the lands granted to him by Alexander, and his son was later able to claim that he had always remained loyal to the King of France.

Meanwhile Kirke's fleet had sailed back to Tadoussac and transferred to its holds another year's supply of furs. At Tadoussac they had the good luck to meet Etienne Brûlé, a man who had spent twenty years among the Indians, spoke their languages, and knew the country better than anyone alive.* Brûlé had been in Canada from the age of fourteen and had no wish to live anywhere else. He believed that New France was finished and had no intention of being shipped back to Europe in a prisoner

---

*This great explorer and renegade from the earliest days of New France is treated fully in *Pirates and Outlaws of Canada*.

exchange. Like La Tour, he entered the British service and piloted the privateers upriver until they could anchor just out of cannon shot of Champlain's fort on the headland of Quebec.

Kirke sent a message to Champlain under flag of truce, demanding his surrender. And the governor of New France, having neither powder, shot, nor even food to sustain a seige, surrendered on honourable terms for repatriation to France. The few soldiers at the fort surrendered with him and were repatriated. The handful of colonists who operated tiny farms in the area remained and, like Brûlé and La Tour, agreed to serve the English.

Sir Lewis (also called Louis) Kirke remained at Quebec as governor and collected boatloads of furs from the Huron and Montagnais Indian traders, as Champlain had done. Other ships of the squadron returned to Tadoussac and continued to monopolize the furs from the northern Indians. The Kirkes thus achieved a total monopoly of the fur trade of Canada, something that no company before their time had ever managed to do.

In the words of one historian, the Kirkes "reaped a fortune in furs." Perhaps. It is true that they monopolized the fur trade for at least five years, perhaps six. But they were not acting entirely on their own behalf. They were agents of a wealthy cabal of London merchants, including powerful members of the Court, and those merchants may well have reaped most of the fortune, though they later accused Sir David Kirke of embezzling some of the company's profits.

Except for Charles La Tour, hovering as a kind of outlaw on the extreme southern tip of Nova Scotia, New France was now entirely in English hands, its conquest complete. The Newfoundland historian D.W. Prowse described the virtually bloodless conquest as the most brilliant naval exploit in colonial history. But then, in March 1632, at the Treaty of St. Germain-en-Laye, King Charles I returned all of Kirke's conquests to the King of France. Inexplicable? A policy of scuttle, as Prowse called it? Not at all. Charles was on the brink of bankruptcy once again, and he sold New France back to the French for a payment disguised as the dowry of his wife, the French Princess Henrietta

Maria. Even before the treaty was signed, the King had already ordered the Scots colonists out of Nova Scotia. So the chief beneficiary of Sir David Kirke's conquests was the King's treasury. But treaty or no treaty the Kirkes continued to hold Quebec and Tadoussac for another year and so picked up another year's lucrative supply of furs.

As a reward for their services, Sir David Kirke and his company, which now included not only the Duke of Hamilton but also the Earls of Pembroke and Holland, received a grant from Charles I giving them title to the whole island of Newfoundland. Like his father, Charles distributed his royal grants with a free hand. Included in the territory of which Kirke now became governor was a colony founded at Ferryland by Sir George Calvert, Lord Baltimore, also under royal grant. Baltimore had left Newfoundland, as the King's grant noted, but many of his colonists were still there, including an appointed governor, and there were other planters in other harbours. Kirke now made Ferryland his capital and expelled the Baltimore colonists by force, bringing out a hundred colonists of his own. He enforced the payment of rents by colonists in other harbours, some of them established there long before his arrival, and collected taxes at gunpoint from foreign fishing ships. This last exaction brought screams of protest from the French ambassador in London, who claimed, quite truthfully, that his nation had fished in those waters by ancient right. Kirke also issued licences for taverns—indeed he seems to have treated the rum trade as his private monopoly. All this, especially his treatment of Baltimore's colonists, coupled with charges of embezzlement by his sponsors, brought on a complex series of lawsuits that continued for the rest of his life.

Meanwhile in Acadia the King of France had appointed the formidable Charles La Tour lieutenant general. La Tour's father and his father's wife had returned to the son's fold at Cape Sable, and all but two of the Scottish colonists had sailed for home. The two who remained married Acadian wives and entered La Tour's service. All very well, except that the King of France appointed another lieutenant general named Charles de Menou d'Aulnay, whose territory overlapped La Tour's and whose character was that of a medieval robber baron. The two lieutenant generals soon took to raiding each other's trading posts, killing each other's servants, and fitting out private navies to make war on each other.

Charles La Tour at first tried to get Sir David Kirke's assistance. He sailed to Ferryland, where Kirke received him amicably enough. What he promised Kirke heaven only knows, but it wasn't sufficient. Kirke by now was a personal friend of the King of England, and it would have taken more than La Tour could offer to make him disobey the King's orders to leave Nova Scotia to the French. La Tour then turned to Massachusetts, a colony that had earlier shown a lively and predatory interest in Acadia. The governor, like Kirke, refused to intervene personally against the orders of his King, but he allowed La Tour to purchase and outfit a squadron of private warships in Boston and to enlist men from Massachusetts as mercenaries.

Profits from the fur trade in the seventeenth century must have been enormous because Charles La Tour, who had no other resources than fur trading, fitted out four ships, armed them with thirty-eight cannon, and hired crews and fifty mercenaries, all at his own expense. He than sailed against d'Aulnay, who was hovering around the mouth of the St. John River in what is now New Brunswick, trying to capture a small fort that had been built there by La Tour. At La Tour's approach d'Aulnay fled, but La Tour pursued him across the Bay of Fundy and into the Annapolis Basin, finally cornering him at the Lequille River, near the place where Fort Anne and the town of Annapolis Royal were later built. Here there was a brief battle from which d'Aulnay fled, defeated. Soon afterwards he sailed to France for reinforcements and a fresh commission from the King.

The next year he returned, loaded with guns and parchments, styling himself "governor and lieutenant general for the King of France in all the coasts of Acadie." Once again he attacked La Tour's fort on the St. John River. La Tour was away at Cape Sable or one of his other posts and had left the fort in charge of his wife, Françoise Marie Jacquelin. She resisted the siege for three days, then surrendered under flag of truce on condition that she and all those inside would be given safe conduct. D'Aulnay then committed the blackest act of treachery in the history of New France. He seized all the men at gunpoint, offered one of them his life on condition that he act as hangman, and had all the others strung up, one by one, to the rafters of the fort, forcing Madame La Tour to watch the massacre, with a rope around her own neck. He didn't hang her, but within three weeks she too was dead, though apparently not from ill treatment.

La Tour fled first to Boston, then to Quebec. Meanwhile d'Aulnay enjoyed a monopoly in Acadia—but not for long. While travelling by canoe, he was drowned at the narrows that connects the Annapolis Basin and the French Basin, in the tide race where the causeway and tidal power station now stand. Tradition says that d'Aulnay was travelling with an Indian whom he had brutally abused some months earlier and that the drowning was no accident. Maybe. In any case Charles La Tour returned, with the renewed title of lieutenant general, and not only took over d'Aulnay's forts but even married d'Aulnay's widow, a woman who, like his former wife, possessed great strength of character and resolution and knew how to help her husband in time of battle.

Despite a charge of treason a few years earlier when he had hired English colonists to fight on his behalf, La Tour was described in his new letters patent as having "faithfully served the Kings of France for a period of forty-three years." This old freebooter, who ranged up and down Canada with musket and cannon for more than half a century, serving the French when they were in control and the English when they reconquered Acadia, finally died in his bed at the age of seventy-two in his home on the St. John River.

Sir David Kirke, the other great privateer whose career was so entwined with La Tour's, remained at Ferryland through turbulence and controversy, even when his partners in the privateering and trading company replaced him temporarily with another governor. When civil war broke out in England and the cause of the Royalists became hopeless, he offered King Charles I sanctuary at Ferryland, which he hoped to be able to defend with his own ships. He probably could have done it too, because when it was properly fortified, Ferryland was virtually unassailable by sea, but the King preferred to remain in England and face execution rather than desert his throne. A few months before he went to the scaffold he wrote Kirke, imploring him to find asylum for his sister, Lady Hawkins.

Kirke eventually made his peace with Cromwell, and his brother Sir James Kirke even managed to save the company by taking Cromwell's son-in-law into partnership. Brother John remained in London as the company's agent, but when he enlisted four hundred seamen to be sent out to Newfoundland as colonists, Cromwell's government refused to allow them to sail, believing that they were intended to help man a Royalist fleet, still at sea under Prince Rupert.

Eventually Sir David Kirke was recalled to London to face charges brought against him by the heirs of Lord Baltimore—a controversy that was never settled. He died in London, with the suit unresolved, but his wife and sons and grandsons all remained at Ferryland, where they established a large fishing enterprise. Lady Kirke, with her sons George, David, and Philip, owned fourteen boats manned by sixty-six fishermen in 1673, when the Dutch privateering fleet under Captain Jacob Everson attacked Ferryland and sacked the town. But even then the Kirkes stayed on and tried to rebuild their fortune. They were not finally dislodged from Ferryland until Pierre Le Moyne d'Iberville destroyed the English colonies in his great raid of 1696.

Chapter 2
Sailing Against Acadia

THE ANNAPOLIS BASIN, on the south shore of the Bay of Fundy, was regarded from the day of its discovery by French explorers as one of the most desirable places on the Atlantic coast. Champlain and Lescarbot both commented on its beauty and fruitfulness. Even today people from many parts of North America live there by choice. A region coveted by both French and English settlers, perhaps its great desirability is one of the reasons it was subjected to so much murder, rape, and arson in its early years.

In 1613 a privateering raid from Virginia, commanded by Captain Samuel Argall, burned the undefended fort at Port Royal and destroyed all official marks of French occupation, using picks and chisels to efface the names of French captains and the fleur-de-lis emblems from a massive stone where they had been engraved. Between the Argall raid and the final British conquest of 1710 this area was fought over by rival fur-trading gangs and captured and sacked no fewer than five times by privateering fleets from the New England colonies to the south. The privateers usually headed for Port Royal, the Acadian capital, but they also attacked the undefended farming settlements at Minas and Chignecto, near the head of the Bay of Fundy, and the posts on the St. John River as far inland as Jemseg, a fur-trading station nearly fifty miles upstream from Reversing Falls, where the Fundy tides flow in and out of the St. John. There were other raids later, as we shall see, but none so vicious as those conducted by gangs of drunken looters from the waterfronts of Boston and other New England ports during the last half-century of the French regime in Acadia.

A force of some three hundred men landed at Port Royal in 1654, at a time when the little settlement was virtually undefended because England and France were temporarily at peace. Cromwell was ruling England at the time, and his ships, sent to attack New York, then held by the Dutch and called New Amsterdam, supported the raid, carried out mainly by New Englanders. The attack is hard to classify: piracy? undeclared war? privateering? It was certainly done on Cromwell's orders, though the orders were given secretly, and many of those involved were civilians. They captured the small coastal forts, then sailed into the Annapolis Basin, fought a brief battle with the defenders, deported the handful of French troops found there, and allowed the Acadian families to keep their farms. The raid was motivated partly by religion: "rooting out the Papists," but only the *ruling* Papists. The peasants were allowed to keep their religion as well as their hard-won farms on the reclaimed salt marshes.

Charles La Tour, who always managed to be a Huguenot when dealing with the English and a loyal son of the Church when dealing with the Most Catholic King of France, put on his Protestant hat, resurrected his father's title as knight-baronet of New Scotland, and, in partnership with two wealthy Englishmen, received from Cromwell's government a grant to most of what had been Acadia. One of his partners, Thomas Temple, was named governor, and he is generally regarded by historians as the first English governor of Nova Scotia, even though he was essentially a merchant, with his headquarters in Boston, and paid only brief visits to New Scotland. The whole story of allegiances in this era is bizarre: La Tour switched his nationality from French to English several times and his religion along with it; the Kirkes managed to serve both King Charles I and his arch-enemy Oliver Cromwell; and Temple, nominated by Cromwell as governor of Nova Scotia, also had a commission from King Charles II, then living in exile in France. After Cromwell's death and the King's return to England, Temple was created a knight-baronet of Nova Scotia.

Nevertheless, thirteen years after the English had captured Acadia, Charles II, who was deeply indebted to the King of France, signed a treaty returning it to France. The residents of the Boston colonies never really accepted this and neither did Temple. He managed to keep his company in control until 1670, three years after the treaty, but finally surrendered the province to the French.

However, the return of a French governor did not end privateering raids against Acadia. The same Dutch privateering fleet that sacked Ferryland in 1673 and assisted in the capture of New York also captured the French forts in Nova Scotia and New Brunswick, took the French governor of Acadia prisoner, and seized control of the fur trade. And speaking of divided loyalties, this same fleet, which had expelled the English from New York, landed its French prisoners at Boston, where the Acadian governor was held for ransom until Governor Frontenac of Quebec paid one thousand beaver skins.

All this occurred while England and France were at peace. But the excuse of another war, if any such excuse were needed, soon stirred the Boston merchants to yet another attack. John Nelson, nephew of Thomas Temple, was a prosperous merchant at Boston, and in 1690, shortly after the beginning of "King William's War" against the French, he approached the governor of Massachusetts, offering to outfit a privateering fleet at his own expense and capture Acadia, provided he could keep the plunder and enjoy the same monopoly of the fur trade that his uncle had enjoyed a generation earlier.

But the governor had other plans. He agreed that Massachusetts should grab Acadia, but instead of passing it over to Nelson, he invited a corporation of merchants to underwrite the enterprise and placed it in charge of Sir William Phips, an illiterate New England treasure hunter, who a few years before had recovered a fortune from the sea bottom and helped rescue the Stuart monarchy from the brink of bankruptcy. He had been rewarded with a knighthood and a modest share of the treasure.

When Phips failed to raise the seven hundred volunteers he figured would be needed to conquer Acadia, the governor authorized him to use press-gangs, and he made the rounds of the taverns, grabbing whatever men he could find to fill his ships. He anchored his fleet of seven armed vessels off Port Royal on May 11, 1690. Faced by overwhelming odds, the French governor surrendered on terms that his garrison of eighty-five men

could keep their arms and return to France and on condition
that the Acadian farmers would not be molested. Phips treach-
erously violated the terms of surrender and turned his shiploads
of ruffians loose in an orgy of looting. They destroyed the fort,
attacked the church, pulled down the altar, chopped down the
crucifix, and smashed the statutes. So much for popery. They
plundered every farm and private house they could reach in a
two-day rampage, then sailed back to Boston with their prisoners. The Boston merchants were so pleased with Phips that they
made him governor the following year.

About a month after this attack on Port Royal two shiploads
of privateers from New York arrived in the Annapolis Basin.
Furious at finding nothing left worth looting, they turned to
murder, rape, and arson. They set fire to the remaining buildings,
burned one family alive inside their house, and hanged two
Acadian peasants whom they managed to catch. Then they sailed
across the Bay of Fundy and attacked the post on the St. John
River at Jemseg, where the interim governor of Acadia, Joseph
Robineau de Villebon, had taken refuge. He was upriver with a
party of Indians when they arrived and captured his fort. On his
return he organized a counter-attack and drove the killers downriver, but they escaped with his ship as a prize and left him
stranded. He then journeyed up the St. John River by canoe to
its junction with the Madawaska, up the Madawaska, over the
height of land, and up the St. Lawrence to Quebec, arriving in
time to help defend the capital of New France from capture by a
fleet organized and led by Phips.

Meanwhile the Acadian peasants who had escaped up the
Lequille River, as the Annapolis River was then called, came back
to the Port Royal area and began rebuilding. The next year the
French returned, installed Villebon as permanent governor, and
sent two privateer vessels from Port Royal to harass the coast of
New England.

The greatest privateer captain of that war—perhaps the greatest in the entire history of New France—sailed out of Placentia,
the French fortress on the south coast of Newfoundland, in the
years 1689 to 1694. He was John Svigaricipi, a Basque captain

with a talent for naval warfare and a strong, fast ship, very able in pursuit and attack. Svigaricipi was credited with taking "hundreds" of English and colonial ships, most of them probably mere fishing vessels. His most outstanding feat was making a prize of a full British warship, the one hundred-gun *Princess*, an action for which he was decorated by King Louis XIV. Unfortunately we have no details of the battles fought by this brilliant sea rover, just the barest outline of his career and a gravestone preserved in a museum at Placentia, where he was buried in 1694 after being killed at sea, apparently in the attack on Ferryland carried out by French privateers that year. The attack was a failure. The Ferryland fishing masters had taken guns from their ships and erected fortifications on the Isle aux Bois, making it impossible for the French squadron to force its way into the harbour. In a letter to the governor of Massachusetts, who offered them assistance, those independent fishing captains reported that they had fought off "the King's enemies" on two occasions by their own unaided efforts and were prepared to do the same again. However, they were obliterated by an overland attack in 1696, when Pierre Le Moyne d'Iberville led a force of French Canadians and Abenaki Indians from Placentia, capturing and burning every English settlement on the Avalon Peninsula, except for Carbonear Island, where the settlers successfully withstood a siege.

Peace returned in 1697, and all territories were restored to their pre-war owners. But four years later England and France were at it again in the War of the Spanish Succession (Queen Anne's War), which lasted thirteen years and put the final seal of doom on the Acadian colony. Near the beginning of the war the governor of New France made an extraordinary offer to the governor of Massachusetts, suggesting that the two colonies enter into a pact of neutrality, despite the impending war in Europe. Governor Bruillon of Acadia made a similar offer. But Governor Thomas Dudley of Massachusetts rejected the idea out of hand—and brought on his people a series of terrible raids by French Canadians and their Indian allies, including the far-famed Deerfield massacre in which fifty or more people were killed and more than a hundred taken prisoner. (Then, as in the future, any defeat by Indians, even of regular army units, was invariably labelled a ''massacre.'')

Dudley called in the Boston merchants and urged them to equip a fleet of privateers to prey on Acadia and any other parts of New France that they could reach. But especially Acadia. They began ranging north into the Bay of Fundy. By the end of 1702 they had destroyed the French fishery in Nova Scotia (though not in the Gulf of the St. Lawrence or Newfoundland) and had brought fourteen ships into Boston as prizes. In response the French stationed privateers at Port Royal and sailed them against English colonial shipping from Maine to New York, making a great nuisance of themselves, especially along the coast of Massachusetts.

By 1704 Massachusetts was organizing a great expedition to wipe out ''that nest of pirates'' at Port Royal. At the same time the government of Massachusetts offered a bounty of £100 each for the scalps of any Indians over ten years of age. One hundred pounds was enough to buy an adult slave or an excellent team of horses. The privateers did, in fact, return with scalps, though how many isn't clear—perhaps a dozen or so.

The naval force raised by the Boston merchants consisted of three warships with eighty-six guns, an armed shallop, thirty-six whaleboats, and fourteen transports with 550 men. They also carried a great store of rum and in the course of the raid captured French stores of brandy and wine, putting it all to such good use that most of the raiders were roaring drunk for a good part of the month and a half the raid lasted.

This was the famous expedition led by Benjamin Church, the New England Daniel Boone who had made his reputation fighting and capturing Indians and selling them into slavery by the hundreds, mostly to sugar plantations in the West Indies, where they lasted an average of five years before being worked and beaten to death. Church should have been able to take Port Royal with ease, perhaps even Placentia, and end French power on the Atlantic coast. But he didn't even make the attempt. Instead he raided isolated farming communities at Minas and Chignecto, slaughtered cattle, burned houses, barns, and churches, and broke down the dykes to allow the sea to flood the reclaimed crop lands. The whole fleet then gathered at Port Royal and demanded the surrender of the fort. The governor, with 193 men under his command, refused. Church, better at kidnapping Indians than capturing forts, sailed away without firing a shot, returned to Boston with his pitiful string of scalps from Indians over the age of ten, and was received as a conquering hero. But the raid is remembered in Nova Scotia for the sheer vandalism of Church's drunken crews.

By now Port Royal was expanding its privateering fleet, becoming the base for a company of French captains who ranged between Acadia and the French West Indies. That was more than the Boston merchants could endure, so in 1707 they organized an even greater fleet than the last, manned by more than thirteen hundred New Englanders (most of them shanghaied by press-gangs) to confront the strengthened forces at Port Royal, where 185 French regulars, sixty Canadian militiamen, and ninety Indians awaited their coming. The New England forces besieged the fort for ten days and actually tried to carry it by storm under cover of darkness, but the French made deadly sallies out of the fort and laid ambushes for the attackers. When the New Englanders finally sailed away defeated, they left behind nearly a hundred dead.

Massachusetts wasn't prepared to give up so easily. The governor raised another hundred men and sent them off as reinforcements for the expedition. Two months after the first siege they were back in the Annapolis Basin once more. This time they again besieged the fort for ten days and fought valiantly against the French sallies, but in the end they retreated to their ships and sailed back to Boston having accomplished precisely nothing.

The garrison at Port Royal was now almost literally on its uppers, the men half-starved and only half-clothed. They had received no supplies from France in more than three years, but they managed to survive another two years and even fed five hundred prisoners who were housed there temporarily. Their supplies came from the privateers, who managed to capture enough food, clothing, guns, and ammunition from Yankee ships to keep the little French capital alive.

Finally, in 1710, a combined British and colonial force of thirty-five hundred men in thirty-six ships sailed against Port Royal and received the surrender on honourable terms of its 156 surviving defenders. Perhaps because the British were in charge, the terms were honoured, and the little garrison was allowed to march out carrying its flag and guns, dressed in whatever rags of uniforms it still possessed. Rarely in the history of human conflict had so little been achieved by so many against so few.

Chapter 3
Sailing against New France

PRIVATEERS WERE NOT INTENT on slaughter. Capturing ships and annoying the enemy were their *raison d'être*. But there were rare exceptions to this: life-and-death struggles with no thought except survival. And there were instances when equally matched ships tangled and fought it out. One such battle took place in April 1757, the year after the decisive struggle for North America had broken out between the English and the French. That year the armed merchant vessel *Robuste* was freighted for Quebec by the French government, armed with twenty-four guns and a crew of seventy-seven. She also carried 150 soldiers to reinforce the army of New France under General Louis-Joseph, Marquis de Montcalm.

On April 13, Captain Jean Joseph Rosier fell in with "an English frigate of thirty guns in a battery and a half." No privateer would engage a frigate by choice, but this was a case of mistaken identity, as Rosier's own account of the battle makes clear: "At daybreak I saw a vessel on my lee, heading northwards, the wind west-northwest, carrying four principal sails, her mizzen, and mizzen-topsail, without top-gallant masts. She changed her course to my wake, and approached. I put her down for a merchantman, obliged to approach by tacking. Her greater speed brought her, at noon, within a twelve-pound gunshot. Observing her closely I could then see that she was a frigate with a battery and a half of guns, crowded with men, and extraordinarily high in the water. Being unable to withdraw, and thinking it useless to parley, I clewed up by lower sails to await him. When he stood across my course I showed him my colours and, as is customary, fired a shot. He broke out his, accompanied by his full broadside. Then the fight began, and was most bloody, always side by side until 7 o'clock, when our mutual disarray forced us to draw off to set things to rights. I had my main [yard]

and main-topsail smashed, my mizzen [yard] and foretopsail yard
brought down, all my sails in rags, and useless. In this attack I
had 18 killed instantly, and 42 wounded, several mortally, and
several cannon shot just above the waterline.

   "Our plight seemed so bad that on making examination of
the ship I agreed with my staff that we should turn back because
of the impossibility of making repairs at sea. Consequently I set
my course for Perthuis, or the River of Bordeaux, the wind being
favourable, continuing all day and the next night under easy
sail.

   "Around noon on the 15th my lookout saw a vessel about
four leagues to leeward which was manoeuvering so as to approach me. My few sails did not permit me to avoid him; by 6
o'clock in the evening he was within range of a long-gun. He
showed a white flag and fired a shot [but] not observing that he
showed any special sign of need, I kept on my course. I took his
bearing at sunset, and thought he was in my wake, and the flares
and rockets which he was firing made me think he was in pursuit. At nine he was within earshot, and hailed me. I answered
him. He said to me, in a compassionate tone: 'Poor prisoner, I
advise you to surrender and not make any resistance. I will give
you good terms.' His exhortation was followed by his broadside into my stern, which was exposed, his sails giving him an
advantage over me. Consequently I manoeuvred my ship so that
she was broadside to him. Then the battle became general, stem
to stern, and was more savage, though less fatal, than the former one. In this attack, which ended at 1 o'clock in the morning, I had my main [topmast] and mizzen topmast smashed,
my sails more destroyed than the earlier ones, 5 men killed and
11 wounded. My enemy, drawing off, allowed me to make
repairs, which I did promptly. I refitted my mizzen and foretop-
gallant yards, these being the only ones I could rig to keep me
under way, which I did.

   "At daybreak my enemy, who had watched me all night,
manoeuvred to rejoin me, which he managed by 11 o'clock. I
recognized him as the same frigate with which I had had my
first affray. I counted his guns, which were 15 on each side, and

some of my officers assured me that they had seen cannon on his forecastle and quarter-decks. The engagement began anew, and did not cease until 6 o'clock, when he hailed, and I answered. He said to me, 'Yield, gentlemen, yield. You will be treated as you deserve. We will grant you good terms. We are an English King's frigate, so be contented.' Then he hoisted a square flag to his foretop. I answered, being unable to hoist a square flat like him, because I had no mast standing, that I was flattered to have conversation with my peers, that I still had powder and shot, that I much regretted I had no canvas to show him a course contrary to that which he would oblige me to take, and that if he would continue to do his duty, I would continue to do mine. I gave him three *Vive le Roi*, my broadside of guns and musketry, at which we continued until half-past seven. My enemy, as crippled as I, was pumping water out of all his scuppers, and was steering with sweeps. I assumed his rudder was useless, and at the same time discovered that mine was also damaged. I had it repaired promptly. It was now out of the question for either to yield to the other. Our condition permitted us to think only of ourselves. The following night put us out of sight of each other.

"I worked hard to manage the repairs. At daybreak I saw a ship ahead, approaching us. We came together at ten, and I made him out to be a privateer of 16 guns, and several swivels, with a large crew. He opened fire, but drew away after an hour, setting his lower sails before a following wind, discouraged by our response and our gunnery. In those last two attacks we had 3 killed and 8 wounded. At noon I sighted the land near Oleron. At eight that evening I dropped anchor a league from Chassiron.

"My state is much to be pitied. I have my mizzenmast standing, and that without its topmast, and my bowsprit, not a piece of rigging in working order from stem to stern, at least fifty shots near the waterline and a great number in the hull. I believe on both sides 3,000 shots were fired, and 15,000 rounds of musketry, which I verified by counting the cartridges remaining. I had 29 soldiers and seamen killed, and 61 wounded. . . ."

The captain then goes on to commend the ship's officers and officers of the regiment, who had shown great courage during the battle, some of them while wounded. Some of those wounded had been shot in the thigh. In those days, if the bone was shattered, this injury would require amputation, with only a 50 percent chance of survival. A passenger, who was going to Quebec on government service, also died of wounds.

The captain explained that he had put up as gallant a fight as possible, "not being ignorant of the importance of my cargo to the King's service." Shipping into Quebec was indeed at a critical point that year. New France was very nearly starved into submission two years before the famous battle on the Plains of Abraham, and some three hundred people actually died of starvation in what was left to France of her former Acadian colony.

There is an interesting postscript to this skirmish in the battle for Canada. John Stewart McLennan, the Cape Breton historian who wrote a monumental history of Louisbourg, researched the British public records and the British press of 1757, looking for confirmation from those on the other side of the battle. What he found was that no frigate of the Royal Navy was in a position to have taken part in this battle and that there is no mention of it in British naval records, as there should have been. He did discover, however, a dispatch in the *London Chronicle*, dateline Bristol, May 7. It quoted a letter from an officer on board the Bristol privateer *Caesar*, describing an engagement with "a French frigate of thirty-six guns on the 13th, 15th and 16th of April . . . which was very obstinate and continued seven hours the last day; and when the *Caesar* left her she looked like a wreck, having lost all her masts and rigging." The *Caesar* reported only one man killed and twenty-two wounded (but this is a press account in wartime, not an official report, so we may take those statistics with a grain of salt.) More to the point, the letter reported that the *Caesar* had fired off seven hundred cannon shot and eight thousand musket rounds "besides an incredible number of Largin and Partridge shot." Also "three thirty Hand Grandes out of the tops, which did great execution." McLennan could not identify the "Hand Grandes." Perhaps they were fire pots, which the French captain reported were thrown to his deck from the topmasts of the English "frigate," though, according to his account, they did no serious damage, being caught and thrown into the sea by the promptness and bravery of his officers.

In any case, it turned out that this battle royal was between two privateers, with approximately equal gunning, each of which believed the other to be a naval frigate.

Privateers were absolutely crucial to the defence of New France in the unequal fight with the British, in which the French colonists were outnumbered by at least ten to one, and the British always had superiority at sea. Morpain, captain of the Port of Louisbourg, commanded his own privateering vessel. Doloboratz was engaged as commander of another privateer to carry out the French attack on the British outpost at Canso. These two were the only ships of war sailing out of Louisbourg in 1744.

After successfully attacking Canso, Captain Doloboratz went on a privateering cruise along the coast of New England. He was well armed with twelve cannon and twelve swivels but quickly fell prey to a ship named the *Prince of Orange*, commissioned by the Colony of Massachusetts. There was much gunfire, but no one on either side was killed or injured in the battle. That same summer the Canso privateers captured nine vessels on the Banks of Newfoundland and one Irish merchant ship, but the English got much the better of the engagement. They sent out a raider named the *Kinsale*, armed with forty-four guns under Captain Robert Young. She arrived at St. John's, Newfoundland, June 23, having taken five ships en route, then raided the entire French shore between Cape Ray and Placentia, putting all the French fishing stations to the torch, including the fortified station of St. Pierre. She then turned her attention to the French fishery north of Cape Bonavista, where she sank or captured a number of French ships and took eighteen thousand quintals of fish, together with eighty tuns of oil.

During this war the New England colonies laid the foundations of the great tradition of privateering that served them so well against Louisbourg, and, a generation later, against the British in their War of Independence. The shipyards of Rhode Island, Massachusetts, and Pennsylvania worked at top speed building privateers and managed to get forty-nine of them at sea in the first year. One of them, sailing out of Boston, was reported at Louisbourg to have taken seventeen ships and seven hundred prisoners and to have sunk a thousand French fishing boats.

Most of the damage must have been to the French floater fishery in the Gulf of St. Lawrence. All the French fishing stations on the Gaspé, as well as in Newfoundland, went up in smoke and flame that year. The following summer the British colonies increased their privateering fleet to 113. They now outnumbered French privateers ten to one.

That was the year General William Pepperrell launched his attack on Louisbourg at the head of the colonial militia. His army of amateur soldiers would never have dared attack the great French fortress except for the support of a huge privateering fleet, commanded by Captain Edward Tyng, the first naval officer to be commissioned by the colony of Massachusetts and the man who had captured Doloboratz the year before. Pepperrell also had knowledge, gleaned in prisoner exchanges (again by way of privateering), that Louisbourg was badly defended, half-starving, and in danger of mutiny.

This amateur army of farmers and fishermen, supported by an amateur navy, sailed for Cape Breton without the support of any regular British troops, army officers, or any elements of the Royal Navy. The head of the British naval squadron in the West Indies gave it about as much chance of success as the Children's Crusade. But when new orders came from England to the West Indies squadron to proceed northward to "attack and distress the enemy in their settlements and annoy their fisheries and commerce," Commodore Peter Warren, British commander-in-chief for North America, set sail with three regular warships, two small armed vessels, and ten transports. A small force, indeed, to protect an expedition against the New World's strongest fortress. But when the British learned that the colony of Massachusetts, with some help from its neighbours, was actually attacking Louisbourg, they dispatched eight more warships to give support. The British squadron arrived off Louisbourg ahead of supply ships from France and imposed a blockade. When the supply fleet did arrive, only one small ship managed to slip through and shelter under the guns of the fort.

Louisbourg was starved into surrender after a siege of a month and a half. Pepperrell had accomplished the impossible by the promptness of his attack, even though his drunken "army" scarcely deserved the name and was certainly incapable of any serious fighting. When they entered Louisbourg, his undisciplined, ragtag militia broke out in an orgy of riot, pillage, and rape, and privateers and militiamen filled their chests with loot. From their point of view the adventure had been a great success, no matter what happened to the rocky island of Cape Breton. And of course, in the peace treaty the English handed Louisbourg back to the French, just as they had handed back Quebec in the previous century.

When the war against New France got going once more in 1756, no fewer than eighteen letters of marque were issued to privateers sailing out of Halifax, carrying among them 232 cannon and crews of 965 men. So attractive was privateering to the unskilled men of the town, that Governor Lawrence complained it was no longer possible to hire local labourers to keep the fortifications in repair. Labourers left town, lured by the promises of prize money held out by the recruiting officers of privateering companies, most of them partnerships entered into by shipowners to spread the risks of loss. New France also outfitted privateers, one of them, the *Caribou*, built at Quebec especially for the job. But in the western Atlantic the French were completely outgunned, both by private and commissioned warships. There was never anything like equality at sea.

In the end New France was defeated in battles fought on land, but it was a bloody, expensive business that need never have happened at all. It was only the arrival of a French supply fleet in the spring of 1759 that enabled Quebec to hold out as long as it did. Had the British wintered their ships at St. John's and Halifax, with orders to blockade Louisbourg and the St. Lawrence River as soon as navigation opened in the spring, there would have been no need for the brutal ravaging of the countryside by General James Wolfe's army or for the bloodletting on the Plains of Abraham. Had the British repeated the strategy of the privateer fleet under David Kirke, Canada would have fallen into their hands intact, and Wolfe would have missed his moment of glory.

Chapter 4
The Spirit of '76

"THE YEARS OF THE PIRATES" still fresh in the folk memory of Canada's Atlantic provinces are, strangely enough, years of glory celebrated in American history. The "pirates" in question were privateers carrying letters of marque from some embryo American state or other, occasionally even from the Continental Congress. But since some of them specialized not in attacking merchant ships but in raiding towns and villages and in campaigns of pillage through the countryside, they are remembered as pirates not only in folklore but in most of the documents of the time.

When the War of Independence erupted in 1775, the rebellious colonies expected Nova Scotia, and perhaps even Newfoundland, to join in their campaign to throw off the yoke of the King. When this failed to happen, they turned loose a swarm of raiders against the "Tories" of the north. Anyone not bearing arms against Great Britain was a legitimate target: his jewellery, money, and silverware free to be seized in a swift night attack, or his house burned at dawn.

The American naval historian D.W. Knox estimates that the American colonies issued letters of marque to some two thousand ships (all but a handful of them converted merchant ships) with eighteen thousand guns and seventy thousand men, not all serving at once but at sea throughout some part of the war. Some ships prowled along distant shores. Some fought out of French ports in the home waters of Great Britain. Others hugged the coastline of North America, raiding fishing settlements as far away as Labrador, carrying off cargoes of salt cod and barrels of oil, sinking small boats, and burning fish stages. Their most lucrative raids were in Nova Scotia, against the wealthy outports and the comfortable farms of the Annapolis Valley.

Though the rebels certainly got the better of the war at sea, they didn't have things entirely their own way. Michael Francklin, Joshua Mauger, and Malachi Salter were all privateering merchants operating out of Halifax in 1758, and Alexander Brymer owned a ship named the *Halifax* that he armed and equipped to raid rebel shipping. The *Revenge* and the *Liverpool* were two others that brought prizes to the Nova Scotia capital.

Then there was the *Lucy*, sailing out of Liverpool after the economy of that port had been all but ruined by rebel depredations. A committee of merchants got together, outfitted her, and raised a crew under Captain Freeman (a name famous in privateering a generation later), claiming they had suffered great losses and hoping to make good some small part of the same. The names of those who bought shares in the *Lucy* crop up again and again in the records of privateering at Liverpool: Tinkham, Freeman, Bradford, and Collins. She sailed with "twenty-three officers and men, three owners, a boy, and a cripple." A cripple? Not, perhaps, as odd as it sounds. He was likely the captain's clerk, keeping the accounts, for the captains of such ships weren't always master mariners and in some cases might even be illiterate.

The most oft-quoted incident of the war on the coast of Nova Scotia (perhaps because it showed the Americans in such a good light) was the rescue at Seal Island, fifteen miles off the extreme southwestern tip of Nova Scotia, of the crew of the British warship *HMS Blonde*. The rock on which she floundered, still known as the Blonde Reef, is one of a group of nasty shoals that make the area dangerous for shipping. A sea was running and she quickly broke up, but all her crew, along with sixty-five prisoners captured from American privateers, reached Seal Island safely, losing all their boats in the heavy surf during the landing. And there they might have remained, trying to subsist on the herd of grey seals (a few of which still bred there, though commercial seal hunters had all but exterminated them) had not two American privateers happened along in the nick of time. These were the *Lively* of Salem, under Captain Daniel Adams, and the *Scammel* of Boston, under Captain Noah Stoddard.

Stoddard was all for leaving the stranded English sailors where they were, but Adams sent his boat ashore with a flag of truce and made a deal with the *Blonde*'s crew, offering to take them off if they would first throw all their weapons into Brig Rock Pond. He proposed to land them at Yarmouth under a flag of cartel. From there they would eventually get a ship to Halifax. Some writers have given Stoddard credit for the rescue—a gross injustice. What really happened was that he sailed back to Salem and raised such a fuss that the local people greeted Adams as a traitor when he arrived, jeering him through the streets, and harassing his family so much that he finally took them to Halifax, sought British protection, and eventually entered the government service, though as a civilian not a combatant.

In Yarmouth the British naval brig *Observer* took about half the *Blonde*'s crew on board and was approaching Halifax when she was overtaken by the American privateer *Saucy Jack*. Thinking the small brig an easy prize, the *Saucy Jack* came alongside, grappled, and was promptly boarded by a huge force of naval ratings and marines. Down came her flag, and the *Observer* escorted her into Halifax as a prize.

In the late years of the eighteenth century the farms of the Annapolis Valley were thriving on trade with the military forts at Halifax, and by the time war broke out wealthy merchant houses at Windsor and Annapolis Royal were shipping out potatoes, apples, meat, fish, and lumber in their own vessels and bringing back bales of cloth, lamps, clocks, chandeliers, china, and silverware for the local trade. The war interrupted the equally lucrative traffic they had enjoyed with Boston, but the hungry maw of the military machine more than made up for the loss: they were enjoying a war boom.

The landowners in the valley were not struggling pioneers but a substantial yeomanry, with valuable possessions in money, jewellery, and silver plate. Some of them were judges, members of the Legislative Council or members of the Provincial Parliament. They supposed themselves safe from surprise attack. They were not, after all, living on the coast, and the coast, in any case, scarcely provided a landing place for raiders anywhere between the Annapolis Basin, which was strongly fortified, and the less strongly fortified Basin of Minas. In addition to the forts there was a supposedly well-organized militia, with muskets, uniforms, and colonels strategically placed and ready to summon them out at the first boom of a cannon. Most of the colonels were retired officers from the regular army, experienced in mustering and managing troops. There was one militia colonel at Wilmot and another at Annapolis Royal.

But none of this stopped Samuel Hall, perhaps the most notorious of all the American "pirates." He moored his sloop *Mary Jane* in an unoccupied cove on the Fundy shore opposite the Gaspereau Valley in the summer of 1778, led his raiders over North Mountain, hid them in the woods, and descended at night on the slumbering hamlets and isolated farms. Hall could not carry off barrels of apples or bales of cloth, for which he would need horses or ox carts. Instead he specialized in more portable goods and is credited with stealing a treasure's worth of jewellery and money from landowners' chests, silverware from their sideboards, and small, well-made items of porcelain. What's more, his raiders got safely back to their ship, which had been left in a dangerous position on an open coast with no safe anchorage. But they never made it out of the Bay of Fundy. A British frigate caught the *Mary Jane* a day or two after the raid.

Hall is one of the few privateers thought to have left behind buried treasure. His loot vanished, the British captain reporting that he'd found no strong-box in the cabin of the *Mary Jane*. Perhaps Hall had buried it ashore. That wouldn't have been difficult because he undoubtedly had the help of local sympathizers and guides. There were no shortage of those in Nova Scotia in 1778, many of them dispossessed Acadians who had returned to their homeland after being stripped of their property and banished in 1755. There have been a number of unsuccessful searches for Hall's treasure, even as recently as the mid-years of the twentieth century. But then Hall may not have left any treasure behind. Perhaps he recovered it. Or perhaps it vanished in other ways. Naval captains in the eighteenth century sometimes managed to convert treasure to their own use—

treasure that under the articles of war they should have turned over to the Crown for distribution. The idea of restoring it to its *owners* seems never to have been considered. Once you lost your property to a pirate or privateer it was regarded as salvage. The King was supposed to get half of it, the captain a quarter, and his officers and crew smaller shares according to their rank.

During the war other landing parties from rebel privateers attacked many small Nova Scotia towns. Barrington, Canso, Chester, and Yarmouth were all invaded briefly. Sometimes the local militia put up a stout defence, sometimes not.

At 3 A.M. on September 13, 1780, Simeon Perkins, a prominent merchant in Liverpool, Nova Scotia, was awakened by his neighbour Snow Parker with the shocking news that the rebels had landed in Liverpool Bay, captured the small fort at the mouth of the harbour, and taken the British pickets prisoner. Perkins hurried his son off to rouse the militia officers and alarm the town, then took his spyglass to the nearest hill just as dawn began to break. He saw two small schooners and concluded that the rebels were scarcely an overwhelming force. Perhaps they could be stopped by a show of resistance. Perkins and his son and three other men posted themselves on the road from Fort Point, where the privateers would have to pass on their way to sack the town. There was a brief exchange of gunfire, and the privateersmen fled, leaving their leader, Captain Benjamin Cole, a prisoner in Perkins's hands. Meanwhile the militia had mustered and was prepared to storm the fort.

Perkins was now able to bargain with Cole, who had no idea that he was the sole prisoner. *All* prisoners would be released, Perkins told him, if the privateers released the captured soldiers and left the harbour peacefully. Otherwise the whole landing party would be surrounded, taken prisoner, and shipped off to Halifax. The bluff worked. Cole's second-in-command agreed to the terms, released the soldiers, and reboarded the ships. The militiamen and the regulars kept their side of the bargain too and did not fire on the vessels as they sailed away.

The best-remembered raid of the war was a piece of unbelievable daring by American privateers, carried out with the help of a spy who knew the local conditions, the state of military preparedness, and the lay of the land. In the dark hours before dawn, August 28, 1781, a merchant named John Roach was awakened by men loudly arguing in front of his house on St. George Street near the centre of Annapolis Royal. He opened a window to find himself facing a musket and two men demanding admission to his house. When he came down to open the door his neighbour came rushing in with the news, "The damned rebels are in the town!"

In the dark of the night two privateer schooners, one armed with twelve carriage guns, the other with ten, had sneaked through Digby Gap (where a guard was supposed to be stationed to give the alarm on the approach of hostile ships) and upstream through the waters of Annapolis Basin and past the fort on Goat Island and the Scotch Fort on Granville shore. They had landed right in the town under the guns of Fort Anne.

The schooners had a guide with them, an Acadian who had been convicted of petty theft at Annapolis Royal two or three years earlier and had been branded on the right hand—a common sentence in those days. According to law, the red-hot iron was to be withdrawn after the victim had screamed out "God save the King" three times.* The man who guided the Americans up the basin and into the fort at Annapolis Royal was said to be seeking out the sheriff who had passed sentence, with the idea of killing him. Perhaps the reference is to John Ritchie, justice of the peace and judge of the Court of Common Pleas, who had been appointed in 1778 and who was taken prisoner by the American raiders. There was no sheriff at Annapolis Royal until 1782. In any case the Acadian guide led the Americans into Fort Anne without opposition. The fort seems to have been unoccupied that night, even by sentries. But in the darkness the Americans mistook their guide for a sentry and shot him dead. He was the only casualty of the whole affair.

---

*There were also many sentences of flogging at Annapolis Royal, all served upon Acadians, who formed the landless labouring class. They were also sometimes sentenced to serve as bond-servants to the merchants whose property they had stolen.

The militia rolls for 1776 show 103 men at Annapolis Royal, under the command of Colonel William Shaw, but none of them put up any show of resistance that night. All three forts seem to have been standing empty. One historian says three men from the regular army were assigned to guard Fort Anne, but if so they were drunk, asleep, or absent. Not a shot was fired, except for the one that killed the Acadian guide. The Americans had planned their raid carefully, had good advance intelligence, and carried it off almost without a hitch. One by one they roused the townsmen from sleep and paraded them at gunpoint into the "moat"—a dry ditch surrounding the fort—with an armed guard standing over them. Women and children were allowed to remain at home.

By daylight the privateers were rampaging freely through the town, looting the merchants' stores and any private house that looked worthy of their attention. They had spiked the guns in the forts* so that their two armed ships, with forty crewmen left on board, had undisputed command of the basin. Requisitioning carts and horses to carry booty down to the King's wharf, the raiders spent the day loading their vessels with everything movable, not only store merchandise and household valuables but even the contents of private pantries and wardrobes, leaving many of the people with nothing to eat and nothing except the clothes on their backs—probably little enough of that too since many of them had been turned out in the middle of the night. Women were allowed to keep the shoes they were wearing but had the silver buckles cut off and carried away as contraband of war. One woman lying ill (said to be Mrs. John Ritchie, wife of the justice of the peace) sent her black slave-woman to the wharf where the privateers were loading the loot to appeal to them for mercy. They sent the slave back with her apron full of sugar, tea, and biscuits.

---

*A soldier spiked a gun by driving a metal plug into its touch hole with a mall. The plug was then sawed off flush with the gun metal so it could not be withdrawn. The only way to restore the gun to service was to drill out the plug with hand tools.

Among the loot removed from the merchants' stores were puncheons of rum, which the privateers opened on the spot and consumed in great quantity. Fortunately the privateer captains had sufficient control of their men to keep the drunken party from degenerating into a riot. No man was beaten. No woman was raped. No house was burned. In the afternoon, on hearing a rumour that the militia was mustering in the valley, the privateers departed hastily, taking with them as prisoners Thomas Williams, the leading magistrate, and John Ritchie. Both were soon released on parole in exchange for American prisoners at Halifax. Ritchie was elected to the Provincial Parliament the following year.

This bold attack on what was supposed to be one of the most strongly fortified places in Nova Scotia should surely have convinced the British of the need to garrison the outports. But it didn't. Their sole interest seemed to centre on Halifax, where they organized invasions of all the rebellious states from Maine to the Carolinas. And so, when the Americans undertook a privateering raid against Lunenburg on July 1, 1782, they again landed almost unopposed. This new settlement, founded by German immigrants under a British plan of colonization in 1753, was situated specifically for defence on a narrow peninsula sixty miles west of Halifax by road (even then there was a road of sorts, passable by mounted riders if not by carriages) or forty miles by sea. The town was difficult to approach without a pilot, even from Lunenburg Bay, and it was almost impossible for ships to approach from Mahone Bay, on the other side, though small boats could come and go by this route.

In 1782 Lunenberg was defended on the east, toward the sea, by a blockhouse and on the west by two forts overlooking the town, with shore batteries that should have been able to defend it from any attack by sea. There were also picket lines for defending musketmen and barracks for troops. As at Annapolis Royal all these defences were empty when the Americans arrived at dawn, having landed just before daylight at Blue Rock Cove near Red Head, three miles east of the town.

Five privateer ships, manned by crews of 150, armed with forty-four cannon, and accompanied by a "rowing galley" (possibly a large landing craft), had put ninety men ashore at Red Head. Magdalena Schwartz, out to milk her cow, discovered them marching towards the town and ran to warn her husband, who ran in turn to alert the defenders. The Americans fired at him, but he escaped unhurt, and the noise of musket fire awakened the slumbering inhabitants. John Creighton, formerly a British army officer, was colonel of militia, his house close by the eastern blockhouse. Hastily summoning five neighbours with muskets, he took command of the blockhouse and began firing at the approaching raiders.

Meanwhile the ships had left their anchorage and sailed around East Head into the inner harbour, where they landed another party of men with four ships' guns. This party then rushed up the hill behind the town, took over the forts, spiked the twenty-four-pounder shore batteries that could have sunk their ships on approach, and rolled the guns off their mountings, downhill almost to sea level.

Other crewmen had hauled their ships' cannon up to the deserted forts and trained them on the town. They now controlled both Lunenburg and the approaches to it by sea. Colonel Creighton and the other defenders in the eastern blockhouse were outflanked and under the attackers' cannon. Their musket fire had wounded three or four of the invaders but to no purpose. They had no choice but to surrender. The Americans clapped Creighton into irons and placed him prisoner on board their flagship, the *Scammel*, commanded by Captain Noah Stoddard of Boston. Stoddard apparently planned and directed the whole operation, and like the raiders who sacked Annapolis Royal, he obviously had detailed information concerning the exact state of the town's defences.

The privateers now proceeded to sack the town, or as the Boston *Gazette* gleefully expressed it, they "fell to plundering with a natural and pleasing vivacity." Indeed there was an element of playfulness in their actions, but there was serious purpose too: they confiscated guns and ammunition wherever they found them. Barrels of gunpowder and tubs of cannon balls intended to supply the forts were removed to the ships' holds. They looted the stores of everything. They seemed to be especially fond of the scarlet uniforms supplied for the militia. Soon they formed a parade, some dressed in the scarlet uniforms, others in bows, laces, and plumed bonnets. The "vivacious" visitors tossed all kinds of merchandise about the streets and looted the shops of supplies of cakes, raisins, and figs, which they generously distributed to barefoot boys who gleefully followed them as though they were a gang of Pied Pipers.

The carnival atmosphere lasted most of the day, helped along once again by the vast supplies of rum discovered in the merchants' storehouses: no fewer than twenty puncheons—not mere casks, mind you, a puncheon was an oversized barrel made of oak, holding as much as a hundred imperial gallons, not of the watered stuff sold today but of proof spirit. The war had made good rum a scarce commodity in the rebel colonies, and this was the world's best, straight from the British Caribbean.

The privateersmen trussed up a local Protestant clergyman, the Reverend Johann Gottlob Schmeissar, who made a nuisance of himself trying to stop the looting, and left him lying in the street, but apart from that and the arrest of the militia leaders, they behaved rather well: nobody was shot, beaten, or raped. Even the black slaves, who surely might have been confiscated as valuable property, were allowed to go free.

Meanwhile people who had fled from town at the first alarm were trying to get help. Two men started for Halifax in a boat by way of Mahone Bay, but somebody else made it over the "road" on horseback ahead of them, and by noon naval ships had left Halifax for Lunenburg—four or five hours' brisk sailing if they had a fair wind.

A mere seven miles overland from Lunenberg to the southwest, at LaHave Ferry, Major Joseph Pernette, a militia officer, received word of the raid around noon from refugees who had escaped the town. He would have started his march by seven or eight o'clock in the morning had there been cannon fire from the town, but there was none. He signalled the local militia by firing off a cannon, collected twenty men, and started off, leaving word that others were to follow as soon as they were mustered. It took more than three hours to cover the seven miles through woods and marshes; he arrived at 4 P.M. and joined

Major Jessen, at the head of another small party of militiamen, on a hill behind the town. At this point the Americans sent a messenger to the gathering troops with word that they would put the whole town to the torch if the militiamen approached any nearer. To emphasize their threat, they set fire to the large house belonging to Colonel Creighton near the eastern block-house. It went up in flames, but the fire did not spread into the town.

Having taken everything of value, the Americans got the local merchants together and demanded a ransom. The Americans suspected that quite a lot of money might have been hidden in the first few minutes of the raid. So the three leading men of the town not under arrest signed a promissory note for £1,000 in favour of Captain Stoddard, payable at Halifax within thirty days. There seems to be no record that the note was ever redeemed, but it very well might have been because the war was virtually over. More than eight months before the raid on Lunenburg, General Charles Cornwallis had surrendered a British army of more than seven thousand men at Yorktown in Virginia, ending the fighting on land. Though Cornwallis had not been defeated in the field and had lost only a handful of men, he was starved into surrender, largely by the outstanding success of the American privateers, who had captured and confiscated numerous shiploads of supplies, including vast amounts of arms, powder, and shot, intended for the British forces. It is said that the only bayonets possessed by General George Washington's army were captured from British ships.

The other factor that brought the war in America to an end was the French navy and a strong expeditionary force of French troops. France sent no fewer than twenty-eight ships of the line to blockade Chesapeake Bay in 1781 and had eight more on the way when a British force of nineteen ships of the line attacked and was defeated. The French fleet involved in this battle was almost as large as the one assembled at Trafalgar twenty-four years later.

Even after the fighting on land had stopped, the war at sea continued. But the British fleet had departed from the American coast, and in 1782 the American privateers were having a glorious romp up and down the Atlantic seaboard, collecting all the loot they could lay hands on before the peace treaty put a stop to it. Meanwhile the British and French fleets were battling for control of the West Indies. The British, French, and Americans signed preliminary articles of peace on November 30, 1782, four months after the Lunenburg raid. Privateering against the Atlantic colonies ceased, though the worldwide naval struggle between Britain and France continued for another seven months, with the final shots fired in the Indian Ocean in June 1783.

The Americans had made such an enormous success of privateering during their War of Independence that it filled them with confidence and plunged them into the disastrous War of 1812. It had taught the Maritimers, and especially their merchants, a lesson they wouldn't forget. Soon, taking advantage of the wars of Napoleon, they would be reaping the rewards of legalized piracy along with the Spanish Main, while their relatives in New England chewed their nails and cursed the stagnation of their foreign trade.

Chapter 5
Godfrey and the Rover

LIVERPOOL, NOVA SCOTIA, is a quiet little town on the estuary of the Mersey River, eighty-seven miles by road southwest of Halifax. It lies at the inner end of a narrow bay that widens suddenly to seaward, with Coffin Island at its centre. The Mersey, which comes pouring out of the great inland lakes, widens into a snug harbour at the point where it meets the sea. There a wide pool, less than a square mile in area, forms what the French call a *barachois*, its entrance guarded by small islands and rocks. To the south of the *barachois* is Fort Point, with its docks and its historic marker, a reminder of the days when Liverpool fought Napoleon and his allies, the Dutch and the Spaniards, and then a few years later battled the greedy Americans, who tried to take Nova Scotia away from the King of England.

Founded in 1760 by emigrant New Englanders, Liverpool was at first just a fishing settlement, but the settlers soon discovered the huge pines and spruces of the inland plateau and began milling logs that floated down from the virgin forests on the waters of the Mersey River. The best of the white pine became ships' masts, not only for the local trade but for export to distant shipyards in New England and Europe. The rest was shipped as squared timbers or milled into lumber locally. Besides its safe harbour and access to the back country, the little settlement had another advantage. It lay half-way between Halifax, its main supply base, and Cape Sable, where ships turned the corner into the Bay of Fundy and the Gulf of Maine. It was well located for trade, peaceful or otherwise, with New England.

But none of this explains why in the closing years of the eighteenth century and the early years of the nineteenth, when warfare was an almost constant way of life and private warships sometimes tipped the scales in the balance of power between great nations, this little town became the privateering capital of

British North America, filled with ambitious young shipowners who made their fame and fortune "in the cannon's mouth." Liverpool's success as a privateering centre came largely from the breed of men who lived there, men who built up a tradition not only of seamanship, of long-range navigation and trading, but also of daring, of taking real risks with their lives and their money. Some of them lost, but others gained both great prestige and great wealth. An aristocracy of risk-takers, a club of men who gambled with life and wealth, met regularly around the tables of the counting houses in Liverpool, while their agents recruited venturesome sailors in waterfront taverns such as the Widow West's (later, the Widow Dexter's).

The earliest privateer from Liverpool of which we have a record was the *Lucy*. She served against the Americans in the War of Independence, with no particular distinction, but some of the people who owned and manned her became famous privateersmen, especially her principal owner, Simeon Perkins, and her captain, Joseph Freeman.

A contemporary of the *Lucy*, the *Resolution*, under Captain Thomas Ross, a Loyalist who had escaped to Canada, fought one of the bloodiest battles in the history of privateering. On July 10, 1780, the *Resolution* met the American privateer *Viper* off Sambro Light, Halifax. The two ships pounded each other with cannon fire for about an hour and a half, until both were badly damaged. In the end the *Resolution* surrendered, with eighteen men dead. But the *Viper* had fared even worse, with thirty-three killed. It was rare indeed that such carnage would occur between privateers: a loss of fifty-one lives in a single battle was virtually unheard of.

The armed merchant ship *Isabella*, attacked in the same war by the American privateer *General Sullivan* (fourteen guns and a crew of 135 men), fought the privateer for two hours "yardarm to yardarm" before the privateer pulled away "in a sinking condition." On her return to Liverpool the *Isabella* reported her losses: two men killed outright, one other who died of an amputated leg, three with disabling wounds (loss of hand, a shattered knee, etc.), and six or seven with slight wounds. The ship had

taken one hundred and thirty-two cannon shots in the hull and
rigging. The "sinking" *General Sullivan* actually limped into port
without her mainmast. She had lost eleven of her crew, a heavy
loss of life by privateering standards.

Simeon Perkins was justice of the peace for Liverpool, a colonel in the militia, and eventually a member of the Legislative
Assembly of Nova Scotia. He had made a fair bit of money out
of the American War of Independence, and when the Napoleonic Wars reached the Caribbean Sea, with Spanish ships fighting on Napoleon's side, he built a large ship especially designed
for privateering: the *Charles Mary Wentworth*. She was fitted with
sixteen cannon, making her nearly the equal of a sloop-of-war,
and carried a crew of sixty-seven men and four boys, under Captain Joseph Freeman, the man who had commanded the *Lucy*.

The *Charles Mary Wentworth*'s first prize was auctioned at
Halifax for £7,460. Her second brought £1,110. In two cruises
she took five ships for a total return of £19,000. Then on her
third cruise she drew a blank because of illness among her crew.
With such success behind him Perkins decided to go whole hog
and fit out his vessel like a fully commissioned warship. He
shipped eighty-two crewmen (eleven of whom were boys between the ages of twelve and fifteen), including a company of
ten marines under a sergeant and a master-at-arms. The crew
drilled constantly in gunnery and in hand-to-hand fighting. But it
all went for nothing. No valuable prizes fell to the *Charles Mary
Wentworth* on her fourth voyage. No hard battles were fought.
The cruise was a financial failure, and the cost of maintaining
the ship was so great that Perkins decided to lay her up, content
with his earlier winnings.

Just as she was laid up, another newly built ship took her
place. Perkins held a share in that one too, the *Rover*. Her captain
was Alex Godfrey, and her first mate was a young man later to
become the most famous privateersmen and the wealthiest shipowner in Nova Scotia, Enos Collins. She sailed to the Caribbean
and returned in less than a month with three valuable prizes,
one with her holds full of Madeira wine and another carrying
eleven hundred barrels of sperm oil. On his second voyage in

the *Rover* Godfrey showered himself with glory, turned a handsome profit, and won the lasting love of an erstwhile enemy. The voyage has become a Maritime legend, and many of the details are recorded in an account that Godfrey wrote on his return.

Failing to meet any worthwhile prizes on the high seas, the *Rover* headed for the coast of Venezuela and began harrying the Spanish coastal shipping. She had done so much damage on her first voyage and was now making such a nuisance of herself that the Spanish governor of Puerto Cabello decided to fit out a small squadron to capture her. He armed three gunboats and a large schooner and sent out a smaller coastal schooner as bait. The small schooner was instructed to lure the *Rover* close to harbour, where the armed ships could pounce on her. Godfrey sailed straight into the trap. He was quickly overtaking the trading schooner when the *Santa Rita* came out of Puerto Bello, armed with two twelve-pounders, ten six-pounders, a hundred sailors, and twenty-five marines. The wind was so light that sails were almost useless, and the *Santa Rita* was towed by two of the gunboats, each carrying a six-pound gun and thirty marines. The gunboats were rowed by black slaves chained to the benches and driven by whips. A third gunboat, identically armed, tried to manoeuvre to cut off the *Rover*'s escape to seaward.

The force arrayed against the little hundred-ton privateer was overwhelming, and Godfrey sent his nephew Henry to the powder magazine to blow up the ship if she should be captured by the Spaniards. "Fall into the hands of God, not into the hands of Spain," Sir Richard Grenville was reported to have said in a similar situation some two centuries earlier. In 1800 Spain still had a bad reputation for torturing and murdering prisoners. Against two hundred and fifteen fighting men, including one hundred and fifteen marines, Godfrey could muster only thirty-eight men and fourteen guns—all of them four-pounders. But he had one advantage. The *Rover* was light, and though the wind was of little help on that day, she could be swung about with the aid of long sweeps worked from the deck. Quickly swinging his vessel at right angles to the *Santa Rita*, he fired the seven guns on that side directly into her deck at point-blank range.

Then spinning through a quarter turn, he brought the seven guns on his other side to bear on the gunboats, hitting one with three guns and the other with four. Chaos broke out on the two slave galleys, and the third beat a hasty retreat. Godfrey then turned his attention back to the *Santa Rita*, his four-pound guns already reloaded and ready for action. He took time to notice that dead and wounded slaves from the two shattered galleys were being thrown into the sea by the marines.

The two schooners then began exchanging broadsides. According to Godfrey, the action lasted for "three glasses," a "glass" being a sand-timer that ran for half an hour. Then the wind came up, and the *Rover* began to make for the open sea. Suddenly, to everyone's surprise, they heard a loud crack from the *Santa Rita*, and her foretopmast fell in a heap of spars and ropes across her bow. She was temporarily out of control, and Godfrey decided to seize his opportunity. He put his headsails aback, swinging his stern close to the rail of the temporarily disabled ship, and led a boarding charge to the deck of the Spaniard. It was a bold move, but it paid off. Fifty-four men lay dead or dying on the *Santa Rita*'s deck. The only surviving officer was the young lieutenant of marines. Without leaders the sailors and marines alike fled below decks.

The ship's flag still flew at the masthead. She had not formally surrendered. But at this point a young lad came running from below, ran up the rigging, toes clutching ropes till he reached the truck and cut away the flag with his knife. It fell into the sea. Then he slid down the ropes to the deck and threw himself at Godfrey's feet, begging for his life. Godfrey prudently took the boy's knife, then reached down and stroked his head reassuringly. He was a compassionate man, with children of his own, and this waif who feared for his life touched his heart at once. He probably knew no Spanish, but he managed to reassure the boy. In any case he soon discovered that he had a small shadow: the young Spaniard attached himself to the victorious captain and refused to be regarded as a prisoner of war.

The *Rover* returned from her voyage to such a reception in Liverpool as few small ships of war have ever enjoyed. She had two prize ships, including the large *Santa Rita*, and hundreds of prisoners, who were sent to Halifax to be held for exchange when the opportunity came. Within a few months, they had all gone free. Simeon Perkins recorded the arrival of the *Rover*, accompanied by the *Santa Rita*, in his diary. Five days later her second prize, the *Nuestra Señora del Carmen*, sailed in with the prize master Lodowick Harrington and a crew of ten. They had nearly starved on the voyage and had put in to Cape Cod for supplies. At auction the two prize ships brought a total of £1,078. Alex Godfrey bought both ships and graduated from privateer captain to merchant-shipowner.

The young Spaniard who had surrendered the *Santa Rita* isn't mentioned in the documents, but he lives on in the oral tradition of the town of Liverpool, where it is said that he refused to be repatriated with the other prisoners and became instead a member of Godfrey's family. In time he too was a trader and shipowner. Indeed he may well have been one of the Liverpool privateersmen who served with such conspicuous success against the Americans a few years later.

The ships of Godfrey's time hadn't made much advance over the ships sailed by the Kirkes more than a century and a half before. Merchant ships were still large, beamy tubs, with as much hold space as possible. There had been some improvement in sail plan but not much. Warships had narrower, faster hulls and were no longer top-heavy with armour, a design flaw that had caused more than one of them to capsize and sink in harbour in the eighteenth century. But all ships were still built by shipwrights who had learned their trade and their designs from fathers and grandfathers. The day of innovative designing, the day of the clipper, was still a generation away.

Guns had improved in range and power, but when mounted on a ship were not very accurate, even within half a mile. They were much more effective when mounted on stone foundations ashore and that was why shore batteries were so dreaded, even by the most powerful warships. The warship was less a fighting machine than a means of transporting armed men from place to place. Captures depending on overtaking your victim until you lay within speaking distance, with the threat of grape-shot or boarding or both if she failed to surrender. Time after time the rigging of the two ships was actually entangled before the duel was decided. But all this was slowly changing. Even then the shipyards on Chesapeake Bay in Maryland were beginning to build something called the Baltimore clipper, not a clipper as we understand it, not a true greyhound of the sea, like the famous *Flying Cloud* or *Cutty Sark*, but moving in that direction. And by the time the next war loomed, this design had evolved far enough to make the small, fast privateer a more effective instrument of war than it had ever been before.

Chapter 6
The Black Joke

THE SINISTER-LOOKING LITTLE SHIP swung at her anchor in Halifax harbour. Built in the United States, bearing a name proudly worn by a long succession of pirate vessels, she had been caught running slaves from Africa, condemned under British piracy laws, and was up for sale. She had been used as a tender to larger slave-carriers rather than as a principal in the illegal trade. Even though slaves were practically stacked like cordwood, the *Black Joke* was too small to handle more than a few score of them at a time.

The only buyer who showed much interest in the ship was a young merchant from Liverpool who had recently opened an office in Halifax. Enos Collins, an impeccable gentleman in a beaver hat, with walking stick and gloves, was no mere small-town shopkeeper. Able and ambitious, he was an experienced seaman who had trodden decks in all weathers and served as first mate on the famous fighting ship *Charles Mary Wentworth*. Collins had returned to Liverpool with enough money to set himself up as a shipowner and trader. But in ten years his small fortune had only grown slowly. He was about to invest a major part of it in a gamble with two Liverpool partners, but like every successful gambler he was close-mouthed about what he was doing. If it paid off, he had every intention of founding an international trading company—perhaps even a dynasty.

The shrewd merchants who crowded the dock looking for bargains among the ships that had been condemned by the Vice-Admiralty Court and ordered to be sold to enrich the King's coffers must have wondered about Collins's interest in the *Black Joke*. She hardly met their standards for a money-maker. Never designed for bulk cargo, speed and manoeuvrability were her only advantages, and those didn't earn many pounds or dollars in 1811. The little ship was a mere fifty-three feet overall and an inch less than nineteen feet on the beam. There was little more than headroom in her hold—six and a half feet. She was registered at sixty-seven tons. Technically a Baltimore clipper, she was two-masted and schooner-rigged, but that did little to describe her. In addition to fore and aft sails on both masts, she carried square sails on her foremast, giving her some of the advantages of both schooner and square-rigger. The most freakish-looking thing was the angle at which her masts were stepped. If her pictures are to be credited, they were raked aft at twelve degrees or more, giving her the predatory look of a pirate vessel. She also had an exaggerated bowsprit that jutted far forward like the snout of a wolverine and carried three big headsails. Her sail plan and dimensions would make the *Black Joke* a poor performer in bad weather, but good for racing, tacking, and coming about, especially in light or moderate winds.

Collins must have had special plans for this ship. A yacht? But he was not yet in the class who indulged in fifty-three-foot pleasure boats. She would make a good gun-runner, but there was no current demand for such a trade. Perhaps he meant to sell her overseas. The other merchants lost interest in their speculations and let Collins have his way. He bought the *Black Joke* at the rooms of the Spread Eagle tavern for the sum of £440, not exactly a steal but a good bargain. He sailed her home to Liverpool on November 10, 1811, without telling anyone about his long-range hopes for the ship. All he would say was "I'll use her as a packet for fast runs up and down the coast." She could, indeed, carry a few passengers and mail, but you'd never get rich in *that* trade. Collins's secret plan was undoubtedly something quite different.

Speed and manoeuvrability, Collins knew, gave a small warship the advantage she needed to capture enemy merchant vessels and run away from enemy cruisers. At the moment there was no demand for private warships in North America, but that might change ovenight. Napoleon was still loose in Europe. The Americans were making threatening noises. It was true that Admiral Horatio Nelson had established British command of the seas, but it was not likely to go unchallenged for long. Meanwhile

Collins would use his speedy little ship as a courier. That way she'd earn her keep while waiting for her big chance. He renamed her the *Liverpool Packet* and applied for the mail contract. She carried her first packages on the initial run from Halifax to Liverpool.

On June 18, 1812, with disputes over maritime trade and impressment of American sailors for an excuse, the American Congress declared war on Great Britain. Britain was fully occupied in Europe, and Napoleon had been encouraging the hawks in Congress to seize what looked like a golden opportunity to push the American border north to the Arctic Ocean. Taking over the continent north of Mexico would be "a mere matter of marching."

It was a time when most Americans believed that the remaining British colonies in North America were itching to throw off the yoke of England as they had done, to join with them in the glorious dream of life, liberty, and the pursuit of dollars. Besides, they believed it was the manifest destiny of the United States to unite the whole continent under a single flag and a single economic system centred in New York.

The New England merchants did not share this dream. Trade, not territorial expansion, was their interest, and the war would play havoc with their trade. They not only opposed the war but continued secretly trading with the enemy. A strange and confusing situation! While their vessels sneaked up the coast as far as St. John, buying and selling goods that might well have been classed as war supplies, other vessels from the same ports sailed out, armed to the teeth, to capture the trading ships of New Brunswick and Nova Scotia.

The war had been going on for nine days before news of it reached Halifax. Then HMS *Belvidera*, a sixty-four-gun cruiser, arrived with the dead, and wounded, and prizes of war. She had been attacked by three American warships but had escaped and captured three American trading vessels.

Collins and his partners decided at once to convert the *Liverpool Packet* to a privateer. But there was a long delay while they waited for a letter of marque. The governor of Nova Scotia considered such a matter beyond his authority and sent the request off to Great Britain. The British waffled, confident in their sea power. Why share prizes of war with private corporations? When they finally issued the letter of marque, they failed to specify American ships as prizes and made Collins and company put up a bond of £1,500 against disputed seizures. Meanwhile the *Liverpool Packet* was commissioned to sail to Boston under a flag of truce carrying civilian prisoners taken from an American ship by the navy. Such prisoner exchanges continued to be frequent throughout the war.

When she returned to Halifax, she was outfitted as a privateer with "five rusty cannons that had been serving as gate posts on the waterfront." Rust or no rust, they were heavy armament. One was a twelve-pounder and the others six-pounders,* big stuff for a ship of her size. Four-pound carriage guns would have been normal armament for a tiny sloop-of-war like the *Black Joke*, but the twelve-pound shot, with its ability to smash through decks and hulls and bring down masts and rigging, served her well over the next three years. By the time Collins had added muskets and pikes, grappling irons for boarding, leg irons and handcuffs for prisoners, she was one of the deadliest little craft afloat.

The War of 1812 was the final flowering of privateering. Privateers had been vital to the American War of Independence, when the fledgling nation had issued letters of marque to no fewer than 515 ships and had captured 1,345 ships flying the British flag, most of them from the colonies of Newfoundland, Nova Scotia, and the West Indies. The Americans confidently expected to repeat their success in this new war. "If it floats, arm it!" cried the hawks in Congress as they issued letters of marque even to whaleboats and single-masted shallops, which could mount nothing larger than a single small swivel gun without danger of sinking themselves.

---

*Cannon were still classed by the weight of their shot. Heavy guns caused so much recoil that small ships could not mount and fire them without the danger of loosening seams and springing planks.

In Nova Scotia it wasn't quite so easy. The British were reluctant to allow colonial governors to wage war. They demanded high bonds of indemnity from privateering corporations. The naval commanders were opposed to privateering altogether. If an auxiliary fleet were needed, they felt the ships should be commandeered and commissioned under the direct orders of the naval commanders. This, however, would have cost a great deal, and in the end wealthy shipowners were allowed to wage war for private gain.

Commissioned as privateers, Collins and company next had to strengthen the decks of their ships to withstand cannon fire and fit bulwarks with ports for the guns. Below decks they had to build steel-clad and, with luck, fireproof powder magazines and shot lockers. Then there had to be quarters for crews ten times the normal size. Extra men were needed not just to man the guns or to board ships that put up a fight, but as prize crews to sail captured ships into port. The glittering prospect of a share in prize money made it easy to get volunteers to fight the War of 1812. Doctors, lawyers, and clerks abandoned their offices. In Newfoundland the outlaws known as Masterless Men flocked to the ports and enlisted. Even a few clergymen left their pulpits to seek their fortunes on the Great Deep. There was no age limit. Any boy big enough to tote a bucket was welcome as a "powder monkey" and might expect half a man's share of the spoils. Better by far than going to school or serving as apprentice to a brickmaker.

Collins and his *Black Joke*, tangled in red tape, were slow off the mark. Not so the Yankees. By the end of July 1812 an estimated 150 American privateers were scouring the Atlantic coast. Perhaps the most famous of them was the *Yankee*, a Rhode Islander that made six raids northward into Canada and eastward into the Atlantic, capturing forty prizes reputed to be worth $5,000,000.

The great braggart Thomas Boyle of Baltimore was also active in the early months of the war. Many of his exploits were certainly imaginary, but it is equally certain that he made a great nuisance of himself. He commanded a fast clipper that was able to snatch prizes from armed convoys, even in Britain's home waters.

It was up to Collins and his partners to redress the balance. They fitted out a whole fleet of privateers, but the little *Black Joke* was the deadliest of the lot. Bristling with arms and crewed by seasoned men, she finally left Liverpool on August 30, 1812, and headed for Cape Cod. She was not the first Canadian privateer at sea. The *General Smyth*, sailing out of St. John, had taken her first prize on August 13, and in cruises lasting ten weeks captured prizes worth £7,119.*

The little *Black Joke* enjoyed certain advantages in addition to her speed and manoeuvrability. Her rig and her deep keeling allowed her to sail closer to the wind than most of her rivals. She was painted black and with sails lowered was inconspicuous against the dark New England shore. Most of her sails could be handled from the deck and hoisted quickly the moment a victim appeared. She took her first two prizes September 7, 1812: the 325-ton *Middlesex*, bound for Boston with a mixed cargo, and the *Factor*, with a load of Port wine destined for Providence, Rhode Island. Next she liberated the *Maria* from Gibraltar, which had been captured by an American privateer; then, in five days, made prizes of five American schooners and sent them to Halifax for auction.

It wasn't just the ship, of course. The man who commanded the *Black Joke* during the first year of the War of 1812 deserves to be as well known to Canadians as John Paul Jones is to Americans. Captain Joseph Barss was a dashing young man in fashionably long hair and sideburns, lean and dark, with the look of an Elizabethan and the character of a Drake or Hawkins. His record as commander of a single fighting ship was rarely equalled, even by the great pirates of the eighteenth century. In October 1812 Barss took eleven vessels in one week off Cape Cod; then, in a single day, made prizes of nine fishing schooners with cargo valued at $50,000. All this was reported with indignation in the Boston and Salem newspapers. Where, they demanded, was the navy of the Republic? Why was it unable to deal with this one small ship? Barss, still hovering off Massachusetts Bay, found

---

*Reckoning inflation at twenty to one, this would be well over $500,000 in today's funds.

himself with such an embarrassment of riches that he began releasing all but the most important prize ships (after confiscating any portable valuables) and saving his crews to man the larger ones. Only five of his biggest victims reached the Vice-Admiralty Court in Halifax that month.

He then sailed home for a refit and more crew members, but was back off Cape Cod by December 10, where, according to the *Boston Messenger*, he captured eight or nine vessels, valued at from $70,000 to $90,000, within twenty days of the time he left Liverpool. The Boston editors fumed. This mere scrap of a warship was running a virtual blockade on the doorstep of America's largest port. They demanded that a fleet be sent out to capture her. They urged immediate work on a canal to bypass Cape Cod—a work actually completed a hundred years later.

Barss and his crew spent a triumphant Christmas with Collins and his partners in Liverpool. Twenty-one ships that they had captured were moored in the Mersey River within sight of the town. After all claims were settled and the Crown deducted its share, the prize money came to over $100,000 (equivalent to about $2,000,000 today)—not bad for three and a half months' work.

In February and March of 1813 Barss sent thirty-three prize ships to Liverpool. But the luck of this great sea rover was running out. On June 11, with most of her men sailing for home in captured ships and only thirty-three hands on board, the *Black Joke* chased a large American schooner, which turned out to be a privateer far more heavily armed and far more strongly manned than she. As the American turned to give battle, the *Black Joke* ran for her life. Barss moved his best gun, the twelve-pounder, to the stern and threw all the others overboard to lighten the ship. But in the stiff wind the bigger ship had the advantage and slowly gained. Barss fired off every twelve-pound shot in his locker without stopping his pursuer. At last, with nothing left to fire and the American still overtaking him, he hauled down his colours. In spite of the fact that the *Black Joke* had already surrendered, the Americans swarmed on board with muskets blazing and killed four of the crewmen before the two captains could stop the fray. They were the only men lost in the battle.

It was a great day for Portsmouth, New Hampshire, when the schooner *Thomas* brought the terror of the seas into harbour, a little wasp of a ship that had captured more than a hundred American vessels and sent some fifty of them to auction. Chivalry on both sides was typical of the naval war of 1812. British and Americans went out of their way to rescue enemy sailors and treated them decently. Prisoner exchanges went on all the time. But Barss and his crew had humiliated too many New England seamen. A mob lined the streets to jeer at the prisoners as they were paraded in irons through Portsmouth. Officials acted no better. They locked Barss into fetters and fed him on hardtack and water. When they finally released him in a prisoner exchange, after months in jail, they forced him to sign an affidavit undertaking not to engage again in privateering against American shipping. It was an undertaking he would have to respect, even though made under duress. Should he be captured again in a fight with an American ship, he would probably be hanged as a pirate. And so Barss shipped instead as master of a trading schooner to the West Indies. By a strange coincidence the ship he commanded was the same one that had taken him prisoner. The *Thomas* had been captured by *HMS Nymph*, condemned, and sold at auction.

Barss took no further part in the war, but his famous little ship was back at sea in fighting trim even before his release. She now flew the Stars and Stripes under yet another name: *Young Teaser's Ghost*. This strange nomenclature arose from the fate of the American privateer *Young Teaser*, herself a successor to the *Teaser*, a small privateer that sailed out of New York in the first months of the war, armed with only two guns and a crew of fifty. When a British cruiser captured her, after five months of privateering, they didn't consider her worth salvaging and burnt her at sea.

The *Teaser*'s crew were sent home in a prisoner exchange, her officers on parole. This was a system in which the paroled officer signed a bond not to take part in privateering for a specified period, a year perhaps or the duration of the war. Officers were supposed to be men of honour, whose parole could be trusted. If they turned out not to be they might be "hanged like dogs."

Among those paroled from the *Teaser* was her captain, Frederick Johnson, who, in violation of his parole, volunteered to sail on the *Teaser*'s successor, *Young Teaser*, a more powerful ship owned by the same privateering firm. This rather remarkable craft was 124 tons, built of oak, sheathed in copper, and painted black, with an alligator figurehead. She was armed with two long guns, one of them on a swivel as a bow-chaser, and three caronades. And she carried a crew of sixty-five. Johnson did not sail as her captain but as lieutenant, or first officer.

The *Young Teaser* made only one voyage. She took two small prizes almost in the mouth of Halifax Harbour on June 9, 1811, and this daring deed was her undoing. She was chased by the *Sir John Sherbrooke*, a powerful Liverpool privateer, and by two small naval vessels, but she escaped from all of them. Then, on June 26, she was cornered by two British warships in Mahone Bay, a short distance southwest of Halifax. First on her tail was the *Orpheus*, a naval frigate which spent the day cruising back and forth to seaward, preventing the privateer's escape from the island-studded waters. In the afternoon the *Orpheus* was joined by *La Hogue*, a seventy-four-gun battleship. The *Young Teaser* kept dodging back and forth among the islands, where the larger ships could not follow her, hoping to escape after dark. But darkness comes late to northern waters at the end of June, and there was still plenty of daylight at 7:30 P.M., when *La Hogue*'s captain dropped anchor and sent off five armed boats, each mounting one gun and loaded with armed men, to attack the privateer. The *Young Teaser* lay becalmed. The attack was timed so that darkness would fall just before the boats reached the privateer—some time after 9 P.M.—making them difficult targets for the *Young Teaser*'s guns. If she decided to fight, her crew would have to man the bulwarks to try to repel boarders, who would be there in overwhelming numbers.

The captain of the *Young Teaser* was still trying to make up his mind whether to haul down his flag when First Officer Johnson went dashing down the companionway to the ship's powder magazine, carrying a "coal of fire." A moment later the deck of the *Young Teaser* blew skyward in a tremendous explosion.

Johnson had escaped hanging by blowing himself and the ship and all but eight of his shipmates to eternity. The carnage was dreadful. Floating corpses and parts of corpses drifted ashore for the next two days. The hulk burned right down to the waterline. Captain William Dobson, standing right at the after rail when the ship blew to pieces under his feet, was one of the survivors. What's more, he wasn't taken prisoner. Somehow he got ashore and made his way back to New York, where he received command of the third *Teaser*, the formidable *Black Joke*.

She made just one voyage under her new name and new flag, failing to take a single prize. Her owners, perhaps disgusted by three successive failures, offered her for sale, and she went back to sea under yet another captain and yet another name, the *Portsmouth Packet*. She still had no luck. Sailing north into the Bay of Fundy, she was promptly cornered by a British warship and forced to surrender. In two voyages under the Stars and Stripes, she had not captured even one ship. Back to the auction block went the old *Black Joke*, her third time in two years, and who should buy her but Enos Collins!

For captain he found a likely young man, a New Brunswicker named Caleb Seely, who had made a reputation sailing out of St. John in the tiny privateer *Star*. Though Seely never equalled the record run up by Barss, he did very well indeed, capturing at least fourteen ships in eleven months. And he may have done much better than this, for some of the records from 1814 have been lost. After a brief and brilliant career in two privateers Seely retired from the sea, became a shipowner, and founded yet another merchant house at Liverpool.

Another Liverpool seaman, Lewis Knaut, now took command of the *Black Joke* and sailed off on one more privateering voyage in October 1814. By this time the blockade of the American coast was so tight that few prizes remained to be captured. American shipping had been practically driven off the seas. In her last two months as a merchant raider the *Black Joke* took only four ships.

Her final score is uncertain. Incomplete records of the Vice-Admiralty Court confirm that sixty-eight of her prizes went to auction. But there were many others. A great storm at Liverpool wrecked some of the ships waiting there to be taken to Halifax. Because she carried such limited manpower, she burned, sank, or released many of her smaller victims. One hundred and thirty might be a reasonable estimate. All told, she was the most successful merchant raider of the War of 1812 and a vital factor in the blockade that strangled the American economy and preserved the independence of the colonies that would unite, fifty years later, to form the nation of Canada.

Collins? Well, he not only founded a great merchant house but also the Halifax Banking Company in 1825. At the time of his death he was reputed to be the wealthiest man in British North America.

Chapter 7
Winners and Losers in the War of 1812

THE *CROWN*, OUT OF HALIFAX, was the smallest of the Canadian privateers. A forty-foot schooner, called by fishermen a jack-boat, she carried a crew of thirty young desperadoes, most of them under the age of sixteen. It's a nice question how thirty people managed to fit themselves into a forty-foot boat, even if many of them were not full grown. The answer seems to be that they slept on deck under sail canvas, an expedient that must have been common on bigger privateers as well. In addition to muskets and cutlasses, this band of apprentice pirates had a nine-pound cannon that must have shaken their ship from topmast to keel whenever they dared to fire it. With almost unbelievable bravado, this tiny privateer sailed out to do battle with the damn Yankees. And sure enough, back she came with a fat prize: the Boston brigantine *Sibae*, which fetched the magnificent sum of £5,062.

Off she went again, looking for more victims, and reportedly sent in several of them before an American privateer with six guns and a crew of eighty men caught up with her. The *Crown* put up a spirited running fight before she finally surrendered. The Americans admired their young enemies, treated them gallantly, and at the first opportunity sent them back to Halifax in a prisoner exchange.

Many other notable privateers sailed out of Liverpool, Halifax, and St. John's during the War of 1812. The most imposing was the *Sir John Sherbrooke*, named for the governor of Nova Scotia. Largest and best-armed of the Collins fleet, the 278-ton *Sherbrooke* was built especially for privateering and was heavily armed with eighteen guns and a crew of 150 under captain and part-owner Joseph Freeman.

Designed to survive an encounter with any American privateer then afloat, this privately owned warship might have been a dangerous opponent even for a naval sloop or frigate. She brought in nineteen prizes in three months for a profit of approximately $50,000. But in spite of her winnings she proved too expensive to maintain as a privateer and on later voyages began losing money. The Collins corporation then decided to convert her into a merchant ship for the West Indian trade. With a reduced crew and somewhat reduced armament she sailed to Jamaica and the Windward Islands, but luck was still against her. An American cruiser cornered, captured, and burnt her in 1814.

Joseph Freeman had a younger brother, Thomas, who served as a prize master on the *Black Joke* (along with the other Freemans, Benjamin, Samuel, and Seth.) After sailing many a captured ship into Liverpool, Thomas Freeman had made enough money to enter the ranks of owners and masters, so he bought a share in a ship of the Collins fleet, the seventy-foot topsail schooner *Retaliation*.

This small ship carried five guns, including a twelve-pound long gun, mounted forward on a pivot so that it could be aimed in any direction except due aft. The long gun (classified like other cannon by the weight of its shot) was the most effective weapon of its time because of its greater range and accuracy. Its one drawback was that it burned a tremendous amount of powder every time it was fired. The caronade, the class of gun usually carried by privateers, could fire shot just as heavy as the long gun but had neither the reach nor the accuracy of its big sister. It was, however, much more economical and very effective in the point-blank battles of the time, when ships lay almost rail to rail blasting away at each other.

Thomas Freeman's *Retaliation* was a gold mine. On his first voyage the young captain took four large prizes, so that the corporation cleared approximately $30,000 on an investment of $2,600. Freeman took his winnings and retired from the wars, but his successor, twenty-five-year-old Benjamin Ellenwood, captured nine more American ships valued at over $50,000. Ellenwood then graduated to a larger privateer, the *Shannon*, also owned by a Liverpool corporation, and sent nineteen more ships to the Privateers' Dock at Halifax. By the age of twenty-six Ellenwood was wealthy and passed the command of the *Shannon* to his prize master, John Brown, who captured three more prizes with her before graduating to the *Rover*. Ellenwood did not live to enjoy his plunder, however. Eight months after retiring from the *Shannon*, he was murdered on Dolby's Wharf in Halifax.

The *Rover* of Liverpool was a captured American privateer, renamed in honour of the ship commanded by Alex Godfrey in his famous battle with the Spaniards. On his first cruise Brown captured thirteen ships in three days, then passed her on to Captain Thomas McLaren of Liverpool, who captured five more before the war ended in 1815.

Though Liverpool was the home port of most of the famous Canadian privateers in this war and Halifax the commercial centre of the trade, other ports in what are now the Atlantic provinces took part. In Annapolis Royal a corporation of local merchants, William Bailey, John Burkett, Thomas Ritchie, and John Robinson, put up the money to commission and arm the fifty-ton schooner *Matilda*. John Burkett Jr. sailed as her captain, with a crew drawn from Annapolis, Granville, and Digby. She sent home thirteen prizes in three months before being captured by the Americans, who later sent her under flag of truce to Halifax with prisoners for exchange.

While still in commission as a privateer she was joined by the *Brooke*, purchased at auction by Phineas Lovett, another merchant of Annapolis Royal, with Daniel Wade as captain.* She was somewhat undermanned for a privateer, with a crew of thirty-five, but covered herself with glory, snatching prizes from even the very mouths of American shore batteries: seventeen of them in the summer of 1813, when Wade retired and was succeeded by Captain William Smith of Halifax.

---

*The ship appears as the *Broke* in most histories, and the captain's name is misspelled "Waid". The spellings given here are those appearing in the application for letters of marque.

Early in the war a number of privateers sailed out of Saint John, New Brunswick, with letters of marque from the governor of that colony. But as the war progressed, New Brunswick developed such an important illicit trade with the New England states that they virtually declared a separate peace, and the governor refused to issue any more privateering commissions to New Brunswick merchants. Some of them managed to get around this, however, by going to Halifax and securing commissions from the governor of Nova Scotia. Their ships then sailed as Halifax privateers, but the money went home to St. John. New Brunswick also took the unusual step of commissioning her own warships, specifically described as privateer-chasers. Their mission: to keep American privateers away from the north shore of the Bay of Fundy.

They didn't succeed too well. This coast, a crenellated shoreline of islands, bays, and river estuaries, became the favourite prowling ground for a fleet of nasty little boats oddly named "shaving mills." Some of these were surely the smallest warships ever awarded letters of marque. They were often mere whaleboats, propelled by oars, with a dozen armed men out to see what they could seize in the way of legalized loot. For armament they would have, at most, a single swivel gun mounted in the bow, with a barrel of powder and a tub of shot to keep it ready for action. Their speciality consisted of raiding isolated farms and hamlets, and the list of their pathetic plunder has an almost comic ring: sheepskins, kitchenware, men's trousers, women's sewing baskets, children's shoes.

Unfortunately, it was not all comedy. One of these piratical jack-boats, the *Wily Renard*, descended on an isolated farm at Sheep Island, New Brunswick, in December 1812, killed a poor settler named Francis Clements, and raped his wife. Captured a few days later, the crew was sent in irons to Halifax, but they were neither prosecuted nor punished for their crimes. They were treated as prisoners of war and released in a prisoner exchange some time later. It was a sad breach of justice, even though the war at sea was generally conducted according to international rules and the "honour of gentlemen."

American privateersmen were as active in this war as they had been in the American War of Independence, and only gradually did the Canadian privateers gain the upper hand. The most far-famed American captain was Thomas Boyle of Baltimore, whose first command, in 1812, was the Baltimore clipper *Comet*, built for the slave trade at a time when every slaver was, by British law, a pirate and fair prey for the Royal Navy. The *Comet*, cross-beamed to allow her to mount heavy armament on deck, carried fourteen guns and a crew of 120. Boyle's success early in the war in capturing ships bigger and better-armed than his own was partly the result of his daring and seamanship, but also because most of his prizes were manned by small peace-time crews of no more than two dozen men and boys, unprepared for warfare and outnumbered as much as five to one.

Many of Boyle's claims to stunning victories against great odds are dismissed by historians as bragging fictions, but enough of them *are* documented to make him one of the leading seamen of his time. On his second voyage he ran into a convoy of two large British merchantmen escorted by a Portuguese man-of-war, heading for Pernambuco, Brazil. Boyle managed to talk the man-of-war out of taking an active part in the battle because the United States was not at war with Portugal. But the Portuguese waffled. Though the warship did not fire on Boyle's privateer, she did fire on his boats when he tried to send out boarding parties. In a night-long cannonade Boyle reduced both merchant ships to mere wrecks and managed to board one of them, but decided she was too badly damaged to be worth capture. In the end he allowed both of them to limp off, still escorted by the warship.

Boyle told this story, with embellishments, to the newspapers and became such a national hero that he was given command of the pride of the Baltimore fleet, the brig *Chasseur*, with sixteen twelve-pound guns and a crew of one hundred men. With this ship he captured many valuable prizes, some of them snatched from convoys under the very noses of the Royal Navy. Convoys were often widely scattered, and their escorts were armed sloops or frigates. Boyle's clipper-built ship, while no match for one of those warships in a gun duel, could outsail most of them. And when not actually in action he could sail under false colours, an accepted stratagem of the time, hoisting the American flag only at the last moment and sometimes gaining the additional advantage of surprise.

In the early months of 1813 Boyle managed to interfere seriously with the supply of the forts at Halifax, while remaining well out of range of its deadly shore batteries. He also plagued shipping bound into the Bay of Fundy, then crossed the Atlantic and plucked prizes right from the English Channel. Not content with this twisting of the Lion's tail, he decided to declare a blockade of the British Isles and sent his proclamation to London in a cartel, as it was called—a ship sailing under flag of truce with prisoners for exchange. The document was directed to Lloyds of London, to be posted, though there is no record that they ever did so. It was couched in the following terms:

Whereas it has become customary with the Admirals of Great Britain, commanding small forces on the coast of the United States, particularly with Sir John Borlaise Warren and Sir Alexander Cochrane, to declare all the coast of the said United States in a state of strict and rigorous blockade, without possessing the power to justify such a declaration, or stationing an adequate force to maintain said blockade,

I do, therefore, by virtue of the power and authority in me vested (possessing sufficient force), declare all the ports, harbours, bays, creeks, rivers, inlets, outlets, islands and sea coast of the United Kingdom of Great Britain and Ireland in a state of strict and rigorous blockade.

And I do hereby require the respective officers, whether captains, commanders, or commanding officers, under my command employed, or to be employed, on the coasts of England, Ireland and Scotland, to pay strict attention to the execution of this my proclamation.

And I do hereby caution and forbid the ships and vessels of all and every nation, in amity and peace with the United States, from entering or attempting to enter, or from coming or attempting to come out of any of the said ports, harbours, bays, creeks, rivers, inlets, outlets, islands or sea coast, under any pretence whatsoever.

And that no person may plead ignorance of this, my proclamation, I have ordered the same to be made public in England.

Given under my hand on board the *Chasseur*, day and date as above.

Thomas Boyle

Boyle got away with this and subsequent exploits right through the three years of the war. After he returned to the western Atlantic, the Royal Navy sent the frigate *Barrosa* in pursuit of him. She got within sight of the *Chasseur* on several occasions, and once the chase was close enough to force Boyle to throw ten of his sixteen caronades over the side to lighten his ship, but he managed to escape.

Boyle's greatest glory was a battle with an armed schooner that he chased and caught near Havana, February 26, 1815. At 1:26 P.M., within pistol shot of the enemy, the *Chasseur* received a broadside of round, grape, and musket balls. Boyle opened fire, and according to his own account of the battle, "At this time both fires were heavy, severe, and destructive." It was then that Boyle discovered that the schooner was far from the weakly manned vessel he had imagined: "I now found that I had a powerful enemy to contend with, and at 1:40 P.M. gave the order for boarding, which my brave officers and men cheerfully obeyed with unexampled quickness; I instantly put the helm to starboard to lay them on board, and when in the act of boarding she surrendered."

Boyle's prize proved to be His Majesty's schooner *St. Lawrence*, commanded by Lieutenant J.C. Gordon and formerly the famous privateer *Atlas* of Philadelphia. By Boyle's account "a perfect wreck," she reported six men killed and seventeen wounded, several of them mortally. The *Chasseur* suffered five men killed and eight wounded, including Boyle.

But the killing and blood-letting were for nothing. The War of 1812 had been ended by the Treaty of Ghent two months and two days before Boyle's most famous sea duel. Like the Battle of New Orleans, also famous in American song and story and also fought after the war was over, the fighting was all a mistake, caused by the incredible slowness of communications.

American history still credits the United States with winning the War of 1812. Even Canadian historians sometimes describe it as fought to a draw, so a few facts are in order. The Americans did not achieve a single one of the objectives they had set out when the war began. Even the "freedom of commerce and of sailors," which was the excuse for starting the war, was not mentioned in the peace treaty. The repeated invasions of Canada by American armies had all failed. Every American army had been driven back across the border, and American territory was occupied by British troops in various places. The northern half of the State of Maine was occupied by troops from Nova Scotia. But above all, Canadian privateers had won the war at sea. They had outcaptured the Americans by four to one. They had virtually put an end to American maritime commerce, both domestic and international. American exports dropped from $45,000,000 the year before the war to $7,000,000 the year it ended. A few American victories in individual naval duels did much for national glory but nothing for the economy, which, by the end of 1814, was in a state of dire depression, while the economies of Nova Scotia, New Brunswick, and Newfoundland were all bursting with war prosperity.

The War of 1812 was Canada's war of independence, when native Canadians, led by small groups of British regulars, fought off the one major attempt to take their country by force of arms. And without detracting from the victories of the tiny armies along the St. Lawrence and the Great Lakes, it must be said that the privateers, mainly those sailing out of Nova Scotia, were the principal line of defence that prevented Upper and Lower

Canada, New Brunswick, and Nova Scotia from becoming American territories and eventually American states.

Newfoundland had taken a smaller part in the war of the privateers than had Nova Scotia or even New Brunswick. Only two vessels are recorded as sailing on privateering voyages out of St. John's. Nevertheless, at the war's end there were thirty American prize ships moored in the harbour there, and some five hundred American prisoners housed in the military barracks ashore. Newfoundland's trade with New England had always been one of her most important overseas efforts, and as soon as news of the peace treaty was received, the governor began issuing licences for trade with the American states. Eleven of the seventeen licences issued that summer went to former American ships.

Privateering in the War of 1812 was the last great burst of a business that had enriched maritime merchants for centuries. The Americans, who had embraced privateering with such success during the wars against France and in their War of Independence, had learned their lesson and were eager enough to sign international protocols by which privateering was to be outlawed. Naval officers had always despised privateersmen, and by mid-century the professionals had their way. A few privateers fought on both sides in the American Civil War, but their effect was not very great. No letters of marque were issued by Britain in the Crimean War, and it was in 1856, at the end of that conflict, that the first international agreement to outlaw privateering was signed, a ban that has stood the test of time. For though ships that had been privately owned fought in both world wars and one square-rigged sailing yacht became a highly effective merchant raider in the First World War, all such vessels were commissioned as regular elements of the belligerent navies, manned by naval officers and men. The days when wars were fought by private enterprise were over.

Part II
Rogues' Gallery

Chapter 8
A Man Called Smith

LIAR, CHEAT, CON MAN, THIEF—Henry More Smith was the most unusual rogue ever to decorate a reward poster in the Maritime provinces. The name was just one of many aliases: Henry Hopkins, William Newman, Henry Moon, Henry More, to mention a few. He had some attractive qualities and could give the impression of being more imp than scoundrel. Nevertheless, he was an unscrupulous criminal who abandoned his young wife without a thought and victimized friends and strangers alike. Though robbery was his calling, Smith seldom rose above petty theft. He owed his notoriety to bizarre behaviour while in jail and to his uncanny ability to escape. Of all Canadian outlaws he is perhaps the most difficult to categorize: madman, gifted hypnotist, or criminal Houdini? He was perhaps all of these things at once. Some of his contemporaries were sure he had entered into a pact with the devil.

Smith appeared at Windsor, Nova Scotia, in July 1812. About twenty years old, "genteel in appearance," claiming to be from Brighton, England, Frederick Henry More (as he called himself) was vague about his past, saying only that he was a tailor but would be glad to get any kind of work. John Bond, a Loyalist who lived at Rawdon, between Windsor and Truro, hired the young man to help on his farm. A pious Baptist, Bond was pleased to find that his new hand was a hard worker and a tee-totaller. In his off hours he shunned the company of other farm-hands, preferring to share prayer time and mealtime with the Bond family. Soon he was leading morning and evening prayers whenever Mr. Bond was away and had won the heart of Bond's daughter, Elizabeth. But her father refused to consent to the match. Charming as young "Frederick" was, Bond considered him below his daughter's station: a man without land, property, or family did not seem a suitable husband for the daughter of an important landowner. But love-struck Elizabeth ignored her father. She eloped with the hired man to Windsor and married him there on March 12, 1813.

Smith then began working as a tailor and pedlar. He did well, making frequent trips to Halifax for materials and supplies; his pack was always well-stocked with watches, silverware, and small household items. No one connected him with the sudden rash of burglaries in Halifax, though he did have a curious travel schedule. He would leave home in the morning, take most of the day getting to Halifax, and be back in Windsor next day. This left little time for legitimate transactions in the city but neatly put him there between dusk and dawn.

If Smith was fast on his feet as a pedlar, he was greased lightning as a tailor, turning out quality garments in record time after he received an order. He soon had a reputation for skill and speed; no one dreamed that he was stealing bolts of cloth from the merchants and fine clothing from the best homes in Halifax. Had it not been for a blunder and a bit of bad luck he might have carried on this scam indefinitely.

In one of his Halifax raids Smith stole three volumes of the Acts of Parliament from the office of Chief Justice Strange. It's hard to say why since it would be almost impossible to sell such books. But when the judge offered an attractive reward of three guineas for their return, "no questions asked," Smith was foolish enough to take the offer, explaining that he had bought the books from a stranger. The chief justice was suspicious, however.

A short time later a young Windsor man was accosted on the street in Halifax by a gentleman. "That's my coat!" the gentleman exclaimed. "It was stolen from my house!" The gentleman called the police and had the young man arrested, but the young man insisted he had bought the coat from his tailor, Frederick Henry More, in Windsor. The man's story checked out, and the judge issued a warrant for More's arrest, but by that time More knew he was under suspicion. He packed as many goods as he could carry and fled Windsor on horseback (whose horse we do not know), leaving behind his young wife and baby. It's unlikely that Elizabeth ever saw her husband again.

In July 1814, now calling himself Henry More Smith, the outlaw arrived in St. John, New Brunswick. Because of the War of 1812 the city was garrisoned, and like many other con men Smith regarded soldiers as easy marks, eager to part with their pay. He made friends among the officers of the 99th Regiment, especially Coloniel Daniel, who owned a carriage drawn by the regiment's finest pair of horses, one of them black. A matched pair would make an even finer show, Smith suggested to the colonel, and by chance he knew of a splendid black horse in nearby Cumberland County. If Daniel would advance him fifteen pounds, he would take a ship to Cumberland, buy the animal, and ride it back to St. John, leaving his own horse for security. It seemed reasonable, and Daniel agreed.

Smith's real plan was to steal a saddle and another horse—a mare pastured near St. John—ride to Nova Scotia, sell the mare, then return to Cumberland, steal the black horse, complete his business with Colonel Daniel, and then slip over the border to the United States. He succeeded in stealing a saddle and bridle from another army friend, Major King, but failed to catch the mare, though he spent a whole night chasing her. He then made his way to a farm some thirty miles away, stole a fine bay, and headed for Nova Scotia. By now he had gone two days without sleep, so he holed up in a barn, leaving the bay tethered outside. He didn't wake until the next day, when the owner of the farm, William Fairweather, saw him leaving his barn. This in itself wasn't suspicious. Travellers often slept in barns, not bothering to wake the owners if the household had already retired, but in this case the traveller hurried off without bothering to pay his respects to the farmer, and on a horse that looked identical to one owned by Fairweather's neighbour, Mr. Knox. Fairweather got in touch with Knox.

Three days later, after a chase of a hundred and seventy milès, Knox caught up with Smith at Pictou, where Deputy Sheriff John Parsons arrested the horse thief on July 24, 1814. Parsons and Knox took him back to New Brunswick, making several stops along the way to restore things Smith had stolen during his flight. They reached the jail in Kingston, New Brunswick, on August 12, and Smith was locked up in the debtor room by Sheriff Walter Bates, a Loyalist from Connecticut who had helped to found Kingston and was now high sheriff of King's County. Later Smith was moved to the unheated criminal room, but without handcuffs or fetters "as he appeared quite peaceable." Next day Bates received a letter from Ward Chipman, clerk of the Circuit Court, recommending a hearing before county magistrates. Smith was examined by Judges Prickett and Ketchum, with Knox, the owner of the stolen horse, attending. He described himself as a penniless, friendless immigrant from England, "the victim of ill circumstance." He'd been hoping to bring his aged parents from England so they could make a home on a little piece of ground he had bought. When asked how he made his living he replied, "By my honesty, sir."

He told the court of the deal he had made with Colonel Daniel but gave the story a new twist. He had missed the boat to Cumberland, he said, so set off on foot, walking all night. On the road he met a stranger with two horses and bought one of the animals, hoping to use it in exchange for the one he planned to buy for the colonel. He produced a receipt with a signature: James Churnan. Shortly after meeting the stranger, Smith said, he was arrested for stealing Knox's horse. He claimed that Knox had kicked him and struck him with a pistol. Despite Smith's sad tale, the magistrates committed him for trial. He made no protest, but once back in his cell he began complaining of pain in his side, caused by the beating from Knox and aggravated by the chill he had received in a rainstorm. He was innocent, he told his jailers, but could only prove it if the scoundrel who sold him the stolen horse was caught.

Next day Sheriff Bates and a companion stopped at Nathaniel Golden's tavern in nearby Hampton. As they were stabling their horses, a man bolted from the tavern, leaped into a saddle, and galloped off toward St. John. Asked about the man, Mrs. Golden said he was a stranger who had visited the tavern two or three times. She believed his name was Churnan. Churnan! The name on the bill of sale! Bates rode off in pursuit but failed to overtake the rider or learn anything about his escape route.

Was there a James Churnan, a partner in Smith's crimes? If so, no trace was ever found of him. Could the escape have been a prank? A dangerous one, you'd think. In any case, "Churnan" vanished completely and was never heard from again.

News of Smith's plight had spread quickly through the region, and there was much sympathy for the young Englishman languishing in jail. This public support became evident when Bates allowed Smith to sell off the contents of his portmanteau to pay his legal fees. People crowded forward to buy "various articles of valuable clothing, two or three genteel coats, with vests and pantaloons of the first quality and cut, a superior top coat of the latest fashion, faced with black silk . . . silk stockings and gloves . . . Bible and prayer book . . . a spy glass of the best kind, and a small magnifying glass in a tortoise shell case. . . ." The public swallowed Smith's story. He had been "handsomely and respectably fitted out by affectionate parents anxious for his comfort and happiness." With money from the sale Smith retained Charles J. Peters of St. John to conduct his defence and paid him an advance of five guineas. But meanwhile he went to work on his own ticket to freedom.

Walter Dibble, a schoolteacher who lived in the courthouse, supplemented his income by acting as jailer, but because he was often confined to his room by ill health, his duties were shared by his nineteen-year-old son, John. Smith went to work on the two Dibbles as well as on Sheriff Bates. The Dibbles noted that the prisoner took a great interest in his Bible, often reading passages aloud. While reading he would cough and sometimes groan. He showed Bates a large swollen bruise on his side, the result, he said, of the beating Knox had given him. He said he was in great pain and was afraid of internal injuries that might prove fatal. Bates responded by "keeping his apartment properly tempered with heat and providing him with such food as was adapted to the delicacy of his constitution." But Smith grew worse. He coughed up and evacuated blood, lost his appetite, complained of chills, headaches, and dizziness. Bates called in a doctor, who prescribed medicine, but Smith continued to grow worse, until by September 15 he was unable to walk and was running a high fever. He could not keep down any food. His life seemed to be in danger.

Among Smith's visitors was the Reverend Elias Scovil. Smith talked much of his approaching death and wept when he spoke of his aging parents in far-off England. On September 23 Bates found Smith lying naked on the floor of his cell, unconscious, and had him carried to his bed and revived with hartshorn, a kind of smelling salts. Members of his family were subject to fits, Smith feebly told his attendants. He probably would not survive the next one.

With a dying horse thief on his hands Bates wrote to Smith's lawyer in St. John, advising him of the situation, and called the doctor again. After examining Smith a second time, the doctor gave his opinion that the patient wouldn't survive another night. The dying man willed his clothing to young John Dibble and his money, a total of £3, to Walter Dibble. The death watch then began, with leading citizens sitting beside Smith's bed in relays. No one, doctor, lawyer, clergyman, or sheriff, had any doubt that he was breathing his last. Mrs. Scovil, the minister's wife, sent her servant Amy to the jail with a comfortable feather mattress for Smith to die on, but when Amy arrived, the place was in chaos.

John Dibble had looked into Smith's cell to see the prisoner feebly writhing in pain. Smith's dying request was for a hot brick to put to his feet. The young man left the cell unlocked and ran to the kitchen to put a brick into the stove. When he returned, Smith was gone. John hurried to tell his father, who was sitting with Rev. Scovil in a room Smith must have passed on his way out. They were frantically searching the building when Amy arrived with the mattress.

"Take it back, Amy, Smith is gone," Rev. Scovil snapped.

Amy hurried to her mistress with the news. "Massa say Smith dead and gone, ma'am."

"Poor man!" Mrs. Scovil sighed, and gave Amy a shirt and winding sheet to lay out the corpse. Only when she returned to the jail did she learn that Smith had escaped. Escaped! Where?

"I don't know, Amy," Scovil replied. "The devil must have taken him."

So well had Smith played the role of dying man that a Mr. Lyon, whom he passed on the road out of Kingston, literally believed he was seeing a ghost. He reported Smith's apparition "scudding past me as fast as quicksilver . . . his feet not touching the ground."

When Bates heard of Smith's departure he too assumed he was dead and enquired at what time the poor fellow had passed away. When he learned the incredible news of Smith's escape, he organized parties to search the roads in all directions, but the searchers found nothing. Next day they learned that a man of Smith's description had taken a ferry across Belleisle Bay, an extension of the St. John River running northeastward from the main channel.

Bates issued posters offering a twenty pound reward for Smith's capture, but soon found that he and Dibble were both under suspicion in the horse thief's escape. The sheriff and the jailer were both Freemasons, at a time when this organization was regarded with some suspicion by outsiders. Smith too was a Freemason, the rumours said, and his fellow masons had connived at his escape. When court convened on the day Smith was supposed to be tried, Bates and Dibble were both indicted for negligence.

After escaping, Smith had outwitted his pursuers. Instead of putting King's County behind him with all possible speed, he went ten miles and spent the night in a haystack on the farm of Robert Bailes. Bailes saw him the following morning but thought nothing of it until the afternoon, when he discovered his house had been looted of eight dollars, a silver watch, a pair of velvet pantaloons, and a pocket-book. He and some neighbours went after the thief and distributed handbills with his description, but they found no trace of Smith, who turned up next day at a farm owned by a man named Green, saying he was on his way to Fredericton to close a land deal and asking for a night's lodging. Green became suspicious when he saw his guest burning some papers and a pocket-book and thought he might be an American spy. Next day he took him to Justice Colwell, but Smith, ever the fast talker, convinced the judge of his innocence and was allowed to go. He then hired an Indian guide to take him to Fredericton. They stopped at a tavern near Gagetown. Sitting in the same room, busily writing handbills, was Robert Bailes. The farmer didn't recognize the scoundrel who had slept in his hay and looted his house, so Smith and his guide enjoyed a leisurely meal. Before leaving, he stole a set of silver teaspoons. Then, at another tavern, he tried to sell the spoons and stole a good pair of boots. He capped the day's activities by stealing another horse from the unfortunate Mr. Knox.

Outraged and afraid that Smith intended to murder him, Knox loudly demanded the culprit's immediate capture. So a general warrant for the arrest of Henry More Smith was issued to every sheriff and magistrate in New Brunswick. The reward was raised to $80. All roads were watched. Knox himself led a fruitless expedition to Nova Scotia in search of the outlaw.

After ten days Bates concluded that Smith had fled to the United States. Actually he was still in New Brunswick, now calling himself Bond, and posing as a constable in pursuit of the notorious Smith. When a clergyman thought he recognized Constable Bond's silver watch as the one formerly belonging to Robert Bailes, Smith played the innocent successfully and spoke with such charm that the cleric let him go his way.

Sheriff Bates had no word of Smith's doings until a tavern owner near Woodstock complained that one of his guests had stolen a suit worth $40, a silk cloak, and several small valuable articles. A few miles from the tavern the same man stayed overnight with a farmer named Robertson, entertained the children by playing the fiddle, and traded Mrs. Robertson some silver spoons for a shirt. This put the posse back on his trail. He was traced to an Indian camp on the St. John River, where he had hired a guide to take him across the American border. After two days the guide had deserted and returned to camp, perhaps doubtful about Smith's intention to pay him and unnerved by the pistol tucked into Smith's belt. Without a guide Smith was forced to use the roads. On October 10 a Dr. Rice recognized him and got some other men to help make the arrest. They collared Smith, and two men, named Putman and Watson, took him to Fredericton to Judge Saunders. There he admitted that he was Smith, the fugitive from the Kingston jail. When asked how he had managed the escape he replied, "The gaoler opened the door, and the priest prayed me out."

Sanders ordered the fugitive put into irons and taken to Kingston. Putnam and Watson had him pinioned, handcuffed, and tied to the centre bar of a canoe. With their prisoner secured and certain to drown if he upset the boat, they started downriver for Kingston. Two days later they reached the farm of Robert Bailes. Delighted to see the villain in irons, Bailes invited Putnam and Watson to spend the night; he would take them to Kingston in the morning. After his guards had gone to bed, Smith asked Bailes to let him go to the privy. Unwilling to trust Smith outside the house, Bailes woke Watson. He too was suspicious, but Smith volunteered a solution. He couldn't run away, he said, if Watson had a rope on him. Watson agreed, tied one end of a rope to Smith's arm, and wound the other around his hand. They were barely outside the house when Smith smashed him over the head with his handcuffs, slipped off the rope, and vanished into the darkness. By the time Watson came to and got back to the house, Smith was long gone.

Next day they shamefacedly reported the escape to Sheriff Bates. Bates didn't blame them. He paid them for their trouble and rode out to Bailes's farm to renew the search. The Oromocto River runs north into the St. John between Gagetown and Fredericton. Bates reasoned that Smith would take this route toward the American border and concentrated all his forces in that direction. Meanwhile Smith had headed north and two weeks later was up to his old tricks near Fredericton. On the night of October 26 he broke into a farmer's shed, where he stole firewood and helped himself to a meal of baked potatoes. Next morning he stole a coat and a large bundle of linens. The loot was awkward to carry, so he stole a pony, saddle, and bridle. Two miles from Fredericton he found an isolated hayshed on a farm owned by Jack Paterson. It looked like a good hideout so he moved in.

For a few days he lived comfortably in the shed, sleeping by day while the pony grazed, riding into Fredericton after dark to steal whatever he could lay his hands on. By dawn he would be back in the shed, stashing his plunder under piles of hay. He was now a widely advertised fugitive, in no position to sell stolen goods. Perhaps he was laying in enough swag to set himself up as a pedlar in the United States. If he could get upriver as far as Woodstock, he'd be only a jump from the border. One of Smith's principal victims was none other than the attorney general of New Brunswick. While that gentleman hosted a dinner party in his mansion three miles from Fredericton, Smith slipped into the front hall and cleared the clothes racks of cloaks and topcoats.

Using the same hideout for too long was Smith's undoing. Walking past his hayshed one morning Jack Paterson noticed that some hay had been spilled out of the door, went inside, and found a sleeping stranger. The stranger woke up, said he'd been on the road late, and hoped Paterson didn't mind his sleeping in the shed. Paterson said he didn't mind at all, but as he walked away he looked back and saw Smith heading for the woods at a dead run. Assuming he must be a thief or an army deserter, Paterson went for help and set off in pursuit. Before the day was over, Smith was back in jail. Paterson then searched his shed and found the saddle, bridle, coats, cloaks, silverware, and other stolen goods hidden under the hay.

This time Smith's escort, which included Paterson, took no chances. Before putting Smith on board a sloop bound for Kingston, the sheriff prepared an iron collar, made with a flat bar of iron, an inch and a half wide, with a hinge and clasp, fastened with a padlock. To the collar, which was put around Smith's neck, was fastened ten feet of iron chain, which Paterson kept a firm grip on for the entire sixty-mile voyage. A strong pair of handcuffs locked Smith's hands in place. The ship docked at Kingston about midnight, October 30, a little more than a month after Smith's escape. His transfer to the prison was delayed till morning, and a large crowd gathered to see him taken to the cells. In Kingston Smith was a great celebrity.

After his earlier escape a search of the cell had turned up broken pieces of a watch and a dinner knife with its blade sawn in two. To ensure that he was not carrying such implements this time,

Bates made the prisoner strip to his "shirt"—a long undergarment that the prevailing code of decency forbade the sheriff to touch. Finding nothing in his clothing, the jailers locked Smith in his old cell. As described by Bates, this cell was "twenty-two feet by sixteen, stone and lime walls three feet thick on three sides, the fourth wall being the partition between the prison rooms." The parition was of timber, twelve inches thick, lathed and plastered. The cell door was two-inch plank, doubled and lined with sheet iron, with three iron bar hinges three inches wide, clasped over staples in the opposite posts and secured with three strong padlocks, with a small iron wicket door secured by a padlock. There was one window through a stone wall, grates without and within, enclosed with glass on the outside. A passage outside the cell led to another locked door and finally to a third. The keys to all locks were kept by Dibble, the gaoler. In addition to all this Smith was kept chained, one end fastened to his leg, the other to the floor. The chain allowed him to reach the wicket and the "necessary"—a hole in the floor—but was too short for him to reach the window. Because his hands were badly swollen when he reached prison, Bates removed the handcuffs. After all, escape seemed completely impossible.

Bates inspected the irons frequently and found everything in order. For twelve days Smith seemed to behave himself. Then, on November 11, a man living near the prison told the sheriff that he and his wife had heard scraping and filing noises in the night. Accompanied by Dibble and several other men, Bates made a careful inspection. Sure enough, one of the bars of the inner grate had been cut through. It could be taken out and replaced so no one would see the cuts. A bar of the outer grate was sawn two-thirds through, the cut hidden by a small, carefully inserted chip of iron. A few more nights' work, and Smith would have been gone.

Bates demanded to know how Smith had done the work; the prisoner obligingly produced a case knife and a small file—relics, he said, of his earlier incarceration. He had cut his chain where the cut would not be noticed, then gone to work on the window. Bates checked to see if the improvised escape tools fitted the cuts in the bars. They didn't. He made a more careful search of the cell and turned up a small saw hidden between stone blocks of the wall. Smith refused to say where he had gotten that tool. A further search of the prisoner's clothes and bedding turned up no more tools, but to be sure Bates fastened a new chain to the prisoner and put him back into handcuffs. He left the cell at 11 P.M. on a Saturday night, satisfied that all was secure. The next night he was awakened again by a message from Dibble: Smith, free of his fetters, had been caught sawing away at the bars of the window. On the way back to his bunk, he had dropped something into the privy.

"Smith, you keep at work yet," Bates said as he entered the cell, astonished to find the prisoner sitting on his bed, free of handcuffs and chains. A search of the cell, including the privy, turned up nothing. They examined his outer clothing again, took the bed apart, replaced the chains and handcuffs, and left, quite baffled. The next day the exasperated sheriff called the doctor and had the prisoner stripped naked in his presence. Sure enough, Smith's "shirt" concealed a ten-inch steel saw blade. Bates assumed that this was the last item in Smith's tool kit, but to make doubly sure, he had the window bricked in, leaving only a four-by-five-inch opening at one corner.

Now began the most bizarre chapter in Smith's story. Till now he had been docile, if somewhat slippery; he soon turned surly and vicious. Perhaps he was faking insanity to escape the gallows—after all, horse thieves were sometimes hanged in those days. But perhaps he really was losing his grip, chained in darkness as he was. Sane or not, he performed feats that almost defy explanation. On November 16 Bates found Smith's cell practically wrecked. He had broken a padlock and used the chains to smash the plaster off the walls. He threatened to burn the prison down. Bates had received a letter from the court in St. John, informing him that the trial might have to be delayed. Witnesses had to be brought from Nova Scotia, and the onset of winter might make this difficult. Meanwhile, the court ordered, the sheriff must use "any severity" necessary to make sure the prisoner did not escape. Taking the judge at his word,

Bates loaded Smith down with forty-six pounds of steel fetters and iron chains, confining legs and arms so that he could move only a few feet and could not even reach his mouth except while sitting on the floor.

For the next month Smith bellowed, howled, and screamed day and night, stopping only when his voice failed. He mixed senseless ravings, threats of bloody violence, and quotations from the Bible with prayers for his wife and friends and his aged parents. Bates, listening, jotted some of it down to present to the court. When the weather turned bitterly cold in December, Bates provided the prisoner with straw and blankets, but the blankets were soon removed when Smith used one of them to try to hang himself, or at least to make it look as if he did. Next he refused to eat, but the hunger strike lasted only four days.

For a while the prisoner fell silent again, and Bates became suspicious. On December 16 he carried out a careful inspection and found that the staple fastening the chain to the floor had been worked loose. It could be drawn out by hand. Also, Smith had contrived to break the iron collar. New fetters were devised, and Smith resumed his ranting. He never spoke coherently now, and the weather became so cold that Bates feared he would freeze to death. He had the chains loosened to allow him more freedom of movement, but strangely enough Smith never seemed to be cold, despite the unheated cell. Bates was amazed to find that even the chains seemed to be warm, as though heated by some supernatural agency. With his limited freedom of movement Smith went on another cell-wrecking spree, and Bates had all the shackles replaced by February 10.

A few days later two men arrived from Nova Scotia with a message from Smith's wife, the abandoned Elizabeth. She wanted to know if she could come to Kingston or if she should sell a colt she owned and send Henry the money. He refused to speak to the messengers. He was, Bates reported, "a lifeless statue, which convinced us that he would go to the gallows without speaking a word." But he spent the night shrieking and howling, disturbing everyone within earshot. He broke chain links and iron collars as fast as Bates could have them replaced. His extraordinary feats filled everyone with wonder. He twisted the iron collar as if it were a piece of leather, and broke it into two parts, which, as Bates pointed out, "no man of common strength could have done with one end of the bar fastened in a smith's vise."

How all this happened was never explained. More hidden tools? Someone helping him? Could Bates have been exaggerating? After all, he *was* still charged with negligence, and a prisoner who (with the help of the Devil) handled steel like putty might have put him in a more favourable light. Still, there were other witnesses, and one of the broken collars was kept for a long time to show to visitors.

On March 5 Smith was allowed his first bath in four months. He ate part of the soap. On March 11 William Dibble resigned his post and left Kingston. He was replaced by James Reid, and Smith at first cooperated with the new jailer. Then on March 24 Reid found his prisoner working away at a stove-pipe hole in the partition, trying to break into the debtor's room. Reid sent a frantic call to Bates, who came running with six or seven men. When they crowded into the cell, they were astounded to find the prisoner free of his chains and doing a bit of shadow fencing with a wooden sword. Short lengths of chain and pieces of handcuffs hung on nails like so many trophies. Smith had torn his coat to shreds. His hands, feet, and face were covered with blood. The sheriff's men fitted new chains, but nothing seemed to hold him. Horse traces, buck chains (used for hauling logs), an ox chain—he broke them all. There was never any mark of cutting on the severed links—or so it was said.

But in spite of all his wizardry Smith did not manage to get out of prison. On May 4, after a night of howling and smashing chains, he went to trial before Judge John Saunders. Sheriff Bates and the attorney general of New Brunswick were present. Before a packed courtroom he continued the display of madness. He took off his shoes and socks, tore his shirt, snapped his fingers, clapped his hands, and said nothing when asked to plead to the charge of horse theft. The judge warned him that faking madness would do him no good, but after some deliberation the jury agreed that the prisoner "stood mute by the visitation of God," and the court adjourned for the day. Next day the prisoner was so violent that he had to be bound hand and foot in the dock. The defence lawyer argued that Smith was a victim of circumstances. The jury did not agree. They found Smith guilty, and the judge sentenced him to be hanged.

He then went back to prison, to steel fetters (which he continued to break) and to a diet of bread and water. At this point, using straw from his bedding and bits of his clothing, he began a new phase of his prison career, constructing puppets and scratching the forms of men and women on the walls of his cell. The puppets were incredibly lifelike, fashionably dressed in costumes devised from his own clothing. By the time he had his puppet "family" completed, he was almost naked. He then incorporated the puppets and etchings into a show that he performed between bouts of screaming. The puppets included a lady and gentleman, a steward, a drummer, and a harlequin clown called Bonaparte. Bates eventually gave him a fiddle so he could play jigs while he made the puppets dance with his feet, and allowed the public to attend Smith's performances.

Bates wrote to the attorney general, describing the performances as "better worth the attention of the public than all the waxwork ever exhibited in this province" and their creator as a man "possessing the art of invention beyond common capacity." The letter was published in New Brunswick's *Royal Gazette* and stirred up great public interest. Bates went to Fredericton in July to attend a Supreme Court hearing. There he learned that the attorney general had decided to drop the charges of negligence against Dibble and himself and had recommended that the death sentence against Smith be commuted. Bates returned to find that Smith had been breaking fetters again, had smashed the glass in his tiny window, and was complaining of dreams in which he was tormented by snakes and toads. But he was making a tidy income charging admission to his puppet show, which by now had become famous. He used his gate receipts to buy materials for more puppets and by August had increased his company to twenty-four.

With the shadow of the gallows removed, Smith became quieter and more talkative. He now told Bates that his real name was Henry Moon, that he was from a good family, and had been educated at Cambridge. He claimed to be fluent in five languages. He had escaped hanging but still faced an indeterminate prison sentence. Perhaps hoping further to impress Bates and to earn a few extra shillings, he now turned his talents to fortune telling, amazing the sheriff, the jailer, and several visitors by recounting incidents from their personal lives that he presumably had no way of knowing.

In August news of a pardon became official. It would be granted upon his appearing in court to enter a plea. Bates offered him a box for his puppets and a new suit of clothes for his court appearance. But when a tailor came to take his measurements, Smith snorted that the man had hands like a blacksmith and insisted on making his own clothes, which he did. He really was a tailor after all. On August 26 he appeared in court, with one of his puppets in hand. There the pardon was granted, but he was told to leave New Brunswick at once or other charges would be brought against him. Through all this Smith continued to act like a maniac. He danced around the courtroom, spoke gibberish, told one judge he looked like a tailor, and asked him for a shoelace. Exasperated, Bates took him back to his cell. That evening he entertained the magistrates with a puppet show, but continued to talk so wildly that they gave it as their opinion that he was a raving lunatic and advised Bates to hurry him out of the province as quickly as possible.

Next morning Bates found a fire smouldering among the straw in Smith's cell. Later that day he set off with his prisoner for St. John and on August 30 saw him on board a sloop bound for Nova Scotia. When the ship docked at Windsor, Smith didn't even bother to take his puppets ashore. They had served their purpose. He didn't bother to visit his wife either. He immediately resumed his life of crime, leaving a trail of thefts that Bates, who had decided to write a book about him, was easily able to follow.

Travelling through Nova Scotia and New England, Smith committed robberies of exactly the same pattern as before. He stole watches, silverware, jewellery, and expensive clothing. On one occasion a stage coach driver stopped his team when a passenger cried out that he had been robbed. The passenger demanded the coach stay where it was while he ran for a magistrate or constable to conduct a search. Shortly after he disappeared, a second passenger discovered that he too had been robbed. As it turned out, the first "victim" was Henry More Smith.

After looting an inn in Connecticut, Smith was lodged in a sturdy New Haven jail, where he again won local sympathy with his tales of woe. He again played the sick man and the puppet master. Before he could be brought to trial, he had escaped. He was recaptured near New York and taken back to New Haven. Handcuffed and chained, he was placed in a cell with two black youths who were also charged with theft. One morning the jailer looked through the wicket door to see Smith (or Newman, as he now called himself) walking about smoking a pipe, with the chains and cuffs draped over his shoulder. "You may take these," he said, handing the irons through the bars. "They're of no use to me." The jailer couldn't open the door. Smith had barricaded it. The sheriff came and ordered him to open up. "My house is my castle," Smith said. "None shall enter alive without my leave."

Furious, the sheriff ordered Smith's two cell mates to open the door. The terrified boys refused. Smith had threatened to kill them if they went near the door. Eventually the sheriff sent for a mason to cut a hole through the wall, and at that point Smith opened the door. He was found guilty of theft and sentenced to three years in the Simsbury Mines, the notorious labour camp that had been a dumping ground for Tories during the War of Independence.

Walter Bates visited Smith twice at Simsbury Mines, but Smith denied knowing him or ever having been in Kingston, New Brunswick. He was French, he said, and had travelled widely in Europe, Canada, and the United States. He had been unjustly imprisoned. When Bates sent him a copy of his book, *The Mysterious Stranger, or, Memoirs of Henry More Smith*, he called it a piece of pure fiction and said there was no such person. Shortly after this he suffered a "convulsion" and was excused from hard labour. For the rest of his term he made rings, Jew's harps, and penknives.

On his release Smith travelled through Massachusetts, Connecticut, and New York, living by thievery. He changed his name and appearance frequently, much to the frustration of Bates, who was still trying to keep track of him for later editions of his book. Eventually he surfaced in Wellington Square, Upper Canada (now Burlington). Augustus Bates, brother of the sheriff, was postmaster there, and Smith called at his home, explaining that Walter Bates was his good friend and leaving a letter for Augustus, who was away at the time. When the letter was eventually opened, no one could read it. It was written in what Bates called "the characters of some foreign language."

Meanwhile Smith was calling on the local merchants, saying he was a businessman from New Brunswick who had succeeded in smuggling thirteen wagon loads of goods over the border from New York. He offered quality merchandise at bargain prices and asked for cash in advance. Surprisingly, many of them fell for the scam and handed over the cash. Smith might have milked the community dry had he not been recognized by a former resident of Kingston. But he successfully escaped with his loot, crossed Lake Erie, and travelled south along the Ohio River, posing as an itinerant preacher, the Reverend Henry Hopkins. At church meetings and revivalist camps Rev. Hopkins attracted large followings and did very well indeed with the collections. But lucrative as the preaching business was, Smith was not content with it. He continued to steal whenever he had the opportunity. His congregations were shocked when, accused of theft, their popular preacher fled in a stolen buggy drawn by stolen horses. He was caught in Maryland and sentenced to seven year in the state prison at Baltimore.

Bates learned of Smith's imprisonment during a visit to New York in 1827. Six years later, in New York again, he could find no trace of the famous criminal and concluded that he had either escaped or died in jail. But the following year he learned that Smith had robbed a New York hotel guest of $200. In February 1835 he was jailed for holding up a mail coach but escaped to

Upper Canada, where, in August of that year, he was sentenced to hang for burglary. The sentence was commuted to one year of hard labour. Smith started to serve his year in the Toronto jail—and at that point he vanished. There is no record of his release, of his death, or of his escape.

Smith is one of those rare figures who flits across the pages of history with no traceable connections. No one knows his true name, where he came from, or where he went. Omar Khayyám concluded one of his quatrains with the line "I came like Water, and like Wind I go." Of no one was it ever more true than of the man who sometimes called himself Henry More Smith.

Chapter 9
The Shiners of Bytown

BYTOWN, UPPER CANADA, was a rough, raw community in the 1830s, wild even by the standards of the North American frontier. No one would have guessed then that the rugged little settlement where the Rideau River joined the Ottawa would one day be the capital of a great country. Even then it was the social and financial centre of the Ottawa Valley, but the Ottawa Valley was the backwoods of a developing colony, and its reputation for violence was unmatched by the most notorious towns of America's Wild West. Gangs of thugs haunted the bars and roamed the streets, savagely assaulting anyone they disliked. They beat and sometimes maimed their victims, even murdered them in broad daylight. They mutilated animals, put buildings to the torch, and pushed society (what there was of it) to the brink of anarchy. Workers and gentlemen alike travelled in groups or carried arms for protection. Women and children feared to go abroad without male escorts. There was little in the way of sanctuary for those who incurred the hoodlums' wrath.

The men responsible for this reign of terror were called the Shiners, under a leader named Peter Aylen, a rags-to-riches timber tycoon who styled himself the Shiner King. Like the gangster czars of a later age, Aylen was ruthless and ambitious, with a lust for power and wealth matched only by his flamboyant, swaggering contempt for law and order. This ruffian didn't look the part: he was charming, handsome, tough as nails, and got what he wanted regardless of the means. An Irish Protestant born about 1799, Aylen arrived in Canada in 1815 as an ordinary seaman, jumped ship at Quebec, fled into the wilderness, and soon found employment in the Ottawa Valley timber industry, where a game young man with a strong back and a quick mind could soon make his fortune. He walked into the logging country at exactly the right time.

Until the wars of Napoleon Canada had supplied a paltry 2 percent of Britain's timber imports, most of it from the St. John River and the lower St. Lawrence. High transportation costs had made the pine forests of the Ottawa, among the world's richest, too remote for development, so Britain, whose own great forests were just a memory, imported much of her lumber from the Baltic states. Two events changed all that. In 1806 Philemon Wright, an enterprising Yankee expatriate, successfully floated a raft of logs down the Ottawa to the St. Lawrence and on to Quebec, proving that top-grade timber could be moved economically to market from the Ottawa Valley. Scarcely a year later Napoleon issued his Berlin Decree, closing continental ports to British shipping. Among other things, he hoped to deny his most troublesome enemy a reliable source of timber for ship-building: the one thing that stopped him from invading England was the Royal Navy. Russia and the United States quickly fell in with Napoleon's scheme and refused to sell timber to Britain.

So Britain turned to the Canadian colonies, and Wright's bold experiment pointed the way. Soon the tall pines of the Ottawa Valley became the masts and spars of the Royal Navy and the British merchant fleet, while Canadian oak provided everything from ships' ribs to barrel staves. Hundreds of men moved north for the timber boom, invading the wilderness domain of hunters and trappers. Speculators and entrepreneurs rode the crest of the boom. One of them, Nicholas Sparks, homesteaded the future site of Bytown when land was cheap, then sold off his property for a fortune. Peter Aylen was another who grew rich on Canadian pine. By the age of thirty the former sailor boy was a millionaire.

The backbone of the new industry was the muscular, hard-handed logger, who cut down trees with broadaxe and crosscut saw, stripped them with hand tools, worked barefoot on log jams and rafts, and floated the timber down hazardous water-ways to market. He spent his winters in the bush, living in a Spartan camp called a shanty, hence the terms shantyman and shantytown. His work was hard and dangerous; his diet, a monotonous fare of salt pork, peas, beans, and biscuits, washed down with gallons of strong tea. Except for the occasional visit of a circuit-riding clergyman, the shantyman was cut off from the world. By spring, sick of the work, sick of the woods, sick of other men's company, he looked forward to the annual timber drive when the logs were floated downriver to Quebec.

The drive began with the thaw, when rivers were swollen by the spring melt. Then the men rolled the "sticks" into the Ottawa's tributaries, floated them to the main river, and there trapped them into booms—huge floating fences of chained logs. The men would assemble twenty to thirty-five sticks into a crib and make a raft by lashing thirty to a hundred cribs together with chains or ropes. The crew—as many as fifty men—rode the raft, using twenty-four-foot oars, or sweeps, for steering and sometimes for propulsion. Every raft had a cookhouse, or "caboose," and a sleeping shed—usually a bark lean-to. At rough stretches the crew would break up the raft and shoot the rapids on individual cribs. They looked on this wild white-water ride as sport, but it was as dangerous, and sometimes as fatal, as breaking up a timber jam. Men could be crushed to death or drowned trying to clear a river channel plugged with logs, or swept away in a fury of white water while riding a crib down a rapids. Even after slides were built to bypass the worst stretches of river, the trip down the Ottawa remained hazardous.

It took four to six weeks to float a raft of pine logs with a cargo of oak from the timber country to Quebec City, and Nicholas Sparks's settlement, soon to be called Bytown, became a welcome stopover. The men piled ashore there, after months of labour, monotony, and celibacy, ready for anything. The town swarmed with loggers thirsty for whisky, women, and the excitement of a brawl. Men from rival camps frequently fought in the saloons, and more formal bare-knuckle bouts were popular, with individual champions slugging it out in the midst of cheering supporters. But the donnybrooks, common frontier pastimes across the continent, were mere roughhouse compared to the organized violence to come.

In the early years of the timber boom most loggers were French Canadians—skilled, reliable men who cut timber in the winter, returned to their farms in Quebec for the summer, and went back to the shanties in autumn. Boisterous, colourful, rowdy at times, they were nevertheless firmly attached to their families and land. Anyone who wanted to run timber had to hire the French Canadians—that is, until the coming of the Irish.

Though Canada had successfully fought off the Americans (with British help) in the War of 1812, Upper Canada still seemed extremely vulnerable to American invasion—hence the Rideau Canal, an alternative route linking Upper and Lower Canada by way of the Cataraqui, Rideau, and Ottawa rivers. Locks and dams had to be built, and several miles of dredging were needed for the 126-mile link between Kingston and Bytown (named for Colonel John By, the army engineer in charge.) Before digging could even begin, thousands of trees had to be uprooted—a monumental task carried out in virgin wilderness with hand tools. The work called for an army of labourers that could not be recruited in the Canadian colonies. Those Canadians not already felling trees for a living were too busy hacking farms out of the bush to go off and work on the canal. By had to import his workers from New York State, where the Erie Canal had just been completed; hundreds of Irish navvies who had done the work with pick and shovel were now looking for jobs.

Like thousands of their countrymen, these Irish had fled their homeland to escape the poverty, oppression, and political and religious intolerance of English rule. Full of hope, they had arrived in the "land of the free" to find themselves exploited and despised. Nicknamed "micks," "paddies," and "hooligans," they were expected to take without complaint whatever menial work was on the go, at whatever wages they were offered. Few had even rudimentary education, and many carried old-country feuds and prejudices with them to North America.

The Irish, inured to the hardest work, got the Rideau job done despite the most deplorable living and working conditions in mud, mosquitoes, and disease. The Irish ghetto was in Bytown's east end, or Lower Town, nicknamed Corktown, a squalid frontier slum built on a reclaimed marsh and separated from the main settlement by the canal. Within sight of the mansions of the timber tycoons the Corktowners lived in flimsy shacks or caves dug into the mounds of earth left by the canal construction. Some historians have suggested that the damp, gloomy burrows were attempts to duplicate the sod huts of Ireland. It is hardly surprising that Corktown was devastated by the cholera epidemics that swept through the region in the 1830s. While the Irish sickened and died, the wealthy families of Upper Town, high and dry in their stately homes, only shook their heads and lamented that they could not afford to clean up the disease-ridden marshes and weirs of Lower Town.

Politically, the Irish had no voice at all. Only a few landowners voted, and the Irish were squatters, without land rights. The Anglo-Scottish establishment regarded them with contempt, while the French Canadians saw them as job-grabbing foreign intruders, bringing with them a well-deserved reputation for brawling and drunkenness. The Irish, in turn, were clannish and defensive and mistrusted all outsiders.

The clergymen sent out by the Catholic Church did little to help the situation. Though some of them were dedicated, well-intentioned men, they were not prepared for the rigours of frontier life or for the peculiar problems of their restless parishioners. A priest who might have been at home in an Irish village was totally out of his element in the Canadian wilderness. There were also wolves in sheep's clothing—a swindler who used his office to line his own purse and "Father" Patrick Polin, who was not a priest at all but an impostor.

When the canal was completed in 1832, the Irish were again looking for jobs, with no labour in demand anywhere except in the timber trade, the traditional preserve of the French Canadians. Most timber bosses didn't want the Irish working in their shanties or on their rafts, but some of the Corktowners got jobs cutting oak, nasty work that the Canadians didn't want. The French word *chêneur*, oak cutter, may be the origin of the name Shiner, though it has also been attributed to the Irish habit of polishing shovels until they were shiny and ready for use as cooking pots, or of slicking their hair with soap.

With every hand against them and without Church or civil authority strong enough to restrain them, the Shiners vented their frustration in drinking and fighting. They fought anyone and everyone: Frenchmen, Orangemen, loggers, raftsmen, farmers, and townspeople. When no enemy was available for a beating, they beat each other. Guns were rare in Shiner violence. Their preferred weapons were fists, boots, rocks, and shillelaghs, as well as a nasty device called a Limerick whip, a willow withe tipped with a drilling chisel. Carousing through Bytown in gangs, the Shiners accosted anyone who fell foul of them, jeering at passersby and frequently beating up helpless victims. Any social event was an excuse for the gangs to gather and start a riot.

Though accustomed to rowdyism, Bytown was in no way prepared to deal with the brutality of the Shiners. There was only a token police force, part-time volunteers who soon learned to avoid Corktowners wherever they appeared. Anyone brave or foolhardy enough to cross the Shiners was likely to have his house set on fire. The nearest jail was fifty miles away in Perth, and Hull, just across the river in Quebec, provided instant sanctuary for outlaws. The officers of the British garrison on Barracks Hill were reluctant to interfere in civilian matters unless ordered out by the government to quell a riot.

Shiner violence began while the canal was being built, when Irish navvies and French Canadian loggers would drink Bytown dry before turning bars and alleys into battlegrounds. The first fatality was an Englishman named Thomas Ford, killed in a brawl on St. Patrick's Day, 1828, but it was not until the mid-1830s that the violence became organized and purposeful. At first the Shiners were just leaderless ruffians, with no goals beyond a grand drunk and a good fight. But as competition between timber barons increased, some of them began to employ Shiners not for their marginal skills as lumbermen but as hired thugs who could intimidate their rivals. At this vicious game the most successful was the bright young millionaire Peter Aylen.

By 1834 Aylen owned property and timber operations throughout the Ottawa Valley. He had a mansion in Bytown and a luxurious country home in Aylmer, Lower Canada. He was not only wealthy but influential, one of Bytown's leading citizens. But money and social standing did not satisfy him. He wanted nothing less than control of the timber trade, and in pursuit of this dream he recruited an army of unhappy, impoverished Irishmen, who were practically begging for a leader. The timber baron began entertaining Shiners in his home, buying their loyalty with food, whiskey, and women, including prostitutes whom he brought in from Montreal. He gave Corktowners jobs on his rafts and promised them that with his help they could drive the French out of the valley. In return the Shiners did all of Aylen's dirty work, which began with cracking heads but soon escalated to arson, robbery, and murder.

Aylen did not hide his association with the Shiners. He tried, with indifferent success, to get other timber barons to hire only Irishmen. He caroused through the streets with the Shiners, as one eyewitness reported, "armed to the teeth, a bold wild reckless outlaw . . . who neither feared God nor honoured the King." He joined their wild, marathon drunks. A favourite prank at a Shiner party was to stage a mock funeral with a hopelessly drunk prostitute who would be stripped naked and laid out on the sidewalk surrounded by candles in full view of the shocked townspeople. Aylen did nothing to curb such outrageous behaviour. If anything he encouraged it. His chief lieutenants were some of the most brutal and feared men in the town. Besides his second-in-command, Andrew Leamey, there were Martin Hennesey, Aylen's giant bodyguard; Thomas Burke, a known killer; seven brothers named Slaven, notorious fighters; Bobby Boyle, whose specialty was arson; and someone with the nickname Jimmy the Wren, described as a "fierce, wild heathen." In a street fight Jimmy the Wren was as deadly with a rock as most men with a gun. The wren, in Celtic folklore, is the Devil's bird, and perhaps that's where Jimmy got his name.

On January 5, 1835, a Shiner foe named Charlie McStravick was murdered on a Lower Town street in broad daylight by a man named Curry. Curry was arrested but easily escaped and was helped to flee the country. When a farmer named Little had a dispute with the Shiners, his house was wrecked by an explosion. Fortunately, it was empty at the time of the blast, and the only casualty was the Shiner who planted the bomb. He was blown to pieces, but a shoemaker was able to identify his boots. They belonged to a man known as Hairy Barney.

As Shiner atrocities mounted, unpunished and even unprosecuted, the Bytown establishment pleaded in vain for military intervention. Aylen, finding he could get away with his crimes, stepped up his campaign of terror. The Shiners, confident in his leadership and in their newly found power, were willing to do whatever he asked—the only man in Upper Town who had ever shown an interest in them. As the spring drive of 1835 approached, stories reached Bytown from the shanties. Camps were invaded, men beaten and killed, horses hamstrung: Aylen's Shiners had unleashed their war against the French. On the river they boarded rafts manned by French Canadians, beating the crews and throwing men overboard. If the pirates couldn't handle a captured raft, they broke it up, destroying thousands of dollars worth of prime timber. In river communities, including Bytown, any man from Quebec was likely to be jumped and beaten in a saloon or brothel. Some were ambushed on the bridge between Bytown and Hull and thrown to their deaths in the Great Kettle, a cauldron of churning water below Chaudière Falls. Before the season was over, the French-Canadian community was reeling before the Shiner onslaught. It wasn't that the Québècois were pushovers. With three hundred years of frontier tradition behind them, they did score some minor victories. But in a wide-open contest of savagery and violence they were outmatched.

The French-Canadian champions included Joseph Montferrand (the "Big Joe Mufferaw" of folklore), probably the most formidable man on the Ottawa River. Though known as a kindly soul with the reputation of a good Samaritan, Montferrand's real claim to fame was his skill as a fighter. Six foot two, with ox-like strength, Montferrand had sledge-hammer fists and was as fast and deadly with his feet as with his hands. In single combat or general *mêlée* Big Joe was a force to be reckoned with. He once trounced the Royal Navy heavyweight champion in a blood-spattered seventeen-round match at Quebec City. Sometime later, when the Shiners were on the rampage, he walloped Big Martin Hennesey in a saloon fight that might well have been called the battle of the titans. According to legend Big Joe's greatest moment of glory was the Battle of Chaudière Bridge. Trapped by a gang of Shiners on the narrow bridge between Bytown and

Hull, Montferrand fought like a Canadian Horatio. Seizing one attacker, he swung him like a flail, knocking down anyone within reach. The fallen he threw over the side like so many rag dolls. The Shiner gang fled, and Big Joe stepped off the bridge, battered but victorious.

But it would take more than one man's heroics to halt the rise of Shiner power. Magistrate George W. Baker tried to stop Aylen's rule by arresting him for assault in the beating of Daniel McMartin, a respected lawyer. With their boss locked up in an army guardhouse, the Shiners rioted. The garrison had to be called out to prevent them from setting fire to the hotel where McMartin was convalescing. Hearing that Aylen had been taken to a riverboat for transport to Perth, the Shiners boarded the vessel and beat up the crew. When they failed to find Aylen on board, they proceeded to wreck the small ship. Actually, he had been taken overland by a strong guard to Perth, where he served a short term in jail. Baker also arrested five of Aylen's men, three for raping an elderly Indian woman and two for threatening to kill witnesses to the crime. But for Aylen these were minor setbacks and did little to curb the violence. Baker wrote in a letter, "No person whatever can move by day without insult, or at night without risk of life. I have not travelled without arms since 14th May."

In June 1835 a Shiner named Matthew Power decided to settle an old score with Joseph Galipaut, owner of a tavern popular among French-Canadian loggers. Two years earlier Galipaut had shot Martin Hennesey, when the Irish giant rode a horse into Galipaut's saloon looking for trouble, and had blinded him in one eye. When Power attacked Galipaut, he was gunned down by the straight-shooting tavern keeper, and while Galipaut waited in jail for trial, the Shiners burned down his tavern. Only a providential rainstorm kept the flames from spreading to the rest of the town. As soon as Galipaut was released from jail, he took his family and fled, knowing he was marked for death by the Shiner goon squads.

In July a constable named Dixon tried to arrest one of the Shiners on a charge of rape. While a crowd of townspeople looked on, three Shiners beat Dixon senseless. No one dared to intervene. Clearly the amateur policemen and the part-time civil authorities were unable to cope with Aylen and his well-organized gang of terrorists. Even the Ottawa Lumber Association, formed to protect the interests of the timber barons, seemed to be ineffectual. While Shiners were cracking heads in Bytown and pirating rafts on the river, the association was giving priority to timber slides and dams. Chief supervisor for this work was Peter Aylen.

In the summer of 1835, with the gangs in control of the streets, Aylen attacked the landowners on their home ground. Leading a large band of Shiners, he crashed the annual meeting of the Bathurst District Agricultural Society, a gentlemen's club that was the pride of the establishment. As the Shiners trooped in, each man plunked down a dollar for membership. They made the meeting hall look like a Corktown shebeen, drinking whiskey, exchanging lewd jokes, and intimidating the legitimate members. When it came time to elect officers, the Shiners voted out the old executive and put in one of their own, with Aylen as president.

In October 1835 a group of men from the Upper Town formed a vigilante organization, the Bytown Association for the Preservation of Peace. They armed their own patrols, temporarily kept the Shiners in check, and by 1836 were raising funds to pay constables and prosecute criminals. They also tried to establish an official armed militia, the Bytown Rifles, but internal dissent and lack of support from the regular army killed the project. At that point the vigilante organization began to lose power and before long Aylen's men were once more effectively unopposed. They demonstrated their renewed power by attacking the funeral procession of a deceased foe, putting the mourners to flight, and dumping the corpse into a ditch. George Baker wrote in despair: "How strange it seems that one man should have the power to keep the whole town and neighbourhood in disorder, but it is so."

Aylen was indeed the architect of disorder; but for all his charm, money, and connections he was really just a gangster, with no political power. His money and his army of thugs had not given him the control he craved over the town and the lumber industry. On January 2, 1837, he made a grab for such power. Leading some fifty Shiners into a township meeting, he demanded they have the right to vote in a council election. If he succeeded, he could take over the local government just as he had the Agricultural Society. His demand had political plausibility: votes for the downtrodden Irish. But the township meeting did not go well for Aylen. James Johnston reminded him that only men who held real estate free of mortgage could vote; this was the law, and it could not be changed. Angered by such resistance, the Shiners started a riot. They erected a picture supposed to be that of St. Patrick and announced that they would beat up anyone who failed to remove his hat in respect. One victim was Johnston, who was severely beaten when he tried to go to the rescue of a friend.

On St. Valentine's Day the Bytown outlaws committed an outrage that united the whole countryside against them. Led by Mike Gleeson, they attacked the wife and daughters of an Orangeman named Hobbs. The women had been shopping in the town and were about to return to their farm in a sleigh when the drunken Shiners moved in with sticks, beating them mercilessly. Mrs. Hobbs, who was pregnant, tried to jump from the sleigh, but her clothing snagged and she was dragged along the frozen ground while the pursuing Shiners continued to hit her. When the terrified family finally escaped, the ruffians vented their frustration on the team of horses. The next day, when Hobbs came to town, he found the animals shorn of their ears and their tails, and one with a knife wound in its side.

This senseless, brutal attack roused the farmers of the region. Almost to a man they were demobilized soldiers and Orange Protestants. A week after the attack they descended on Bytown en masse, armed with guns, clubs, and pitchforks and looking for Gleeson, who had thus far evaded arrest. Shiners quickly spread the alarm, telling the Catholics of Lower Town that an Orange mob was about to murder them in their homes. Thus alerted, dozens of otherwise peaceful and law-abiding Irish joined the Shiners to repel the Orange attack. Desperate intervention by the magistrates just managed to prevent a full-scale battle. They persuaded the farmers to retreat and put Gleeson in the lock-up under guard.

On March 9 there was another potentially fatal confrontation when a party of twenty constables arrived from the town of Richmond to arrest Aylen for assault. Again the Catholics mustered to defend themselves from an imagined Orange invasion. George Lyon, a prominent citizen of Richmond, arrived just in time to talk his neighbours into retreating rather than starting a pitched battle. Even as the Orangemen were drawing off, the Shiners were stalking old foes. It was rumoured that Hobbs was in league with the Richmond men and was staying at the home of James Johnston. Sixty Shiners crowded around Johnston's house that evening and called for Hobbs to come out, but they dispersed when Johnston appeared, armed with two pistols. Two hours later they were back, led by the Shiner King himself and some of them armed. This time Johnston barricaded his door, while some of the drunken mob began shooting at his windows. When they tired of this sport, they left. The occupants of the house were shaken and battle-weary but uninjured.

In spite of all the bravado Shiner fortunes were beginning to turn. Aylen now faced numerous charges resulting from Shiner riots. On one occasion three magistrates, Baker among them, burst into Aylen's house to arrest one of his henchmen for assault. He threatened the three that he would "make them sweat for it."

On March 25 the Shiners were on the offensive again. Thomas Burke, Patrick O'Brien, and James Macdonald ambushed James Johnston on the Sappers' Bridge over the Rideau Canal. Johnston jumped down the twelve-foot canal bank, but the snow that cushioned his fall also hampered his escape. While he floundered, two of the Shiners shot at him and pelted him with stones. The third leaped down the embankment to beat him with a whip, but his cries for help attracted townspeople who drove off the attackers. He suffered a fractured skull but recovered. The authorities were now better organized and acted swiftly to arrest Burke, O'Brien, and Macdonald, sending them to Perth under armed escort. Aylen boasted that he would free his men, and on May 1 a gang of Shiners stormed the Perth prison. They liberated the three, who escaped. However, all of them were soon recaptured in New York and sentenced to three years' hard labour for attempted murder.

The people of Bytown, including many of the Irish, were by now fed up with the Shiners. Not only was the town a dangerous place to live, but if anarchy continued to rule the Ottawa Valley, there was danger that Britain might turn back to the Baltic for timber. The army began to take more of a hand in peacekeeping, and when they were called away to deal with the Mackenzie and Papineau rebellions, special constables were sworn in to patrol the streets and keep order.

On the river the much-abused French Canadians played their trump card. They blockaded such strategic points as Carillon and the Long Sault, which were in Quebec territory, where the Shiners would be outnumbered and at a disadvantage. Neither Shiners nor rafts belonging to Aylen were allowed through the blockade. Shut off from market, Aylen capitulated, sold his Bytown property, and moved to Aylmer. He was never brought to book for any of his major crimes but remained a rich and respected citizen until his death in 1868, living proof that money could excuse just about anything. Andrew Leamy established a sawmill in Hull, prospered, and became wealthy. Martin Hennesy never gave up his violence; he died with his head bashed in by an iron poker in a barroom brawl. Mike Gleeson, according to local legend, was trapped by farmer Hobbs in a blacksmith shop, where Hobbs proceeded to cut off his ears. He was subsequently nicknamed "Croppie."

Bytown remained a tough timber town for many years thereafter, and gangs of hoodlums calling themselves Shiners continued to be a nuisance well into the 1840s. But the real Shiners—the canal diggers, oak cutters, and raftsmen—either moved on or settled down. They had lost their war, but as class distinctions lessened and time eroded racial and religious intolerance, they traded notoriety for respectability and gave the lie to the old stereotype of the Irishman with a penchant for drink and fit only for hard labour and cracking heads.

Chapter 10
The Brook's Bush Gang

ON A DRIZZLY DECEMBER NIGHT in 1859 a tall Irish gentleman stepped uncertainly onto the ice-crusted boards of an old wooden bridge in the provincial city of Toronto. A thin layer of snow had been turned to a slippery shell by freezing rain. The man wore a thick greatcoat over a light hunter's coat, silk vest, and shirt, and was fortified from within by a warm bellyful of whiskey. He could hear the rush of the Don River as it churned under the ice, and though the night was dark, there were pools of light around the lanterns on the bridge. As he started across, he saw shadowy forms moving in and out of the light, people he thought he knew and had reason to be wary of. Moments later a woman was walking beside him, smiling, taking his arm to help steady him on the slick surface. Perhaps she clung to his arm a little *too* tightly. They talked briefly, then, in a moment of swirling violence, she snatched a weapon from her belt, swung hard, and struck him on the head. He crumpled, dazed and bleeding, while she rifled his pockets, and two men, or perhaps three, joined in the assault. The man cried out as they beat him, stripped him of his greatcoat, and tore off his vest. He was either too drunk or too stunned from the blow to resist while they bound his arms and legs; he may not even have heard the order "Throw him over!" He crashed like a stone through the thin ice, and while the cold black water pulled him under, the gang on the bridge gathered under a steaming lantern to divide the loot.

Toronto in the 1850s was a small city surrounded by woods and water, trying to live down its "Muddy York" image. Though not yet "Toronto the Good," it was already a bastion of British Protestant law and morality. A small wealthy establishment lived in its fine mansions, and a crowd of desperate poor inhabited its slums. Urban growth had brought unemployment, poverty, alcoholism, and prostitution. Not all the immigrants in the two decades following the Mackenzie Rebellion could find work as tradesmen or labourers. Of those who braved the outlying frontiers, trying to hack farms from the bush, many failed and retreated to the city. There, in saloons, shebeens, and whorehouses, the poor and the desperate temporarily forgot their woes or plotted ways and means to steal their daily bread.

By far the most common form of larceny was highway robbery, not as it was practised in England by such legendary mounted highwaymen as Dick Turpin but by bandits who haunted the roads on foot and were known as footpads. Today they would be called muggers. Few footpads used guns—many could not afford them. They tended to use knives, cudgels, or their bare fists. A popular weapon, easy to acquire, was a "tag," a hefty rock tied in a piece of cloth and wielded like a blackjack. The footpad's victims were farmers, tradesmen, merchants—anyone in the wrong place at the wrong time.

These small-time crooks often preyed on each other as well as on the general public and squandered most of their loot in drinking and gambling. The Toronto police arrested them when they could. The courts imposed fines and jail terms. But it was easy for a felon to slip out of the city, beyond reach of the police. East of the Don River, west of the Humber, north along the rough highway called Yonge Street, all was farmland and bush, where a criminal could hide out or work on a farm for room and board. As for the general citizenry, they tended to ignore the ruffians in their midst—at least those of them who had not been robbed or assaulted. They read brief accounts in the police reports and kept a decent distance between themselves and Toronto's underworld. That is until the disappearance of John Sheridan Hogan MPP.

Hogan had led an active and sometimes controversial life. He had arrived in Canada, a twelve-year-old Irish lad, in 1827, became a newsboy for the *Canadian Wesleyan* in Hamilton, and worked his way up to printer and then journalist. In 1842 he had been arrested twice in Rochester, New York, in connection with the destruction of the American steamer *Caroline*, burned by Canadian militia in 1838 after the Mackenzie Rebellion. He was acquitted, but his arrest and trial had made him briefly the centre of an international dispute.

Hogan studied law and was admitted to the bar in 1844, but was far more successful as a journalist than as a lawyer. He wrote for the prestigious *Blackwood's Magazine*, was parliamentary correspondent for several newspapers, and founded his own weekly, *The United Empire*. In 1855 he wrote a prize-winning essay on Canada for the Paris Exhibition. The same year he became chief editor of the *British Colonist*, a leading Toronto paper. In 1857 he won election to the Assembly from Grey County as a member of the Reform Party. With Oliver Mowat and Thomas D'Arcy McGee, he was regarded as one of its rising stars. Then, on December 1, 1859, he disappeared.

Hogan, a bachelor, kept a room in a Toronto hotel but often stayed with Mrs. Sarah Laurie on what is now Bay Street. Their relationship has been called "domestic." Mrs. Laurie, a widow, cooked for Hogan and mended his clothes. He helped support her children. If more than that was involved, they kept it quiet. On November 30 Hogan stayed overnight with Mrs. Laurie. Next evening, after drinking one glass of whiskey (all she would allow him), he left the house around 8:30, supposedly to keep an appointment with a new editor at the office of the *British Colonist*. That was the last time she saw him alive.

His disappearance at first passed unnoticed. He had no family in Toronto and few friends. He kept an erratic schedule, and his professional associates saw nothing unusual about a prolonged absence from the city. Mrs. Laurie worried when he did not return from his appointment but was reluctant to go to the police. It was *two months* before the newspapers began asking "Where Is Mr. Hogan?" Detectives went to several Canadian and American cities where he had supposedly been seen, and a $500 reward was offered for information. Rumours circulated that he had run away or that he was in financial trouble and had killed himself. But this did not fit his character at all, and the police suspected murder. *Sixteen months* after Hogan last said good night to Sarah Laurie, John Bright and his three nephews were duck hunting from a skiff in the marshy delta of the Don

River when they found the rotting body of a man caught on a snag in the shallow water. They towed the corpse to a wharf, where two policemen hauled it ashore and took it to the "dead house" behind city hall.

Though the head was reduced to a skull, police soon knew that they had the body of John Sheridan Hogan. His tailor recognized the hunter's coat. Sarah Laurie summoned up enough courage to visit the morgue and pointed out repairs she had made to Hogan's clothing: a patch sewn on his shirtband, a safety pin that held up his underpants. She clinched the matter by informing the police that he had a pair of webbed toes: the corpse had the same oddity.

Discovery of the body and speculation that Hogan had been murdered made the front pages in Toronto. The papers covered every detail. The *Globe* even printed a grisly account of the post mortem: "The deep muscles retained their reddish colour. The whole skull was entirely denuded . . . eyes quite shrunken. The teeth were generally very perfect. . . . The brain was converted into a soft cheesy mass. . . ." And much more in this vein.

While Toronto buzzed with the story, police began their investigation. If Hogan had been murdered, who did it and why? The trail would be a cold one after sixteen months, but Detective James Colgan thought he knew the answers even before the investigation began.

East of the Don River, not far from Toronto's New Gaol (the Don Jail) was a twenty-acre woodlot known as Brook's Bush. This bit of wild land, with a dilapidated barn and rickety stable, had for some four years been home to a band of criminals known to police as the Brook's Bush Gang. The men and women who frequented this robbers' roost on the eastern edge of Toronto lived by thievery and prostitution. In lean times they stole livestock (mostly chickens) from neighbouring farms. "Gang" was perhaps a misnomer. There was a core of hardened criminals but also a shifting population of petty hoods and whores who did their business in the city, returning to the bandit camp to drink and sleep. Drifters came and went as individuals were arrested, jailed, or released. At the time of Hogan's murder there were probably about twenty, but the Bush sometimes harboured forty or fifty people without legitimate means of support.

Toronto police had long been aware of the gang's existence and knew the ringleaders, but major convictions were rare. Brook's Bush was outside Toronto, beyond their patrol area. Cases were often dismissed for lack of evidence. As a result the Brook's Bush Gang behaved as though they had a free hand in the city: the occasional fine or a month in jail was little more than a licence to steal. And steal they did! They robbed houses, waylaid pedestrians, picked pockets in bars, and lured unwary victims to their lair in the Bush. After a drink of shebeen liquor and a tumble with a "soiled dove," the visitor would be relieved of his pocketbook and any other valuables. The Don Bridge, at King Street, became one of their favourite haunts. People entering or leaving the city by the bridge were often accosted by loitering thugs and whores.

Detective Colgan had only to put a few simple facts together. The body had been found at the mouth of the Don, probably washed down from upriver, perhaps from the bridge where the gang had been known to waylay travellers. Robbery seemed the likely motive: the Bush was a nest of thieves. But Colgan had neither evidence nor witnesses, and he certainly didn't expect any of the gang to volunteer information. Then he learned that Ellen McGillick, a prostitute who had once been a member of the gang and was now a police informer, had been hinting that she knew something about the crime.

Colgan was well acquainted with McGillick, having arrested her several times. She was about thirty, dark-haired, bright-eyed, and scarred by smallpox. She had turned to prostitution in her late twenties when deserted by her husband. Strangely, she considered Colgan a friend, perhaps because they came from the same town in County Meath, Ireland. Yet, on one occassion, when he was arresting her for stealing a watch, she pulled a knife and stabbed him in the chest, apparently aiming for the heart. The wound was superficial, and she was not prosecuted for attempted murder. Instead, she became a "blab," the contemporary term for informer. At various times she testified against members of the Brook's Bush Gang, and if lawyers expressed doubts about her evidence, as they often did, she would turn to the judge and say, "Your Worship, have I not always told the truth, bad as I am?"

Colgan found McGillick living in a shack on Stanley Street in Toronto's slums. At first she refused to talk about Hogan. If she had said anything about the case while in jail for streetwalking it had just been drunken chatter. But she did admit that she lived in constant fear of the Brook's Bush Gang, who didn't care much for blabs. She was certain they'd try to kill her if she testified against them again. She especially feared Jane Ward, the harpie who was the gang's unofficial leader.

A native of Yorkshire, twenty-five-year-old Ward had been a prostitute since her teens and had severed all relations with her family, who farmed near Hamilton. No "whore with a heart of gold," she had been repeatedly charged with robbery and had served a term in the Kingston penitentiary. By all accounts she was passionate and vindictive, the Dragon Lady of Brook's Bush. According to the *Globe*, she ruled the gang and "all alike feared her when her blood was up."

To allay McGillick's fear of Ward and the Brook's Bush hooligans, Colgan put a guard on her shack and continued his interrogation. After three days of harsh questioning and a promise of immunity from prosecution (and who knows what else) he had her version of the murder. She said that on the night of December 1, 1859, she had left Brook's Bush for Toronto in the company of several people, including Jane Ward, James "English Jim" Brown, John "English Jack" Sherrick, and Hugh McEntameny. She parted company with them as they entered town, but two hours later she saw them struggling with a man on the bridge. She heard the man cry out, "Don't take off my coat; she's got all my money." Then she heard Ward say, "Pitch him over, goddamn him, and he will tell no tales." At that order Brown picked up the victim and tossed him into the river. The man was tied up and possibly weighted with a large stone. McGillick, who claimed to have witnessed it all from behind a beam, stepped out and asked Ward what the matter was. Ward answered, "Don't hold me. I'm after taking a few dollars from a man." When McGillick asked about the "tag" hanging from her belt, Ward said, "The one I struck with that will never tell another tale."

Other members of the gang soon joined the killers on the bridge and lined the rail to see if Hogan might reappear. When Ward said, "He is tied too tight to swim," the whole gang left for the Bush, satisfied that Hogan was dead. In the draughty old barn Ward drank herself into a stupor and passed out. While she was senseless, two hangers-on, Charles Gerde and Mary Ann Pickly, robbed her of her $40 share of the $160 the killers had taken from Hogan. There was no honour among thieves in the Bush.

Next morning Brown and Sherrick returned to the scene of the crime. Brown saw bloodstains on the railing where he had thrown Hogan over, so he whittled away the evidence with his knife. This done, the gang considered themselves free and clear, but Ward complained that she had not slept properly "since that man was thrown into the water" and had had "no peace or luck since it took place."

McGillick's story was all Colgan needed for a wholesale arrest of the Brook's Bush gangsters. Some sixteen people, including Ward, were held for questioning. Brown was thought to have fled to Owen Sound, but Colgan nabbed him in a saloon near the Don, drinking with a bandit named William Reid, wanted for robbing a farmer of $300. Sherrick was a little harder to track down. The police were informed that he was in jail in Auburn, New York, charged with horse stealing, but this proved to be a hoax. He was actually in Kingston, serving time for a robbery committed at Whitby, twenty-five miles east of Toronto. Hugh McEntameny, the third man in McGillick's story, had died the previous winter in Toronto's General Hospital, the victim of a "debauched life."

With his suspects locked up, Colgan went looking for more evidence. A thorough search of Brook's Bush turned up nothing until a tip from a local shebeen owner led him to an old well. In it was Hogan's silk vest, the first "exhibit" linking the gang with the murder. One of Hogan's killers had given it to another gang member who needed something presentable for a court appearance. Later it had been tossed into the well. The vest had been crudely altered to fit a larger man than Hogan, but Sarah Laurie identified it as his.

Colgan then took McGillick to the Don Bridge and had her point out the place where Brown had carved away the bloodstains. He cut out the section of railing and sent it to a laboratory for tests. Ward would later argue that there were so many cuts and carvings on the rail that this piece of evidence was worthless. But the lab did find traces of blood that had seeped into the cracks, though it could not be positively identified as human blood.

Most of those arrested were questioned and released, but Ward and Brown were held for a preliminary hearing before Magistrate George Gurnett, a tough-minded old Tory with ties dating back to the Family Compact. The hearing began April 8, 1861, before a courtroom packed with people anxious to get a look at Ward and, especially, Brown, the man who had allegedly thrown Hogan to his death. Thirty-one-year-old Brown, from Cambridge, England, had arrived in Canada in 1852, and worked as a labourer before falling in with the Brook's Bush Gang. Surprisingly, his police record was almost spotless. The only charge had been disorderly conduct, a misdemeanour. Unlike most of his accomplices he could read and write, but he was cursed with what the *Globe* called "a repulsive countenance, with a brow villainously low. His face is not improved by the cancer in his nose."

As the hearing began, Brown seemed confident, even amused, while Ward appeared haggard and worn. The prisoners were not represented by counsel, and questioned witnesses themselves. While Sarah Laurie was testifying, Ward broke into tears, the first time she had shown any emotion. Laurie recalled Hogan telling her that on two occasions he had been stopped on the bridge by the Brook's Bush Gang, "and had some difficulty getting through them, but [he] immediately added that they knew him well, and was sure they would not hurt him. I told him he ought to be cautious as he went up and down."

None of the prisoners questioned Laurie, but when McGillick took the stand, Ward astonished the court by throwing her hands above her head and crying out, "May God forgive you, Ellen McGillick, for the false oath you are about to take with that Testament in your hand. If I am guilty of what you say, may God punish me this day. I call God to witness that I never did what I am charged with. May God forgive you, Ellen McGillick, for the false oath you are about to take and for what you have said." Later in the enquiry she repeated it all in a second outburst.

Brown refused to question McGillick. "What's the use of asking her any questions?" he said. "She will take a false oath and swear to anything against me. On the 29th of November I was working for a farmer in the country. On the 8th of December I went to work at Mono Mills and was there till Christmas. . . . She will swear anything false to salt me." He became especially angry when McGillick stated that during the struggle on the bridge Hogan had said, "I know by your size that you are Brown, the bully of Brook's Bush." Brown vehemently denied ever meeting Hogan at any time and called McGillick a liar. Her story did seem melodramatic at times, and over several days of hearing Ward pointed out contradictions and changes in her testimony. "She has made a few mistakes, and has corrected them," Colgan admitted.

Sometimes the argument between Ward and McGillick resembled a bawdy house brawl, and the magistrate instructed the constables to keep the women apart so they could not scratch each other. One argument developed over a scar on McGillick's head. She swore that two months after the murder Ward had accused her of talking to "certain parties" about the affair and attacked her with a knife. She showed the court the scar, and a doctor gave his opinion that it was the result of a knife wound. Ward insisted she had never hit McGillick with anything but her fist and said the wound was inflicted when another woman of the Brook's Bush Gang broke a dish over Ellen's head. That, said McGillick, was an entirely different episode and she parted her hair to show a second scar.

Mary Ann Pickly, the woman who had allegedly fleeced Ward while she slept off her drunk, testified that she had heard

McGillick "wish to God" that Ward would commit a crime that would send her to the penitentiary. According to Pickly, McGillick wanted revenge for the abuse she'd suffered at Ward's hands and also hoped to get money from the police.

Some of the evidence compounded the mystery. A heated exchange took place between Brown and Dr. T.C. Gamble, an important witness for the prosecution. Dr. Gamble, an elderly and respected physician, had seen a scuffle on the bridge that fateful night while returning from a visit to a patient. Being an old man, he did not try to interfere and thought, when he heard a splash, that someone had thrown a large dog off the bridge. As he walked past, one of the group asked, "Who are you?" He replied, "I'm old Dr. Gamble," to which one of the gang added, "and a damned good old fellow too." He did not know at the time that murder was afoot, but he did recognize Brown. At home he mentioned the incident to his wife, but she could not recall it at all.

Brown and Ward angrily denounced the doctor's testimony. "Where did you ever see me before?" Brown demanded. "You never saw me in your life. I know nothing about you."

"Oh, I know all about you," the doctor said. "It was not a moonlit night, but the lamps were shining brightly. I am seventy-two years of age and have got what is called the 'second sight,' which people generally get in their old age. . . ."

"When did you see me?" Brown demanded.

"You have been pointed out to me on the street," the doctor replied. "Any man who saw your nose would easily know you again."

Exasperated, Brown replied, "If you got another glass of whiskey, you would swear anything you were told."

Dr. Gamble placed the incident at ten o'clock; McGillick, at nine o'clock. Laurie said that Hogan was sober when he left her house at 8:30, but McGillick said he was drunk when the gang met him. A man named Alexander Williamson testified that Hogan had been with him on the fatal night, drinking until after midnight, and that the MPP was so drunk he could not stand up without the support of a tree. Williamson said he had sent Hogan to his hotel in a cab and that was the last he saw of him. The cab driver, who might have been able to verify Williamson's story, could not be found. Did Williamson have his dates wrong? That seems the most likely explanation.

John Sherrick arrived in Toronto from the Kingston penitentiary on April 16. His appearance excited Ward, who exclaimed, "There is Jack at last!" She had been insisting that he could shoot down McGillick's testimony. He did indeed have an alibi. He could produce witnesses to testify that he had not been in Toronto at the time of Hogan's death, if it had happened on December 1, 1859, as alleged.

Though McGillick's stories of the outlaws' violence seemed exaggerated, a statement from Ward provided a grim insight into life at Brook's Bush. She was indignant at the suggestion that she would take a dead man's money: "If I had wished to rob a murdered man, I could have taken the money from the black man who was murdered three or four years ago in Brook's Bush." What black man? Who knows? This seems to be the only reference to the killing.

Such statements, together with the evil reputation of the Bush, doubtless influenced the findings of the preliminary enquiry, even though McGillick was suspected of perjury. Ward, Brown, and Sherrick were all charged with murder and sent for trial. Sherrick and Ward were tried first, on April 29.

Representing them before Chief Justice Sir John Beverley Robinson was James Doyle, a young lawyer defending his first murder charge. He produced an able defence. He brought witnesses to swear that Sherrick had been working on a farm some fifty miles from Toronto on the day of the murder. This first evidence that McGillick might be telling something other than the "whole truth" was followed by the revelation that Sherrick and McGillick had once been lovers and that Sherrick had ended the relationship. He played on the jilted lover theme enough to discredit McGillick's testimony.

The jury did not regard McGillick's testimony as reliable and found Sherrick not guilty. They also gave Ward the benefit of the doubt, perhaps because only McGillick had testified to her presence on the bridge but perhaps also because there was a reluctance to send women to the scaffold.

That left James Brown. The state's strongest case was against him and perhaps that is why they held him for trial on October 8, at the autumn assizes before Chief Justice William Henry Draper. Brown was so sure of his acquittal that he brought his street clothes into court to wear on his discharge. But he was the one who had been identified by Dr. Gamble. And unlike Sherrick he could not produce an alibi. To his horror the jury found him guilty. Doyle appealed the conviction and argued the case eloquently, but the conviction was confirmed. Doyle then fought to have the death sentence commuted to life imprisonment, and many Torontonians who doubted Brown's guilt signed a petition for clemency. But the government was determined to have a hanging, and his execution was scheduled for March 10, 1862.

That morning more than five thousand people crowded along Front Street and from Berkeley to King to see Brown hanged on the west wall of the jail. Men who owned wagons sold standing space at a shilling a head. Boys playing hookey from school ran shouting through the crowd. A woman prisoner, watching from her cell window, screamed as Brown stepped up to the scaffold, his arms pinioned and a white cap on his head. There were hymns and prayers, and Brown joined in. Then he addressed the crowd: "My friends, I want to say a few words to you. I have been a very bad man, and now I am going to die. I hope it will do you good. I hope this will be a lesson to you, and to all people, young and old, rich and poor, not to do those things that have brought me to my last end. Though I am innocent of murder, I am going to die for it. Before two minutes are gone, I shall be with my God, and I say with my last breath, I am innocent of murder. I never committed a murder in my life, and shall be before my God in a few minutes. And may the Lord have mercy on my soul." (This, at least was the *Globe*'s account. It sounds suspiciously like many other "last words" from the scaffold, which reporters were known to "edit" for the edification of their readers.) Brown spoke in a low voice. Only a few of those nearest the wall could hear him. Then the hangman, wearing a "frightful mask" and covered from head to foot so that no inch of skin was visible, fixed the noose. The trap was sprung, and the body dangled for half an hour before it was cut down and carted off for burial.

It was the last public hanging in Toronto and had been conducted with all the ritual and panoply of a human sacrifice at an Aztec temple of the sun.

John Sheridan Hogan, the prize-winning journalist and promising politician, had suffered a tragic and senseless death. Perhaps the same could be said for English Jim Brown, the common labourer turned petty outlaw. The evidence against him was shaky and many people in Toronto believed he was telling the truth when he declared his innocence on the scaffold. Others felt that Brown's accomplices should have accompanied him to the gallows.

As for the outlaw village at Brook's Bush, it was already at an end before the hanging. While the trials were under way, people from Toronto had moved in with saws and axes to cut down the trees and level the buildings and put an end to the most notorious lair of footpads, robbers, and prostitutes in the history of Toronto the Good.

Chapter 11
The Confederate Raiders

DURING THE AMERICAN CIVIL WAR, which began in 1861, the British North American colonies were officially neutral in accordance with British policy. Britain had no intention of being dragged into the American war, but there was a great deal of difference between neutrality on paper and neutrality in fact. Both in Britain and Canada there was a good deal of sympathy and support for the southern Confederacy. This did not mean support for slavery. Britain had long ago declared the slave trade to be piracy and had freed the slaves in all British colonies by 1834, some of them much earlier. But Britain and British North America did not swallow the Yankee argument that the war was about slavery. They believed the real issue was economic domination of the South by the North. So while she refused to recognize the Confederate government in Richmond, Virginia, Britain continued to do business with the Confederacy and allowed her shipyards to build warships for the Confederate navy. One of them, the *Alabama*, sank or captured more than sixty Union vessels before she went down in flames after a spectacular sea fight near the coast of France.

Angry politicians in Washington argued that Britain's declaration of neutrality was really indirect recognition of the Confederacy, leaving the door open for the use of British territory by the rebels. And indeed this was what happened. Though southern slave owners had regarded Canada as the most hateful of countries: the "vile, sensuous, animal, infidel, superstitious Democracy of Canada," to which escaped slaves were welcomed at the northern end of the Underground Railway and where John Brown had received support and had plotted his ill-starred insurrection, by the time the shooting actually started, Canada was strongly pro-Confederate and opposed to the designs of Yankee land-grabbers. William Seward, American Secretary of

State, had already proposed annexation of British territory, and many people on both sides of the border suspected that he was more of a power in the land than President Abraham Lincoln, whom his critics portrayed as a weak and ignorant leader. Lincoln had even managed to alienate the abolitionists in Canada when he made it clear that in spite of his personal feelings the war was a struggle to "save the Union" at any cost, with or without slavery.

Almost from the start, neutral Canada was involved in the long and bloody conflict. Fearful of American invasion Britain shipped troops to Upper and Lower Canada (now Ontario and Quebec) and strengthened fortifications. Thousands of young Canadians left home to fight in the war for the Union or the Confederacy, depending on their personal inclinations. Partisan newspapers kept up a lively and heated argument over the evils and merits of North and South. Hard-line Loyalists, whose forefathers had fled from Yankee persecution, gloated over the disintegration of the Great Republic and even speculated that some of the states bordering on Canada might rejoin the British Empire. And the son of the attorney general of Newfoundland wrote a prize-winning poem in Latin to commemorate the death of the brilliant Confederate General Thomas "Stonewall" Jackson.

As the Union blockade began to strangle the Confederacy, Canadian blockade runners became increasingly active, running guns and medical supplies down to the hard-pressed armies of General Robert E. Lee, taking cash and cotton in exchange. If caught, they would lose both ship and cargo, but enough of them got through to make the trade profitable.

Northern draft dodgers, called "skedaddlers," fled to Canada, where they roamed the countryside working for room and board, sometimes earning a reputation for petty theft.

Illegal recruiters, called "crimps," prowled Canada, hunting cannon fodder for the Union armies. The crimp earned a fee for every man he could lure into a Yankee uniform. British soldiers and sailors serving in Canada were favourite targets because they were already trained and could be encouraged to desert for higher pay and the chance to see action, but most of the men "crimped" were civilians. Some were restless youths who went willingly, perhaps with dreams of adventure and glory. Others were shanghaied while drunk, drugged, or even beaten sense-less. Crimping became such a scandal that John A. Macdonald organized a special detective force to track down crimps, with loyal soldiers used as bait, but the more resourceful recruiters escaped prosecution by luring their quarry over the border before enlisting them. American courts viewed crimping with a lenient eye and imposed penalties as light as $100 fines, but British deserters heading for the United States could expect harsh treat-ment if caught in Canada: flogging, hard labour, a shameful "D" tattooed on the chest, even death.

As the tide of war turned against the South, as Vicksburg fell, and as Lee began his retreat from the awful disaster at Gettysburg, the Confederates increased their activity in Canada. Canadians were used to Northern and Southern spies stalking one another on the streets of Halifax, Montreal, and Toronto, and the rebels were encouraged by Canada's Confederate sym-pathies. After all, the Canadian parliament had actually applauded the news of a Confederate victory at Chancellorsville, Virginia.

The beleaguered rebels even began to envision a second front, a drive southward from Canada, "a fire in the rear of the Union forces," as they expressed it. This would bring the war home to the Yankee heartland, drawing Union troops away from south-ern battlefields, and encouraging Northerners to demand an end to "Lincoln's war." Failing this, they hoped they might goad the North into an attack on Canada, thus drawing Britain into the war as a reluctant but powerful ally. To prepare for this new theatre of war, the Confederates sent agents and commissioners to every region of British North America. In Halifax they engaged Nova Scotian skippers to run the Yankee blockade, most of them the sons and grandsons of privateers who had sailed in two earlier wars. In distant Victoria a Southern Association met around the beer tables of the St. Nicholas Hotel, planning privateering ventures with ships they didn't have. Some of the schemes, though not all, had the personal blessing of Confederate President Jefferson Davis.

As the plight of the Confederacy became more desperate, the rebel plots became correspondingly wild. Southern agents sneaked from Canada into the cities along the border, where they started fires, hoping for a holocaust. But the plan failed: all their fires were contained and extinguished. One arsonist, R.C. Kennedy, was hanged for torching Barnum's circus in an attempt to burn down New York City.

Few incidents were more explosive than the *Chesapeake* affair. Like the earlier *Trent* affair, in which a Union warship stopped a British vessel at sea and forcibly removed two Confederate diplomats, the *Chesapeake* incident brought Britain and the North close to war. The coastal steamer *Chesapeake*, which had helped to capture a Confederate privateer some months earlier, left New York on December 5, 1863, on her regular run to Portland, Maine. Among the passengers were sixteen Confederate agents who had travelled to New York via St. John, New Brunswick. Their leader, John C. Braine, claimed at different times to be a native of New Brunswick, England, and Kentucky. Sickly and penniless, he had been jailed in Indiana for sedition but had later turned up in Halifax, where he spent the summer of 1863 raising money for the Confederate cause by selling phoney book subscriptions. He then moved on to St. John. Another major conspirator was John H. Parr of Canada West.

In the dark early hours of Monday, December 7, while the *Chesapeake* was chugging past Cape Cod, Braine and his men broke open a chest full of weapons and took command, though not without a struggle: they overpowered the watch, wounded the first mate and first engineer, and killed the second engineer. Unarmed and outnumbered, the rest of the crew put up no resistance. Braine clapped the captain in irons, and since none of the conspirators knew how to run a ship, he forced the wounded engineer back to work, while an unwilling passenger acted as pilot.

Braine and Parr helped themselves to the captain's money and the ship's papers. They planned to unload passengers and crew in Canada, sell the cargo, sail to Bermuda, and fit the ship out as a privateer. At Grand Manan Island in the Bay of Fundy they picked up Vernon Locke, an expatriate Canadian from

South Carolina and Braine's chief lieutenant. Locke had an out-dated letter of marque that he hoped to exploit in the privateering adventures. They then steamed to within six miles of St. John, where they set the captain, the passengers, and most of the crew adrift in a lifeboat. While the castaways rowed for shore, the rebels weighted the dead engineer's body and dumped it over-board.

In St. John the outraged captain hurried to the American consulate to report the seizure. The alarm spread quickly, and Union vessels were soon hunting the *Chesapeake*, which by now the rebels had renamed the *Retribution*. They sold most of the cargo (which included a load of bootleg liquor) in Nova Scotia but had trouble getting enough fuel for the long run to Ber-muda. In Nova Scotia the leaders of the plot were separated from their ship. First Locke went ashore on business, promising to rejoin the ship at Halifax. Then Braine went ashore at Liver-pool, where an American official tried to arrest him. He escaped with the help of Confederate sympathizers, but the ship sailed for Halifax without him. Parr sneaked the *Chesapeake* past two American warships into St. Margaret's Bay, where he went ashore, trying to buy bunker coal. The two warships entered the bay, cornered the ship, and took her into Halifax. There the Vice-Admiralty Court found in favour of her original owners, but most of the raiders went free. Only Locke was extradited to the United States, not for seizing the ship but for the unrelated crime of slave trading. Braine and Parr slipped through British hands and carried on their privateering careers, seizing at least one steamer and two schooners before the war ended.

Though the *Chesapeake* affair shocked many Canadians, the colonies remained generally sympathetic to the South. And believing that Canada might yet be the key to victory, the Confederates shifted their attention to the Great Lakes. This great cluster of inland seas, patrolled by a single American war-ship, was practically an open border, which the Confederates hoped to exploit in a series of naval raids on port cities such as Buffalo, Chicago, and Milwaukee. One of their particular tar-gets was the liberation of Southern prisoners of war held in wretched camps that were reputedly as bad as the Confederate hellhole at Andersonville. One of the worst was the camp on Johnston's Island in Lake Erie, near Sandusky, Ohio, where captured Confederate soldiers were dying of epidemic disease and starvation and were left half-naked in the northern winter. The plan was to empty this camp of its prisoners, take them across the lake to Canada, and there form them into guerrilla bands for border raids. Alternatively they might be able to fight their way through Northern lines to the South. A pipe dream perhaps and a dangerous one because of its total disregard for Canadian neutrality.

The Confederacy sent one of its ablest agents, Jacob Thompson, to carry out the delicate mission. A native of North Carolina, Thompson was a wealthy planter who had served as Secretary of the Interior with President James Buchanan and as an aide to the Confederate General Pierre Beauregard. Jefferson Davis personally chose him for the job and entrusted him with a large sum of money. Thompson's assistant, lawyer and slave owner Clement C. Clay, had served in both the United States and Confederate senates, but was described by one acquaintance as impractical and lacking in judgement.

Unofficially attached to the Confederate team was George N. Sanders of Kentucky, who met the other agents in Canada and claimed to be authorized by Davis himself, though Davis later denied it. Sanders had travelled widely in Europe, had met the great Italian revolutionary Giuseppe Garibaldi, and had shared drinks with the French novelist Victor Hugo. He had served as consul in London under President Franklin Pierce and had been an advisor to President Buchanan. Despite such a background those who knew Sanders well regarded him as unprincipled—and untrustworthy.

There had been other attempts to liberate Johnston's Island but none so daring as the raid Thompson organized in the autumn of 1864. The plan hinged on seizing the *USS Michigan*, the lone warship stationed by the Americans on the Great Lakes. Thompson's chief assistants were John Yates Beall, a renowned Confederate privateer, and Charles Cole, a Canadian who claimed to have been both a captain under the Confederate General Nathan Forrest and a lieutenant in the Confederate navy. Cole's job was to scout the territory, learn the *Michigan*'s schedule, and make friends with her captain and crew. Beall was to secure a vessel that the rebels could use to surprise and capture the *Michigan* while her officers were lulled into a state of somnolent inebriation by Cole. The *Michigan*'s guns would then be used to liberate the prisoners on Johnston's Island.

Cole quickly gained the confidence of the *Michigan*'s officers, dined with them, supplied them liberally with wine and spirits, and learned that though Captain Carter was unhappy with his backwater command, he was not a likely candidate for a bribe. Cole was also using Thompson's money to entertain a young woman. Known as Annie Brown, she was probably a common prostitute, but some writers have cast her as a Union spy. Her part in the story is not clear. One version has her acting as courier between Cole in Sandusky and Thompson in Toronto. Another suggests that she might have been a double agent to whom Cole drunkenly revealed his plan to get the Michigan's crew well into their cups on the night Beall was to lead boarders from another vessel to capture the warship, after which the *Michigan*'s guns would be used to liberate the prisoners on Johnston's Island.

Whatever the case, someone betrayed Cole's plans to the Americans. If it were not the shadowy Annie, then it was an informer in Thompson's organization. Alerted to the plot against his ship, Captain Carter sent men to arrest Cole in his hotel room a few hours before the scheduled drinking party and readied the *Michigan* for battle. Ignorant of Cole's arrest, Beall was in Windsor. Having failed to buy or charter a ship, he resorted to the age-old policy of pirates and stole one. The *Philo Parsons* was a small steamer used as a packet on the run between Detroit and Sandusky. On September 18, 1864, the day of Cole's arrest, a stranger approached Purser W.O. Ashley and asked if some friends of his could be picked up at Sandwich on the Canadian side of the Detroit River. Ashley agreed, and the "friends," one of them Beall, boarded the *Philo Parsons* on the morning of the nineteenth. Sixteen tough-looking men came on board as passengers at Malden, carrying a large trunk. The *Philo Parsons* then crossed the lake to Middle Bass Island, where the captain went ashore to visit his family. She continued her voyage without the captain, making another stop at Kelly's Island, where three more men joined the company. Then, as she steamed toward Sandusky, Beall announced that he was a Confederate officer and took over the ship.

Ashley reported: "I was standing in front of my office when four of the party came to me, and drawing revolvers they levelled them at me and said that if I offered any resistance I was a dead man. At the same time the old black trunk flew open, and in less time than it takes to tell it the whole gang were armed to the teeth with revolvers, hand axes, etcetera. They then stationed two men to watch me, the remainder rushing into the cabins, threatening to shoot everyone who offered any resistance."

The rebels quickly herded the passengers and crew into the hold, firing their guns to show they meant business. The pilot reported that when he told one of them to go to hell, "He shot at me, the ball passing between my legs." With the ship secured, Beall ordered the pilot, fireman, and engineer back to their posts. He next discovered that fuel was low, and with time to spare before the appointed hour for boarding the *Michigan*, he turned back to Middle Bass Island. There the raiders forced the owner of the fuel depot, at gunpoint, to load the ship with wood. While this was going on, a hysterical boy rushed into the captain's house crying that thieves were murdering his father and stealing the wood supply. The captain hurried to the wharf, only to be met at gunpoint and put under guard.

Before the refuelling could be completed, another vessel, the tiny *Island Queen*, tried to attach a line to the *Philo Parsons*. Some of the crew boarded the larger ship and were attacked and beaten by the rebels. When the *Island Queen* tried to pull away, one of Beall's crew shot her pilot in the face. Then, armed with axes, they leaped to her deck and hacked their way through the crew until that ship was also in their possession. Beall released most of his prisoners on shore, including twenty-six Union soldiers on leave who had sworn not to raise an alarm for twenty-four hours. He then towed the *Island Queen* a few miles offshore and scuttled her.

So far everything had gone well for the rebels, but as they approached Johnston's Island, they saw a chilling sight through their telescopes. The *Michigan*, steam up and decks cleared for action, was sitting in a commanding position before the prison island. Cole had obviously failed, and the Yankee warship was ready to send any challenger to the bottom. The Confederates discreetly withdrew. The *Michigan*, failing to recognize the small steamer as the promised Confederate privateer, did not give chase. The *Philo Parsons* now headed back toward Detroit. On the way she met another vessel, and the raiders considered attacking her, but dropped the idea when they realized they were in Canadian waters. At Fighting Island they released their remaining prisoners, keeping only the pilot. At Sandwich they looted the ship of everything they could carry off, including a piano, then scuttled her. Loaded with booty, they set off for Windsor, inviting the unfortunate pilot to join them in a "great spree."

Thompson was disappointed with the failure of his lieutenants but was determined not to give up. Late in October a former Mississippi steamboat captain, using funds provided by Thompson, purchased the steamer *Georgian* in Toronto and turned her over to Beall at Port Colborne. Pretending that the *Georgian* was to be used in the timber trade on Lake Huron, her new owners planned to arm her secretly with cannon and a ram. Beall still hoped to sink the *Michigan*, then turn to privateering with his new ship, capturing Yankee vessels on the lakes. But the *Georgian* never fired a shot for the Confederacy. Canadian police intercepted a cannon that had been stolen from a foundry in Guelph. A search of the Grand Trunk Railway station in that town turned up other war materials marked for delivery to Spanish River on the north shore of Lake Huron. In Toronto they raided a munitions factory in the basement of a house. A trapdoor led them to a large cache of gunpowder, shot, and torpedoes. Canadian authorities finally caught up with the *Georgian* at Collingwood on the south shore of Georgian Bay, where she lay crippled by a broken propeller, and the Confederate scheme for a naval battle on the Great Lakes came to an inglorious end.

The most spectacular of all Confederate operations based in Canada was not an act of piracy but a land raid, which for a few hectic weeks made British North America a tempting target for the powerful Union army. The central participant in this drama was a twenty-one-year-old theology student from Kentucky, Bennett H. Young. The son of wealthy slave owners, Young was well on his way to being a Presbyterian minister when the war started. He enlisted in the Confederate cavalry and rode with the famous Morgan's Raiders until he was captured in 1863. Imprisoned at Camp Douglas, near Chicago, he escaped to Canada and enrolled as a theology student at the University of Toronto, but was soon on his way back to the Confederacy. In Halifax he met Clement Clay, who was on his way to meet Jacob Thompson in Montreal, and Young proposed to the Confederate agent an idea for guerrilla war against the states bordering on Canada. Young was suggesting a series of lightning strikes out of Canada, not only bringing the horrors of war to the Yankees' backyards, but also perhaps capturing some badly needed money for the South. With a handful of men, he pointed out, the raiders could take control of a town, loot the banks, terrorize the citizens, and escape to Canada, leaving the town in flames behind them. The plan seemed feasible provided they did not break any laws on the Canadian side of the border.

Clay liked the idea and so did Sanders, whose son had just died in a Northern prison camp. Thompson opposed it as a worthless adventure without military significance, but his objections were overruled by the Confederate government. The desperate men in Richmond, Virginia, promoted Young to lieutenant and gave him authority to do whatever he thought necessary in this venture. He was authorized to "collect together such Confederate soldiers who may have escaped from the enemy, not exceeding twenty in number" and to "execute such enterprises as may be indicated to you." Young had no trouble finding his men. Canada was swarming with escaped prisoners of war, many of them wanting nothing more than another crack at the "damn Yankees." Clay and Young made it clear that their main purpose was not robbery, but that any "money, treasury, or bank notes" that they might capture were to be turned over to the government of the Confederacy, "or to its representatives in foreign lands." Later some members of the rebel band would have second thoughts on this matter.

The first target was St. Albans, Vermont, a small railroad town just east of Lake Champlain and about sixteen miles south of the Quebec border. Young had selected it during a scouting mission through Vermont and northern New York. From Clay he received $1,400 to outfit his men and cover their expenses. Clay also promised that if they were arrested in Canada after the raid, he could have them released through his contacts within twenty-four hours.

During the third week of October 1864 men began arriving by twos and threes in St. Albans. Despite their Southern accents no one seems to have doubted their story, that they were Canadians on holiday from Montreal with nothing more dangerous in mind than hunting and fishing at Lake Champlain. They took rooms in the hotels and bantered with the locals about the availability of guns in the town. They questioned liverymen about the horses in their stables. They were all horse fanciers, more or less. One of them, possibly Young, allegedly introduced himself to the wife of Governor J. Gregory Smith and toured the governor's own stables.

At 3 P.M. October 19 the raid began. Eyewitness reports do not agree on exactly what happened. The shocked citizens of St. Albans were too shaken to recall the events precisely. Lieutenant Young, either standing on the porch of his hotel or mounted on a stolen horse, drew a navy Colt revolver and announced: "I am an officer in the Confederate army. I have been sent here to take possession of this town, and I'm going to do it." As he spoke his twenty men went into action. While one group herded terrified citizens to the town green, where they could be kept under guard, three others entered the banks with drawn guns and looted them of more than $200,000. It was the first daylight bank robbery in North America, and the raiders' modus operandi became a blueprint for post-war out-laws such as the James and Younger gangs.

Inside the banks the Confederates bullied and threatened the staff and clients. They claimed to have a hundred men in their party and swore they would burn St. Albans to the ground. One private citizen was relieved of $400. Several others were forced at gunpoint to swear allegiance to the Confederacy. One of the raiders told his frightened victims that the attack was revenge for General William T. Sherman's atrocities in Georgia. Those on the town green heard the same message from one of their guards: "You damned Yankees, we'll treat you like you do our people in the South. We'll show you how it feels."

In her house on a hill above the town Mrs. Smith, the gov-ernor's wife prepared to defend herself with an empty rifle. Fortunately she didn't have to go through with the bluff. A Union army captain, George Conger, who was home on leave, slipped away from his guard and hastily organized resistance. He had gathered some forty men, with arms of various kinds, by the time the Confederates emerged from the banks, sacks and pockets stuffed with loot. As Young led his troop out of town on stolen horses, they tossed bottles of Greek fire—early versions of the Molotov cocktail—at several of the buildings, but most of the bombs failed to explode and the fires that did start were quickly extinguished. Conger's men were now mobi-lized, and they opened fire on the retreating rebels. In a brief running gun battle the Confederates killed one man, wounded several others, and lost one of their own. Encouraged by the governor's wife, who wanted the entire band dead or captured, Conger led a posse in hot pursuit. The furious Vermonters ignored a barn fire that Young had started to distract them, but a burning covered bridge held them up long enough to allow the raiders to escape into Canada.

When they crossed the border, the rebels assumed they were safe, but Conger's party, too angry to waste time with customs officials, thundered past the checkpoint and onto Canadian soil. The pursuit continued. About midnight, at Phillipsburg and Frelighsburg near Montreal, the Vermonters captured several of the raiders, including Young. The Confederate officer was badly beaten by the enraged posse and probably owed his life to a British major who arrived on the scene with a company of Canadian militia. The officer advised the Americans that they were in violation of British neutrality and demanded custody of the prisoners. One of the Vermonters waved his gun and scoffed, "We don't give a damn for your neutrality!" But common sense prevailed. Perhaps awed by the British officer, Conger backed down and turned his prisoners over to the Canadian authorities.

Meanwhile the frontier was buzzing with false reports and exaggerated accounts of the raid. Wires hummed between Montreal and Washington. Military and civil leaders heard shocking tales of a town in flames and scores of casualties. Viscount Sir Charles Stanley Monck, Governor-General of Canada, anxious to convince the United States government that his country was not hostile to the North, ordered the arrest of those raiders not yet caught. In all, fourteen of the rebels, including Young, went to jail.

In the United States General John Dix and General Joseph Hooker talked openly of an invasion of Canada. Robert E. Lee, the champion of the South, was critical of the raid as a misuse of his soldiers. Residents of the bordering states expected Confederate guerrillas to come swooping down from Canada, killing and pillaging like the raiders who had earlier carried the black flag through Kansas and Missouri. Farmers loaded their guns and prepared to defend their homes as their grandfathers had done in the border wars of the American Revolution. From Maine to Detroit the Americans tightened border security as best they could and looked on Canada as hostile territory.

The British colonials, including many who sympathized with the South, were outraged by the Confederate government's blatant abuse of Canadian neutrality. Public opinion shifted in favour of the Union. But Young did not feel that he had committed a crime. From his jail cell he wrote to the Montreal *Evening Telegraph*: ". . . the citizens of Vermont, and not our party, will be found to be the violators of Canadian and English law." Other raiders wrote taunting thank-you notes to the citizens of St. Albans.

Privateer schooner *Black Joke* (the *Liverpool Packet*) sailed out of Liverpool and Halifax in the War of 1812. In the whole history of war at sea, no small ship ever equalled her record as a merchant raider. (Bowater-Mersey Limited)

Captain Joseph Barss of Liverpool, Nova Scotia, Commanded the schooner *Liverpool Packet* (the *Black Joke*) the most successful privateer of the War of 1812. (Redrawn from a contemporary portrait.)

Surviving portraits of Enos Collins show a silver-haired banker of eminent respectability, reputed to be the wealthiest man in British North America. His fortune was founded on loot from the War of 1812, in which he was the most successful privateer owner on either side. (Redrawn from a contemporary portrait.)

Privateer brig *Rover* sailed out of Liverpool, Nova Scotia in 1800 against Napoleon and his Spanish allies. She is shown here engaging a French squadron off Canada's east coast. She later captured the flagship of a Spanish squadron especially fitted out to sink or capture her. (Bowater-Mersey Limited)

An alleged likeness of Henry Moore Smith. The authenticity of this portrait is still questioned by historians. (The New Brunswick Museum)

Timbermen of the Ottawa Valley, a century ago, on their raft cookhouse. (PAC #8405)

Toronto's Don Bridge, where the Brooks Bush Gang murdered John Sheridan Hogan.
(Metropolitan Toronto Library)

John C. Braine (left) and John Yates Beall (right) Confederate agents and privateers who
led raids from Canada. The North executed Beall for treason.
(U.S. Department of the Navy, Navel Historical Centre)

The St. Albans Raid — Confederate guerillas from Canada robbing a bank in St. Albans, Vermont during the American Civil War. (St. Albans Historical Society)

The St. Albans Raiders in jail — Five of the captured raiders, and their clergymen, Rev. **Stephen F. Cameron** (standing at left) posed for a photographer in the kitchen of the Montreal jail. **Lt. Bennett H. Young** is seated at right in cavalry boots. Sitting front row centre is **Lewis (or Stephen) Saunders**, cousin of George N. Saunders, an important Confederate agent in Canada. (St. Albans Historical Society)

Donald Morrison, the Canadian "Rob Roy", about the time of his capture. (Metropolitan Toronto Library)

New Advertisements.

$1,000 REWARD!

WHEREAS, on the 6th day of May, instant, JOHN D. B. OGILVY, Esq., Deputy Collector of Customs and Indian Agent, was wilfully murdered on board the schooner "LANGLEY" at Bentinck Arm.

One Thousand Dollars is hereby offered for the apprehension of

ANTOINE LUCANAGE,

commonly known on the coast as "Antoine," who is accused of the murder of the said J. D. B. OGILVY. The reward will be paid to any person handing over the said "Antoine" to any Police authority of the Colony of British Columbia.

By His Excellency's command.

C. BREW,
Chief Inspector of Police.
New Westminster, 26th May, 1865.

DESCRIPTION OF "ANTOINE."

Height about 5ft. 10in., very thin, pitted with the small-pox, light hair and eyes, about 35 years of age, stoops slightly when walking, speaks English well, slight foreign accent, slight moustache and whiskers.

my30-tc

John D. Ogilvie, the customs officer murdered by Antoine Lucanage. (British Columbia Provincial Archives)

Charcoal, the Blood outlaw, defiantly refuses to look into the camera in this picture taken shortly before his execution. The hat hides a pair of handcuffs. (Glenbow Archives)

Medicine Pipestem, the man Charcoal shot. (Glenbow Archives)

Canadian gangster Alvin Karpis (hands bound) is arrested in New Orleans. FBI boss J. Edgar Hoover is in the foreground. (UPI photo)

Norman "Red" Ryan, the bank robber known as the "Canadian Jesse James." (Metropolitan Toronto Police Museum)

While Young and his men languished in jail awaiting trial, Clay and Thompson quarrelled. Thompson had taken no active part in the raid, indeed had been opposed to the whole idea, and he worried that its aftermath would be disastrous to his mission in Canada. Clay, fearing arrest, denied involvement. Since he had promised the raiders legal protection, he gave George Sanders $6,000 for their defence, but on a visit to their jail cell he denounced them as a gang of thieves and wished all of them, except Young, in hell. Clay also wanted all the money that was still in the hands of the uncaptured raiders. This was a considerable sum. Only $86,000 had been recovered. A small amount of cash that spilled out of pockets and saddles along the escape route from St. Albans had been picked up by Canadian and American farmers, some of whom dutifully turned it over to the authorities. But more than $100,000 was still unaccounted for. Disgusted by Clay's apparent betrayal, the raiders refused to trust him with their "prize of war." Some of them apparently tried to turn the loot over to Thompson, but he refused to have anything to do with it. There is evidence that some of the money was used up in legal costs, but the bulk seems to have disappeared with the men who held it. It is unlikely that any of it ever reached the Confederate treasury.

The government in Washington demanded extradition of the prisoners on charges of murder, robbery, arson, horse theft, and assault. The extradition trials, which began in Montreal on December 5, were a sensation. In spite of growing anti-Confederate feeling, the rebels were treated like heroes. They were moved from their cells into the jailer's own house, where Sanders provided them with the best of food, wine, and, it was rumoured, female companions. Young played chess with his guards and subscribed to the St. Albans *Messenger* so he could read the colourful accounts of his raid. The defence team included some of the best lawyers in Canada East, headed by John J. Abbott, a future prime minister.

Abbott, who had no personal liking for his clients, insisted to the court that they had carried out a legitimate act of war on the orders of their government and that the responsibility for the attack rested not with them but with their leaders in Richmond. He had difficulty obtaining documentary evidence to support this argument because President Lincoln refused to grant special couriers passage to the Confederate capital, and Monck refused to take any action at all. Indeed Monck was so anxious to placate Washington that he appointed the clerk of the Crown to work with the prosecution. In spite of such difficulties Abbott won an acquittal, and the raiders were saved from death on a Yankee gallows. There were appeals and further trials, which finally ended when Young was discharged by the court in the autumn of 1865. By that time the war was over. As partial compensation for the raid the Canadian government gave the town of St. Albans an *ex gratia* payment of $70,000 in cash and gold.

Young returned to the South but was not granted the amnesty extended to other Confederate army officers. He had to flee to Europe but later returned to practise law in Kentucky. In 1911 he attended a "St. Albans reunion" in Montreal and met some of the people whom he had robbed. He maintained until his death in 1919 that his raid had helped the Confederate cause. He also wrote a book, *Confederate Wizards of the Saddle*, glorifying the exploits of the Confederate cavalry.

The Canadian connection with the War Between the States did not end with Lee's surrender to Grant at Appomattox on April 9, 1865. On April 14 Abraham Lincoln was assassinated by John Wilkes Booth, an actor who had been a friend of the privateer John Yates Beall. Late in the war Beall had been taken prisoner in New York while trying to sabotage a train carrying Confederate officers to a Union prison. Beall was executed for treason. Booth had visited Montreal in 1864, and it was reported that he plotted Lincoln's murder there, not for political reasons but for personal revenge. It is even said that he went on his knees before the stone-faced Lincoln to beg clemency for Beall, but this may be an embroidery of the facts. Those who believed that Lincoln was the victim of a conspiracy held the Confederate agents in Canada high on their list of suspects. Thompson, Clay, and Sanders were all named as possible conspirators, but papers that might have proved their involvement in the assassination disappeared.

Ironically, Lincoln and Thompson had once been friends, and one of the President's last official orders allowed the Confederate agent to escape arrest. With the Confederacy in ruins Thompson fled from his Toronto headquarters, bound for Europe. While crossing through Maine on his way to Halifax, he was recognized by government agents, who telegraphed for presidential permission to arrest him. Lincoln decided to let the rebel go. He told his assistant secretary of war, Charles A. Dana, "When you have an elephant by the hind leg and he's trying to run away, it's best to let him run." This was only hours before he went to the theatre where Booth killed him.

The argument that Young, Beall, and the other Confederate raiders based in Canada were carrying out legitimate acts of war is tenuous at best. Strictly speaking, they were outlaws. Their motives might have been patriotic, but they had no licence to make war from Canadian soil. Their methods discredited their own nation and in some cases were not acts of privateering but acts of outright piracy. In twentieth-century terms they might be called terrorists. Their operations had one unexpected result: by placing the British colonies under the Yankee gun, they focused attention on weaknesses in British North America that could be cured only by a strong union. So the dying Confederacy helped sway opinion in the direction that soon brought about the birth of the Canadian nation.

Chapter 12
Viscount Monck and the Reno Gang

BANDITS HAVE NEVER SHOWN MUCH RESPECT for borders, and on many occasions during the nineteenth century they caused severe strains in the relationship between Canada and the United States. By far the most notorious of the border-hopping bandits were the Renos, a brotherhood of hard-riding, gunslinging desperadoes who terrorized the American Midwest in the post-Civil War years and robbed trains before Jesse James ever thought of the idea. Three of the gang eventually came to roost in Canada, where, according to legend, they hid a fortune in plunder.

Several gunmen, burglars, and road agents worked with the outlaw gang at various times, but the Reno brothers themselves, all natives of Indiana, were the principal members of the band. Frank, the leader, was born in 1837, John in 1839, Simeon in 1843, and William in 1848. A fifth brother, Clinton, was nicknamed ''Honest Reno'' because he alone did not live by the gun. The father of the clan, an unlettered Kentuckian, was one of the most prosperous farmers in his county, but farming apparently did not appeal to his four wayward sons, who would rather raise hell than knuckle down to hard work.

During the Civil War the Reno boys worked a lucrative bounty-jumping scam. They would enlist in the army, collect a bounty for signing up, then desert and enlist again elsewhere. After the war they moved into the little town of Rockford in Jackson County, Indiana, and made it their headquarters. A newspaper in nearby Seymour reported that ''Jackson County contains more cutthroats to the square inch than Botany Bay.'' Through bribery and intimidation the Renos quickly took control of Rockford and terrorized Seymour. They were notorious card cheats and were known housebreakers and highway robbers, but few people dared oppose them. Those who did saw their houses and barns go up in flames or simply disappeared. When local pickings grew thin, the Renos began raiding treasury offices in other counties, always striking just after the tax collector had made his rounds and the safe was fat with public money. Then, in October 1866, Frank Reno "invented" train robbery when he led his brothers and a few associates in a raid on a train near Seymour and rode off with $13,000. The Renos' method of commandeering the engine and express car and systematically robbing the passengers of money and valuables was copied by numerous Western outlaws, including Frank and Jesse James.

A few robberies later, when it became obvious that local authorities were either too afraid or too well bribed to do anything about the Renos, the railroad and express companies hired the Pinkerton Detective Agency to run the outlaws down. Allan Pinkerton placed agents in Seymour and Rockford and began gathering information on the bandits. Shortly after the treasury office of Davies County, Missouri, was burglarized, Pinkerton men literally kidnapped John Reno and delivered him to jail. Frank Reno swore he would rescue his brother before he could be taken to prison but did not. He later wrote John a letter explaining that he had a plan set up, but the men who were to have helped him missed their train. In his autobiography John Reno recalled his entrance into the Jefferson City Prison: "When we arrived at the prison gate, I looked up and read in large letters over the entrance: 'THE WAY OF THE TRANSGRESSOR IS HARD Admission, twenty-five cents.' But I was on the dead-head list and went in free."

The remaining Renos, with an ever-changing cast of accomplices, continued robbing banks, trains, and treasury offices. In one job they knocked over a bank and a train in the same town. The boldness of their crimes was surpassed only by the gang's flair for violence and brutality. They pistol-whipped uncooperative victims and shot a troublesome train conductor. A witness to one of their robberies was gunned down in broad daylight while the town looked on. When an express-car clerk refused to cooperate, the outlaws seized him by the arms, shouted "One, two, and to hell you go," and threw him out the door of a fast-moving train. A woman whom they mistakenly thought had a large sum of money hidden in her house was hanged by the neck and almost strangled to death before the outlaws were convinced she had nothing to steal.

As the bandit boss of his region, Frank Reno jealously guarded his hunting ground from trespassers. In September 1867, when a pair of free-lance thieves robbed a train of $8,000 without inviting the Renos in on the job, Frank sent a few of his boys to beat them up and then informed on them. As a result the unlucky pair went to prison, and Frank got his message across: in Indiana only Renos could rob trains. This did not mean, however, that he couldn't expand his own operations.

Early in 1868 Frank Reno and three others, including Mike Rogers, a leading citizen and "pillar of the Methodist Church" in his hometown of Council Bluffs, Iowa, pulled robberies in two small Iowa towns, netting over $20,000. Pinkerton agents traced the robbers to Rogers's home in Council Bluffs and arrested them as they were trying to burn the money—the only evidence linking them to the crimes—in a kitchen stove. They were locked up in the county jail at Glenwood, Iowa, but sometime before the morning of April 1 they managed to knock a hole through a wall and escape. They left a message scrawled in chalk on a wall for the guards and the Pinkerton men: "APRIL FOOL!"

Frank Reno hurried back to Indiana to reassemble his gang. With his brothers Simeon and William, Mike Rogers, and Charles Anderson, a Detroit-based safecracker, he stopped a train near Marshfield, Indiana, on May 22 and rode off with his biggest haul ever: $97,000 in cash and government bonds. In the course of the robbery they shot and wounded a conductor who pulled a gun and threw an express clerk, who tried to grab a weapon, out of the train. The man hit a sandy embankment and was not seriously hurt. Within a week of the hold-up Simeon and William Reno were caught in Indianapolis and taken to a jail in New Albany. It was not considered wise to hold them in Seymour, where a strong anti-Reno vigilante group was forming. The advocates of Lynch law had already snatched six known members of the Reno gang from the hands of police and strung them up without benefit of trial. They had sworn to continue their deadly work until the last outlaw dangled from a tree.

Sensing it was high time for a change of scenery, Frank Reno, Mike Rogers, and Charles Anderson fled to Windsor, Ontario, where Anderson had a house and many friends. (One story has it that Simeon Reno joined the trio, but this is an error. He was secure in the New Albany jail when his brother took up residence in Canada.) At that time Windsor was a favourite sanctuary for American outlaws on the run. The town's Turf Club was a popular meeting place for thieves and killers. Langdon Moore, an American bandit who visited Windsor, described it in his memoirs as a Canadian Dodge City, where one could meet in any bar some of the characters who made the West wild.

It did not take the Pinkerton agents long to trace Reno and company to Windsor. They simply trailed a small-time thief named Jack Friday, who was a known associate of the Renos. Friday led the detectives to the hideout in Windsor, and the sluggish wheels of bureaucracy were set in motion. Canada and the United States had an extradition agreement, but the rules and procedures were full of grey areas and legal pitfalls, which a clever bandit with a good lawyer could take advantage of. Reno had a first-class lawyer in John O'Conner, who later became attorney general. While a flurry of letters and telegrams issued from the offices of Prime Minister John A. Macdonald, Governor-General Charles Stanley Monck, American Secretary of State William Seward, Allan Pinkerton, British Ambassador to Washington Edward Thornton, and Magistrate Gilbert McMicken, chief of the Dominion Police, Reno took the offensive. He probably thought a legal showdown would be better than moving on, hounded by Pinkerton men and Canadian police.

Still the master of the bribe, he had himself arrested in Windsor by a Detroit detective, hoping to force his enemies to show their hand before they had a solid case against him. He knew the Canadians would not deport him or his friends without indisputable proof of the charges against them. The charges, armed robbery and assault with intent to kill, were hotly contested by John O'Conner. In a report to the Governor-General, O'Conner presented evidence that Reno and Anderson were not even in Indiana on the day of the Marshfield robbery. They had been seen in Windsor and later at the race-track in Chatham by several people, including the chief constable of Windsor. The robbery victims who identified Frank Reno, O'Conner said, had to be mistaken. These witnesses all agreed that it was dark when the robbers boarded the train, and the outlaws were disguised. And one of them admitted that Frank Reno could easily be mistaken for his brother Simeon. As for the charge of assault with intent to kill, O'Conner challenged the Crown to prove there had actually been an intent to kill. The bullet, fired by an unidentified bandit, had passed through the conductor's coat, wounding him slightly. O'Conner argued that "he who fired the shot, intended that the ball should so pass; and as a necessary corollary, he did not intend to kill or murder." In other words, the trigger-happy bandit wanted to shoot the coat, not the man who was wearing it.

Reno's scheme almost worked. Twice he and his friends were taken before Windsor magistrates and twice they were discharged. But Pinkerton and Seward were not easily discouraged. They persisted in their demands for custody of the suspects and reminded Macdonald and Monck of the assistance Americans had given the Canadians in disrupting Fenian activity along the border. The Canadian officials finally decided to dismiss O'Conner's long-winded alibi and hold Reno and Anderson for an extradition trial. Rogers, who was not identified by anybody at the scene of the robbery, was released.

O'Conner still managed to have the trial delayed day by day, expressing his concern that "these men are hunted by private detectives for speculation—that if surrendered they will not be tried, but delivered over to a mob, called a vigilance committee, to be murdered in the same manner as six other men have already been served." This point was well taken, in the opinion of Lord Monck. The Governor-General, who alone had authority to sign extradition warrants, would not do so until he had assurances that the prisoners would be fairly tried in a court of law and not executed by vigilantes. He made this clear in several letters and telegrams to Macdonald, Thornton, and Seward.

Frank Reno, meanwhile, was not idle in jail. He made one try at escape but was foiled when guards discovered a six-foot-by-fourteen-inch hole in the wooden floor of his cell. Reno probably expected help from the Windsor underworld. The town's criminal population had been swelled by an influx of thieves and desperadoes, hungry for a share of the $97,000 heist, which Reno was said to have stashed somewhere in Windsor. In fact he and Anderson were drawing from the loot to pay their legal costs. It was widely rumoured that a gang of ruffians stood ready to rescue not only Reno and Anderson but also two other outlaws named Morton and Thompson, who had robbed the New York Central Railway of $30,000. They too were being held for extradition. But the rescue never came off, and Reno resorted to other, darker means.

First he tried to bribe the teenage son of one of the magistrates conducting the extradition hearings: he offered the boy $6,000 in gold if he would influence his father in their behalf. The plan backfired when the youngster reported the bribery attempt to his father. Reno then tried to have Allan Pinkerton assassinated. Reports conflict as to whether the assault took place in Windsor or Detroit, but as Pinkerton stepped from a ferry onto a wharf, Dick Barry, a known outlaw, approached him and drew a gun. Reacting with the speed of a much younger man, the forty-nine-year-old detective seized the would-be killer's gun hand and jammed a finger behind the trigger, making it impossible for Barry to fire. Pinkerton wrestled the man to the ground and held him until a sailor came to his aid. Washington was outraged by the murder attempt, and Seward, a personal friend of Pinkerton, thought he might intimidate the Canadians into hurrying things along by sending a gunboat to Windsor. The vessel stayed ten days and was removed after loud protests from the Canadian government.

Shocked by Reno's treacherous behaviour and assured many times over by Seward that every precaution would be taken for the prisoners' safety, Monck finally decided it was time to send the train robbers home. On October 19, 1868, he wrote to Macdonald, "I think, having taken all precautions in our power for securing the prisoners from 'Lynch law,' that we have no valid [illegible] for delaying the issue of the warrant." A few days later, on a Saturday evening, the sheriff of Essex County delivered Anderson and Reno, in handcuffs and irons, to Allan Pinkerton. A crowd of about fifty rough characters had assembled on the Windsor dock, but any ideas they might have had about rescuing the outlaws were dampened by the presence of a large force of Dominion Police and a strong American escort. The prisoners were placed without incident on board the tug *Seneca*. The real danger lay on the other side of the river, where both outlaws and vigilantes were waiting to wrest Reno and Anderson away from the police for their own respective purposes.

To foil these equally lawless groups, the Americans started the *Seneca* upriver along the Canadian shore toward Lake St. Clair, giving the impression they were heading for Michigan City, Indiana. But once they passed Belle Isle, they turned around and went down the American side, bound for Cleveland. From there the guards would take their prisoners to New Albany by a secret route. That was the plan Monck had arranged with Seward. However, as the little tug was passing Detroit in the darkness, she collided with the steamer *Phil Sheridan* and was cut clean in two. The *Seneca* went down in a minute, leaving her fifteen passengers and crew in the water. The manacled outlaws would have gone straight to the bottom had it not been for Captain Patrick Foley of the *Seneca* and Pinkerton agent John Curtain, who held onto the helpless men while struggling to keep their own heads above water. The crew of the *Phil Sheridan* rescued all of the men and landed them at the Detroit dock. Reno and Anderson were locked in a heavily guarded jail while officials arranged for a special train to transport them to Indiana.

For the moment it seemed the crisis was over. Seward wrote Ambassador Thornton "a very handsome letter," expressing his appreciation for the manner in which the case had been handled. Thornton passed the pat on the back to Lord Monck, who in turn extended it to Macdonald. Magistrate McMicken seemed to be heaving a sigh of relief when he wrote to Macdonald on October 27, "Re, Reno and Anderson. The agony is over and by tonight they doubtless will be safe in New Albany gaol."

The Renos—Frank, William, and Simeon—as well as Anderson were indeed in the New Albany jail, but they were not safe. The vigilance committee, having no intention of honouring Washington's deal with the Canadian governor, had determined that as far as the Renos were concerned, "the agony" wasn't over yet.

Upon delivering his charges to New Albany, Allan Pinkerton had inspected the jail and immediately advised the sheriff, Thomas Fullenlove, to transport them to a stronger prison in Indianapolis. Fullenlove refused. New Albany was a law-abiding town, unlike Seymour, where citizens lynched outlaws as regularly as they hung out the laundry. Fullenlove insisted on keeping the prisoners in his jail, and there they stayed until December 13, 1868.

At 11 P.M. December 12 "a train of mystery" pulled out of Seymour. Inside the single car were fifty-six men armed with guns and clubs and wearing red flannel hoods. When the train rolled into New Albany at 3:30 A.M. on December 13, the mob poured out of the car and silently took over the sleeping town. The few people found on the streets were taken prisoner. Armed parties patrolled a few strategic blocks while most of the men headed for the jail. They found jailer Chuck Whitten on guard in front of the building, warming himself by a fire in the gutter. Before Whitten knew what was happening, the raiders jumped him, took his gun, and left him hog-tied in a chair in the sheriff's office. The angels of death poured into the jailhouse.

The leader took a few men to the upstairs room where Sheriff Fullenlove was sleeping with his wife. Awakened by the noise below, Fullenlove met them at the door. The vigilantes demanded the keys to the cells, but Fullenlove surprised them by barging through their ranks until he got outside. "I am the sheriff!" he cried, "the highest peace officer in the country and if you respect the law you will not dare to shoot me."

He was wrong. As he ran to the street to raise an alarm, over a dozen shots were fired at him. Two or three struck his right arm. As he staggered, one of the vigilantes clubbed him to the ground with a gun butt. "Don't kill him," the leader ordered.

"Take him into the house." The masked men tried to frighten Mrs. Fullenlove into handing over the keys, but she was no more cooperative than her husband. The vigilantes finally locked Fullenlove, his wife and children, and Whitten into a room while they ransacked the office. They found a ring of keys but were furious that none of them would open the jail door. Then Tom Matthews, Fullenlove's deputy, appeared with a gun on the other side of the bars and declared he would shoot anyone who tried to break in. Hardly intimidated, the vigilante leader held up five nooses. Four, he said, were for the three Reno brothers and Anderson. The fifth was for the deputy if he didn't "behave himself" and open the door. Matthews hesitated, then when the lynching party threatened to break down the door and hang him, he opened up. After tying up Matthews, the vigilantes went straight for the Renos and Anderson, ignoring the other prisoners who cringed in terror in their cells.

Frank was the first to be dragged out and hanged from a rafter, gasping, "Lord have mercy on my soul." Simeon and William Reno followed. William, youngest but biggest of the outlaw brothers, fought like a cornered bear and seriously injured several of his attackers before they got a rope around his neck. He died pleading innocence of any crime. Anderson was the last to go. When the rope he swung from broke, dropping him to the floor, he pleaded for his life and prayed to God for help. "It's too late now for prayers, Charlie," the vigilante leader said. Using a fresh rope, they strung up Anderson again. To make sure the job was well done, members of the mob hugged the dangling bodies and, swinging like apes, broke necks and crushed windpipes. When the last corpse had stopped twitching, one vigilante suggested that every prisoner in the jail be lynched. But the leader, satisfied that their job was done, called his men together and got them quickly out of town.

Nothing was ever done about the mass lynching, though the identities of several of the hooded men were known. State and local officials were too glad that the Renos' reign of terror was over. Ironically, a new wave of crime swept Indiana as outlaws, posing as vigilantes, robbed and murdered with impunity, taking care to select known or suspected Reno friends and sympathizers as their victims.

In Canada there was outrage and disgust. The Renos were nobody's heroes, but the Canadian sense of law and justice had been betrayed. Lord Monck wrote to Washington, demanding an apology for "the shocking and indefensible lynching" of the Renos and Anderson. Anglo-American relations, already touchy in the wake of the Civil War, were once again strained, and there was speculation that Britain would cancel all extradition agreements with the United States, making Canada a safe haven for American criminals. The U.S. Senate hastily passed a bill providing federal protection for extradited prisoners, and Seward enclosed a copy of that bill with the official apology he sent to Canada and Britain.

Little of the money stolen by the Renos in their brief career was ever recovered. The loot from the Marshfield train robbery, which Frank Reno, Charles Anderson, and Mike Rogers had allegedly carried into Canada, was of considerable interest to law officers and treasure hunters. Some of it was spent on legal fees, some to cover living expenses, and no doubt many dollars were squandered in saloons, brothels, and gambling dens. In the spring of 1869 Allan Pinkerton informed Magistrate McMicken that about $16,000 in bonds stolen at Marshfield had been circulating on the Chicago black market. This still left the lion's share of the plunder unaccounted for. Mike Rogers might have taken it, but this doesn't seem likely because he was soon in prison for burglary and counterfeiting. When searchers could find no outlaw booty in the woods around Seymour, they looked to Windsor as the most likely site of a hidden fortune. Many people hunted for the lost hoard, but no one found it.

Long after it was all over, a Pinkerton agent named Pat O'Neill, who had taken up journalism as a second career, attempted to debunk the story of the massive Reno loot hidden somewhere in the Windsor area. His attempt was not very convincing. There was no doubt about the size of the haul and no doubt about the fact that it was still hidden when Reno and Anderson were hustled across the border to their deaths. But for all practical purposes the money might just as well have been a myth, because the only people who knew where the riches were stashed had been choked to death by a commitee of their victims.

Chapter 13
The Canadian Rob Roy

FOR ALMOST FOUR YEARS young Donald Morrison had followed one of the toughest, dirtiest trades on the North American frontier—the unglamorous job of the cowboy. The workload was Herculean and the pay Spartan; no Eastern romantic put up with the cowboy's life for long. Morrison loved it. Throughout the early 1880s the burly, strong-minded Scot roamed the cattle country from Texas to Saskatchewan, working or drifting as suited his independent soul. As a novice he had choked on dust while "riding drag" behind bawling herds. Later, as experience earned him promotion, he had marked trail and kept an eye peeled for rustlers while "riding point." He knew the horror of a stampede and the loneliness of the line rider's shack. He had never complained about sleeping on the ground or living on the monotonous fare of chuckwagon cooks: sourdough biscuits, beans, and a concoction called son-of-a-bitch stew. Morrison could ride and rope with the best of them, and he knew how to handle a gun. After four years of the cowboy's life he had accumulated substantial savings. He might never have left his free life on the prairie had he not received a letter from home late in the summer of 1883.

Home for Donald Morrison was a two-hundred-acre farm on the shore of Lake Megantic in the Eastern Townships, ninety miles south of Quebec City, near the border of Maine. It was a Gaelic-speaking community hacked out of the wilderness by Scottish settlers. Donald's parents, Murdo and Sophie, natives of the Isle of Lewis in the Outer Hebrides, had arrived in Canada in 1838, having been forced like thousands of their countrymen to emigrate to make room for sheep to supply the English textile mills with wool.

Sponsored by the British American Land Company, they homesteaded in Lingwick, where their children were born (Donald about 1858), then on the farm near Megantic. The youngest of the Morrisons, Donald helped his father and brothers haul rocks, cut trees, and pull stumps—drudgery that was a commonplace of most pioneer life in Canada. He escaped by riding off to the wild West, but even after four years as a cowboy he could not ignore his parents' letter. The family farm was in trouble; they needed him at home.

He returned to find his father $700 in debt and desperately in need of help to manage the farm. Donald did not know that his father was sinking into senility and had already quarrelled with his older sons over money. Donald paid off the debt and took over the lion's share of the work. For two years it went well. Father and son worked together to make the farm productive. But Murdo became increasingly critical of Donald's expenditures on improvements and of the time and money his son spent at the American House, a popular Megantic tavern. Donald was used to spending his money as he saw fit, and after a week's hard work he enjoyed a Saturday evening in the saloon. He resented his father's badgering and his refusal to turn full control of the farm over to him as promised. By the third year they were hardly speaking to each other. Donald refused to sink more of his savings into the farm, so his father borrowed $300 from Donald's brother, Murdo Jr. When that was gone, he went to a money-lender, Major Malcolm B. McAulay.

A native of Ross in the Highlands of Scotland, McAulay had come to Canada as a child. At eighteen he had volunteered for the Union army, and by the end of the War Between the States was a lieutenant colonel. He then returned to the Eastern Townships, where he made a fortune in real estate, construction, the lumber trade, and as a money-lender. He held major's rank in the militia and was regarded as a leading citizen but was heartily detested by the farmers for his usury and land grabbing. When Murdo Morrison asked for a loan in 1886, McAulay smelled prey.

The financial swamp that bogged the Morrison farm was complicated, to say the least. Murdo needed money to keep it going. He was in debt to three of his sons. The brothers wanted their expenses paid and claimed something for the labour they had put into the farm. Donald's claim was $900. Murdo signed a mortgage with McAulay for $1,100, half of which he received up front. The other half was "to be applied against the mortgage when due." Murdo would pay full interest on the loan, though he had received only half the amount. It was a legal swindle, designed to grab the land, but Murdo willingly placed his mark on the agreement of which he couldn't read a word. He then paid back some of the money he had borrowed from Murdo Jr. but had nothing for Donald. Angry, Donald sought legal help. Sherbrooke lawyer B.C. McLean advised him to sue, explaining that the suit would force the farm to auction. Donald could then buy it and have McAulay's shady mortgage reduced to second-mortgage status on the grounds that Murdo's sons had a prior claim. Trusting his lawyer, Donald agreed to the plan.

On September 18, 1886, title to the Morrison farm went on the block. The only bidders were Donald Morrison and Major McAulay. It was no contest. The major showed up with more money than Donald could hope to raise and bought the farm for $1,000. Donald spent the next few months trying to fight the mortgage and the sale in court. He lost on both counts. Eventually he could no longer get legal assistance because he could not pay his lawyers. He took his claims to McAulay but to no avail. In March 1887 McAulay had the Morrisons evicted.

Donald Morrison moved his parents into a cabin near Marsden, just west of Megantic, then moved back to the empty farmhouse. On the land he found a number of stripped logs that McAulay had contracted to sell for telegraph poles. He cut them up for firewood. The enraged major had him arrested and assessed a hefty $50 fine. When he returned to the farm, Morrison found that McAulay had ordered his clothing and furniture to be seized. He promptly charged the money-lender with illegal entry and theft but could produce neither lawyers nor witnesses, and after three postponements the charges were dropped. "That was burning me to the very heart," Morrison said later, "that this man got off scot free no matter what he did while I was punished for every little thing."

In June 1887 Donald was forcibly evicted from his house by the police, but he let it be known that anyone who tried to live in it would do so at his peril. McAulay, anxious to be rid of the troublesome property, offered it for sale. No Scot would buy it, but a French Canadian named Auguste Duquette came up with the $1,600 McAulay was asking and moved his family to the farm. Duquette knew about the McAulay–Morrison feud but expected no trouble. McAulay assured him that Morrison's claim was a dead issue. In fact, Donald Morrison was not seen in Megantic for some months, and rumour had it that he was heading west once more. Actually he was in Montreal looking for lawyers to help him regain his property. They all told him the same thing: he *had* been badly treated; he *had* been badly counselled by McLean; but there was nothing he could do about it now. He thought otherwise.

On April 3, 1888, a stranger approached Duquette in his fields—a tall Scot with a thick moustache who warned him to clear out within ten days. On April 16 the stranger returned, this time with a companion, and repeated the warning. Duquette replied that he had bought the farm legally and intended to stay, but he was worried enough to talk to McAulay, who promised to have Morrison arrested if the harassment continued.

Three weeks later, on May 8, the Duquettes woke up in the middle of the night to find their barn in flames. A timely breeze kept the fire from the house, but they lost the barn and some of their animals. On May 17 a bullet shattered the kitchen window and sent the terrified family diving for the floor. Duquette peeked outside and saw a shadowy figure aiming a rifle. A moment later a second bullet whistled into the farmhouse, and Duquette hit the floor again. The only casualty was the family's grandfather clock, its face smashed and its hands stopped at 9:30. Duquette reported the attack to the police and moved his family to a neighbour's house. Ironically, the neighbour was Murdo Morrison Jr. Duquette then went back to the farm, promising his wife he would get help. But no neighbours would agree to share his vigils, and after a trip to town he returned to find the house a smoking ruin.

No one could prove that Morrison had set the fires or done the shooting. He told friends that he had nothing to do with either and that he could bring witnesses to swear he had been miles from Megantic on the nights in question. Someone else, for whatever reason, was terrorizing the Duquettes, he said, but authorities in Megantic thought it unlikely. On June 6 Coroner A.G. Woodward held an inquest into the events. Several witnesses, including Murdo Jr.'s wife, said they had heard Donald threaten to drive the Frenchman off his farm. A man named McDonald had loaned Morrison a rifle. Woodward issued a warrant for Donald Morrison's arrest, charging him with arson and attempted murder.

Morrison, who felt he had done nothing wrong, had no intention of giving himself up, but thought it best to lie low until things cooled off. Local police made a half-hearted search but were frustrated by the Scots' wall of silence. Irish and French Canadians in the area were also uncooperative. Many of them knew what it was to be gouged by a money-lender and were already hiding and feeding the fugitive. They admired what they took to be his defiant stand against McAulay. As a Montreal *Star* editorial later put it: "The people of the Scotch settlements declare they have suffered for years the greatest injustice at the hands of unscrupulous moneylenders. Till the Morrison outbreak, the hostility of the people did not show itself. He is the first to declare his enmity, and his friends and countrymen, who claim to have suffered the same as him [sic], consider it their duty to stand by him."

McAulay considered Morrison a dangerous criminal and feared for his life. After all, if the young fool had shot at the innocent Duquettes, what might he do to the man who had swindled the damned farm from him in the first place! He demanded Morrison's arrest. But who would attempt it in the face of local opinion and after the poor showing by the police? The answer came from the barroom of the American House. There a certain Lucius Jack Warren was heard to boast that if the timid constables would keep out of his way, he could take care of Morrison. Warren was an American who fancied himself a gunfighter in the mould of Wild Bill Hickok and Wyatt Earp. He was not popular in Megantic, but that did not bother him. He cared little for the opinions of a bunch of farmers. Megantic was merely his Canadian business headquarters. Posing as a hunting and fishing guide, Warren made his living as a smuggler, running bootleg booze into Maine and Vermont. But he hinted to his drinking pals at the American House that he had done a few deeds more spectacular than rum running. He wore a gun and assured everyone he knew how to use it.

On June 18 Justice of the Peace Joseph H. Morin swore Warren in as a special constable and gave him a warrant for Morrison's arrest. Over the next few days Warren made the rounds of the taverns, his gun on his hip, bragging that he would either take Morrison alive or drop him in his tracks. When he wasn't drinking and talking, Warren practised his fast draw in the yard behind his hotel. The noise of gunfire disturbed the usually quiet village as he blasted away at imaginary outlaws. Donald, keeping to the woods, heard from friends about the American who had sworn to bring him in dead or alive. He had no wish for a confrontation. He had met men like Warren in the Western cowtowns, braggarts who talked themselves into dangerous situations, where they had either to shoot or lose face. He stayed away from Megantic until Friday, June 22, when he believed Warren was out searching for him with the regular police, and then ventured into the village to buy supplies.

What happened next was like a scene from a Western movie. As Morrison walked down the main street in the early afternoon towards the American House, word swept through the community that he was in town, and people scurried for cover, then watched to see what would happen. Warren was drinking beer on the veranda of the pub when someone told him that Morrison was coming down the street. Peering out, he saw a rugged-looking Scot, walking stick in hand, approaching. He asked Nelson Leet, the hotel owner, "Is that Morrison?" Leet said it was. Warren disappeared into the hotel momentarily, perhaps to check his gun, perhaps to steel himself with a shot of liquid courage. When he came out, he took his stand on the sidewalk, confronting Morrison and calling on him to halt. "Stand clear!" Donald ordered as he stepped off the sidewalk to go around the American. Again Warren blocked his way and told him to surrender. "Stand clear!" Donald repeated, shifting the cane to his left hand.

For a minute they exchanged challenges, Warren with a gun on his hip and a warrant in his pocket, Morrison with a gun in his coat and a cane in his hand. After Donald's third "Stand clear!" Warren's hand dropped to his holster. Instantly Morrison whipped the Colt .45 from his pocket and fired. Warren staggered back, then fell facedown in the street, his gun drawn but unfired. Morrison, who had killed him with a single shot through the neck, looked down at the body, its hand reaching for the gun that lay in the dirt a few feet away, then calmly walked out of town. A few days later, disguised and discreetly keeping to the rear of the small group of mourners, he attended Warren's funeral.

In the American West, where Donald had learned how to use a Colt, shootings were so common that cowhands, with grim humour, called them "death by natural causes." Had Donald killed Warren in similar circumstances in Texas or New Mexico, it would have been called self-defence, and no charge would have been laid. But in Canada men did not carry the law in their gun holsters. After a coroner's inquest a new warrant was issued for Morrison's arrest, this time for murder, and the huge reward of $2,000 was offered on the wanted posters. Local police had neither the will nor the manpower to search hundreds of square miles of forest and bush for the outlaw, so they sent to Sherbrooke and Quebec City for reinforcements.

At the same time the Scots in the Eastern Townships patched together a shadowy network, called the Morrison Defence Organization, to protect him from the police. It had its agents in every community of Highlanders and every homestead of sympathetic farmers. Morrison had become a folk hero. The Scots called him their own Rob Roy, after the legendary seventeenth-century outlaw, Scotland's answer to Robin Hood. They also compared Morrison with Louis Riel, the French-Canadian leader

recently hanged by the Canadian Tories. Farmers of all national-
ities fed Morrison, sheltered him, and kept him informed of
police movements. French-speaking or English-speaking officers who tried to gather information found those who would
talk knew nothing or offered false leads or could speak only
Gaelic.

Morrison did not quit the area, though he could have crossed
into Maine with ease and taken a train to the cattle country,
where any experienced cowhand could find work with no questions asked. But like many other outlaws, including the notorious Billy the Kid, whose story is not unlike Morrison's, Donald
stuck close to home. He seemed to believe that sooner or later
justice (as he saw it) would prevail.

The police were not the only people looking for the elusive
Morrison. A reporter from the Montreal *Star*, Peter Spanyaardt,
had been nosing around Megantic for four weeks, trying to pick
up leads on the sensational story. More than anything he wanted
an exclusive interview with the outlaw. He fired off articles to
his paper, praising the law-abiding Scots and their lovely Lake
Megantic country and reporting the police failures to catch Morrison. He interviewed and quoted Morrison's friends, something
the hostile Sherbrooke *Gazette* had not done. "We do not
approve of Morrison's conduct," he quoted one farmer as saying,
"but we thoroughly believe that the boy has been badly treated,
and we simply want to see him have fair play, which he cannot
obtain till his side of the story has been published in the public
press."

Spanyaardt's persistence paid off. On August 7, as he sat down
to breakfast in his hotel, a visitor informed him that Morrison
was ready to tell his side of the story. The reporter left his meal
on the table and hurried to the train station for the first leg of a
roundabout journey that would lead him to the outlaw. He
had to jump from the train at a slow curve, where he met Scottish
guides who whisked him along back roads and trails until he
was completely lost. Then a guide put him into a buggy and
drove him along a lonely road guarded by armed men who spoke
to the driver in Gaelic and seemed to dislike the outsider's

presence. The buggy finally drew up at a small farmhouse; the guide went in, and Spanyaardt then waited about five minutes before he was invited inside. There he came face to face with the notorious Morrison: ". . . a tall, gaunt, big-framed Scotchman, with a ruddy complexion and steel blue eyes, high cheekbones, tawny moustache and a rather serious mien, which however was lightened at times by a specially charming smile."

Pacing back and forth while Spanyaardt scribbled in his notebook, Morrison poured out his tale of family quarrels, of McAulay's swindle, of the auction and the evictions. He denied shooting at the Duquettes or burning their house and barn. As for Jack Warren, the man had never identified himself as a constable, had pulled a gun, and he had shot him in self-defence. When asked about surrender, Morrison said he intended to "keep out of the way . . . but if I'm cornered they will never take me alive . . . for there is no justice of me in Sherbrooke." He added that he had sent a letter to McAulay demanding the $900 that the major still owed him. "When the matter goes through the press, so that people can see what the trouble is, I will know better what to do. . . . If he will return this money, I am ready to leave the country."

The interview, written in Spanyaardt's flamboyant style, made sensational copy. Across the country newspapers reprinted it, and the Canadian Rob Roy became national drama, almost a national hero. Not all Canadians agreed. Quebec Premier Honoré Mercier and Attorney General Arthur Turcotte were as disgusted with the lionizing of Morrison as they were impatient with the failure of the police to arrest him. They had little sympathy for a man with one hand on the plough and the other on a six-gun. But how to pluck him out of the wilderness, where every stand of timber was a hideout and every farmer his friend? They tried negotiating with the Defence Organization. If Morrison would surrender and promise in writing not to disturb Major McAulay, they would turn the reward money posted for his capture over to the Scots to cover his legal fees. For three days the Defence Organization considered the proposal, then, suspecting a trap, rejected it. The government was too slow in guaranteeing the transfer of the money, and the idea of McAulay getting out of the mess untouched did not sit well with Morrison.

The authorities responded by raising the reward to $3,000 and sending in reinforcements. Amid much controversy a contingent of Montreal city police joined the manhunt. They weren't much help. They quarrelled with the other policemen, antagonized the local population with threats, and failed to turn up a single useful lead. By December, with Morrison still at large, the provincial opposition and the Montreal press wanted to know whether the city police were tracking down an outlaw or having a holiday at taxpayers' expense. They began calling the expedition the Megantic Picnic. While his men chased a will-o'-the-wisp, Montreal's police chief George Hughes tried to justify what they were doing, and, at the same time, cope with the difficulties of his short-handed department in the city. Meanwhile Morrison tried to "keep out of the way," as he had told Spanyaardt. Loyal supporters hid him in barns and attics or left food where a wandering fugitive could find it at night. He had his narrow escapes and on some occasions must have been but a heartbeat from drawing his gun. There are numerous stories of his close calls, some of them probably true. As is often the case, it is hard to disentangle fact from fiction.

In one story Morrison is visiting the home of an elderly Scottish lady when the police come knocking. He hides under the bed while she answers the door. As she responds to their questions in Gaelic, pretending to have no English or French, she spots one of the fugitive's boots sticking out under the bed. Continuing her flow of Gaelic without a change of expression, she warns Morrison to get his feet out of sight. He does so, and the posse leaves.

Another tale describes a chance encounter between Donald and a police patrol on a lonely road. It is the depth of winter, when every move leaves prints in the snow, but the Defence Organization confounds the police by sending people out to tramp around in the bush, confusing Morrison's trails. The tactic works, but in one instance he runs smack into a party of constables. Keeping his wits about him, he pulls down his cap, wraps his muffler around his face, and boldly walks up to them. Asked whether he has seen any sign of Morrison, he calmly says no and suggests they search the next county, where rumour has it the outlaw is now hiding.

During all the many months Morrison was on the run, he allegedly attended dances, went to church, and even drank in taverns under the noses of the police. It was all too much for the provincial government. In late February 1889 Premier Mercier appointed Judge Callite Aimée Dugas of Montreal to lead an expedition to the Eastern Townships in March with a hundred policemen, soldiers, and prison guards and a few Pinkerton detectives.* The iron fist had arrived among Scots who had been laughing at the police for eight months. Dugas promptly declared martial law and set up checkpoints on the roads. Anyone *suspected* of aiding the outlaw was thrown into jail without charge. Among those arrested were the leaders of the Defence Organization. Police patrols made surprise searches without warrants, rousing families in the dead of night and turning their houses inside out. One party raided the unhappy home of Murdo and Sophie Morrison and carried off a trunk containing their son's letters and personal effects.

Not content to be an armchair general, Dugas moved about the country by sleigh, urging on his men, warning that anyone who helped the criminal would go to prison. His systematic searches covered country miles beyond Morrison's home ground. His men even went down a mine shaft when a barroom prankster suggested Morrison might be hiding there. "Morrison has not been arrested," the Montreal *Star* quipped, "but nearly everyone else in the district has; whether for giving aid or comfort to the enemy or laughing at the expedition is not quite clear." With police morale at a low ebb it must have been a surprise to Dugas when Morrison sent word that he wanted a truce and a chance to talk with the judge. First Morrison arranged another interview with Spanyaardt, one of the few outsiders he trusted and a man

---

*Anyone needing a detective could rent one from the Pinkerton agency in the United States. They specialized in breaking strikes.

intensely disliked by Dugas. Morrison told Spannyaardt that he
did not trust the police and was distraught over the "petty"
arrests of his friends. "My heart bleeds whenever I think of the
wrongs that they [the authorities] have done me, and, besides,
I have lost all faith in justice through my bitter experience of
days agone. Money can do anything, and in the case of the
burning of the farm buildings alone, enough men can be bought
near the Shadagee River at $10 apiece to convict me."

All of which meant that he would not surrender, and he told
Dugas so when they met in an old log schoolhouse on April 11,
1889. He wanted the charges against him dropped and his friends
released from jail. If Dugas could not arrange that, then Morrison had an alterantive plan: Get McAulay to pay the $900 he
owed, and Morrison would leave the country for good. Then
the police could go home, and life would return to normal.
Dugas, however, refused to make a deal. He urged Morrison to
give himself up and promised a fair trial. Morrison said he would
make no deals either. All he wanted was justice. The outlaw
returned to the forest and the judge returned to the hunt, issuing
a sheaf of forty-five new warrants for the arrest of people suspected of aiding the fugitive. While many Scots were hauled off
to jail in Sherbrooke, others fled to the woods to wait out the
crisis.

After the meeting between Morrison and Dugas the Defence
Organization—what was left of it—and members of the respectable United Caledonian Society began negotiating with the
authorities to arrange a truce and an opportunity for Morrison
to surrender under favourable terms. Premier Mercier responded
with a letter to High Constable Adolphe Bissonette, authorizing a three-day truce from Saturday, April 20, to Easter Monday, April 22, after which, if all went well, Morrison would turn
himself in. The Caledonians also had a letter from the Honourable Edward Blake, former premier of Ontario and past leader
of the federal Liberal Party, promising a fair trial if Morrison
would surrender. Everyone believed a truce was in effect when
the outlaw visited his parents' cabin on Easter Sunday. Dugas
himself had gone to Montreal to be with his family. Morrison

knew the cabin was under constant watch, but he understood he had safe conduct and would surrender on terms. The months of running and hiding had left him exhausted. The West still beckoned, but he wouldn't go until he had matters settled at home. He now believed he had friends in high places who would help him get the justice he had been seeking all along.

The premier of Quebec may not have been party to what happened on Easter Day, but somewhere along the line of command Morrison was betrayed. He walked into a trap, led by Silas H. Carpenter of the Montreal police. Carpenter's assistants were James McMahon, a burly detective, and Pierre Leroyer, a latter-day *coureur de bois* who was known around Megantic as an eccentric backwoodsman, a crack shot, and a skilled tracker and hunter, who kept a pet moose for company. Leroyer spotted Morrison as he entered the cabin. Soundlessly he crept up to a window to get a good look at the man who was eating supper with the elder Morrisons. Their man identified and cornered, the police took up positions and waited.

Murdo and Sophie wanted their son to stay the night. After all, there was still a full day left in the truce. But he insisted on leaving. If the truce failed, his presence could be a danger to them. Some time after 9 P.M , with a bottle of milk and a parcel of his mother's biscuits in hand, he said his goodbyes and stepped outside. He had barely cleared the threshold when McMahon shouted, "Throw up your hands!" Morrison dropped the milk and biscuits and drew his Colt. Firing wildly into the darkness, he ran for the woods. A fence blocked his way. McMahon and Leroyer both emptied their rifles at the running figure, then pulled out their revolvers. As Morrison reached the fence, a slug tore through his left buttock and right hip. Crippled by the shot, he fell over the fence. McMahon pounced on him and took his gun. "Rob Roy" was caught at last.

The police carried Morrison to Marsden train station, where they left him lying facedown in pain and humiliation on the floor. One officer was kind enough to give the wounded man a drink of brandy. They took him by special train to Sherbrooke and lodged him in the town's grim stone jail. Doctors discovered that the slug had passed through eleven inches of his body, damaging the right hip bone. They found the spent bullet in his clothing.

As far as Morrison's sympathizers were concerned, he had been taken by treachery in the classic tradition of outlaw folk heroes, tricked with a truce, then ambushed right on his aging parents' doorstep. Peter Spanyaardt echoed the outrage in his paper. Dugas, who had allegedly masterminded the treachery, was unmoved by his critics. The police had grabbed an accused killer, and that's all there was to it. But public disgust over Morrison's capture made it necessary to postpone his trial for many months. In fact, the authorities did not believe they could get a jury to convict him.

It was October 1889, nearly sixteen months after the shooting, before Morrison went to trial. The Scots, with generous contributions from Irish and French Canadians, established a defence fund to provide the best legal talent. His lawyers were J.N. Greenshields and François Lemieux, the celebrated attorneys who had defended Louis Riel. They must have had a feeling of *déjà vu* as they battled against odds for the life of the tall Scot, who limped into court flanked by armed guards. Morrison was charged with several counts of arson and shooting but was tried only for the murder of Jack Warren. For four days in a packed courtroom Greenshields, Lemieux, and a local barrister, John Leonard, fought hard to have their client acquitted. They argued that Warren, an American, could not legally serve a warrant on *anyone* in Canada and that the warrant itself was bogus. Moreover, Warren had boasted that he would shoot Morrison if he ever caught up with him.

One witness quoted Warren swearing that he "would have his Christly soul either dead or alive." In the fatal confrontation with Morrison, the defence pointed out, Warren had not presented the warrant or identified himself as a constable; he had reached for his gun. The shooting was therefore a clear-cut case of self-defence. In an eloquent speech Greenshields told the jury: "Brave men do not commit murder. It is committed for gain, for hatred, but not under the circumstances as those of which we know so well at this present time. The prisoner belongs to a fearless people, the Scots, men who believe that when they have rights, they are ready to fight for the preservation of those rights till their last drop of blood.''

Morrison might well have won his acquittal, but the presiding judge, Justice Edward T. Brooke, broke with professional impartiality and suggested to the jury that Morrison should be found guilty of either murder or the lesser crime of manslaughter. After long deliberation the jury found the defendant guilty of manslaughter, but recommended that Brooke ''give him the lightest penalty which you can consciously [sic] give.'' The recommendation for mercy was lost on Brooke, a hard disciplinarian who was not impressed with Morrison's antics in the months preceding his capture. Like his colleague Dugas, he felt the law was entitled to its pound of flesh. To the astonishment of all, he sentenced Morrison to eighteen years' hard labour in the hellish St. Vincent de Paul penitentiary.

The verdict and the harsh sentence broke Morrison spiritually and emotionally. Withdrawn and sullen, he did not even attempt an appeal. Nor did the man who had lived the rigorous life of a cowhand adapt well to prison. After eighteen wretched months behind bars he suddenly stopped eating. Only when he became too weak to resist force-feeding were his keepers able to get food into him. It was not a hunger strike; Donald Morrison had simply given up. When doctors found him in the early stages of pulmonary consumption, he refused medication. He lingered on, a wasted shell, until June 1894, when his old Defence Organization, armed with petitions and letters, persuaded the government to release the dying prisoner. He was freed on the morning of June 19 and taken to Montreal's Royal Victoria Hospital, where he died the same afternoon at the age of thirty-six. Mourned by hundreds of friends and neighbours, the Megantic outlaw was buried in a glass-topped coffin in a cemetery near his parents' cabin.

To the fiercely independent Scots Morrison was still a champion, and like the original Roby Roy he had his balladeer. Angus MacKay, writing under the name Oscar Dhu, composed an epic

poem entitled "Donald Morrison, The Canadian Outlaw."
Though the poem has little literary merit, at least one stanza
reflects the feelings of the Scottish farmers for their hero:

We'll gang to jail ere ye shall ken
Whether he's in the town or glen,
We'll let you see we're hell and men
Like Morrison.

Chapter 14
Booze and Gold Dust

WITH THE POSSIBLE EXCEPTION OF southern Alberta in the days of the whiskey traders, the wildest West that Canada ever knew was in British Columbia in the days of the Cariboo gold rush, which began in 1860. The Pacific frontier was full of lawless men a decade before they began pouring into the remote wilderness of the Cariboo, and most of them, like their more famous cousins who built the Alberta forts a few years later, were bootlegging liquor to the Indians. Operating mainly from Victoria, the West Coast whiskey traders dealt in the most vicious concoctions ever sold for human consumption. These mixtures usually contained one or more of the various alcohols, if not the potable ethyl alcohol then one of its more or less deadly relatives. Apart from that there was no resemblance to whiskey. What the Indian wanted was something hot, something to burn holes in his stomach and knock him unconscious. And that was what he got. Boatloads of "Tanglefoot" and "Snakehead" were smuggled out of Victoria to be sold in camps and villages up the coast for a dollar a bottle. (The average cost to the whiskey trader was ten cents a bottle.)

The booze trade drew entrepreneurs from all classes, but few achieved the fame of John Butts, nicknamed "The Boy" after Paddy Miles's Boy—a character of Irish literature who was always getting into trouble. There were other traders with incredible strings of arrests and convictions: Whiskey John Livermore, for instance, arrested an estimated two hundred times, with some fifty terms on the chain gang. But none of them attracted as much attention from the police and the press as the eccentric, flamboyant Butts. From the late 1850s to the mid-1860s he amused, exasperated, and enraged the people of Victoria.

A native of Australia, Butts arrived in California during the California gold rush, where he was suspected in a fraudulent gold strike and thrown into a San Francisco jail. Apparently he broke out and made it to Vancouver Island. In Victoria he quickly established himself as a whiskey trader and was arrested several times for selling liquor to Indians. He was also charged at various times with assault, vagrancy, and theft. An imaginative rogue, Butts set himself up as a mission preacher to the Indians. But he would always conclude his fire-and-brimstone sermons by selling grog to his congregations. Between jail terms he ran unsuccessfully for a seat in the colonial assembly and served from time to time as Victoria's town crier. In this role he sometimes got into trouble for publicly insulting prominent people. One man caned Butts for his slanderous announcements and was fined for disturbing the peace, but according to the press Butts was "well served" by the beating.

Butts was known for his antics in court and in jail. "While the light holds out to burn, the vilest sinner may return," he quoted to a judge. "Do not convict me of a charge of which I am totally innocent." Arrested for assaulting an Indian, he assured the court that he had merely pushed the man away to avoid catching smallpox. He repeatedly pleaded that his only ambition was to return to Australia, if only the law would allow him time enough to earn the money for his passage. Described by the Victoria *Colonist* as the greatest curse ever to land on the shores of Vancouver Island, he responded with open letters to the public:

TO THE PEOPLE OF VICTORIA
Having been in jail for the past 12 months, and willing to reform, I purpose cleaning the streets, providing I can get sufficient to pay the expense. Most of the merchants in Yates street have generously responded to my call and have kindly received me. I have left off drinking liquor, and also selling it to Indians, and if a few will kindly come forward and assist me, they will find no longer a nuisance, but a useful member of society in

Yours, gratefully
JOHN BUTTS

However sincere Butts might have been when he wrote this letter, he could not stay away from drinking and bootlegging, and so was repeatedly thrown into jail.

Butts was adept at avoiding any hard labour to which he was sentenced. Sometimes he wound up on the chain gang, with a six-pound bracelet around his ankle, but he usually managed to get out of these situations. On February 14, 1861, he reported that he was unable to walk or even stand. Next day he was transferred to the city hospital, and word came out that he was not expected to recover. The doctors were skeptical. They inflicted numerous painful tests designed to make him use his legs. But Butts hung tough and convinced them that he really was a cripple. For six weeks he enjoyed a rest in bed, reading his Bible and occasionally dragging himself outside by his hands to get a little sun and fresh air. But one keen-eyed doctor detected suspicious movements and had Butts stripped and set in a chair below a balcony. An orderly then poured eighteen buckets of ice water over the helpless victim. He screamed for mercy but did not move. The doctor responded that this was the best treatment for his condition and had the buckets refilled. Butts stood it a second time, but halfway through the third dousing he scrambled out of the way, retrieved his trousers, and hauled himself inside the hospital. Next day the doctor announced that the ice-water treatment would be continued, alternating with boiling water, and a roasting at the hospital's kitchen stove. The treatment worked even before it was resumed. Butts got up and walked out of the hospital, cursing the doctors and promising to carry on as a bootlegger.

The press lamented that he couldn't be shipped across the border to the United States, where he was equally well known, because the people there would "box him up and ship him back." But eventually he did leave, not for California and not for Australia—at least not directly. In September 1866 he went straight from prison to a berth on the *Rodoma*, bound for China, and that was the last anyone on Vancouver Island ever heard of him.

While John "The Boy" Butts was peddling rotgut and playing the fool, two other criminals became central figures in the bootlegging trade. But unlike the flamboyant Butts, One Ear Charlie Brown and Antoine Lucanage were both ruthless killers.

Bully, braggart, horse thief, and swindler, Brown was a regular guest at the Victoria jail in the early 1860s. Violent by nature, he rarely submitted to arrest without a fight. On one occasion he was taken from prison to court after savagely beating an Indian inmate who accused him of selling seawater in barrels marked "whiskey." He was sentenced to the chain gang, and after several months of hard labour made a desperate attempt to escape by jumping a guard, who in the struggle shot off Brown's ear. Three months later, now known as One Ear Charlie, he managed to escape and vanished into the cattle country, where for the next five years he thrived as a rustler.

In the spring of 1867 Brown was in Idaho, where he stole three horses from a ranch and headed back to the British Columbia cattle lands. Two Dutch ranchers who owned the horses trailed him to a camp about four miles from the town of Kootenay. Rather than confronting him themselves they rode to the boom-town of Wild Horse Creek for help. One constable, named Normansell, refused to help them on the grounds that the crime had been committed on American soil, but they found another, Constable Jack Lawson from the Maritimes, who agreed to help them recover the stolen horses.

As they approached Brown's camp, Lawson spotted the outlaw coming toward them on the trail and told the ranchers to wait behind while he rode ahead. Drawing up to Brown, the officer demanded the horses. Brown reached into his coat for a gun, but he wasn't quick enough. Lawson had his own gun levelled in an instant and told Brown to raise his hands, which he did. Then the policeman made a fatal mistake. As he dismounted, he turned his head to call to the ranchers. In that split second Brown pulled his revolver and blew Lawson's brains out. As the terrified Dutchmen spurred their horses and ran for their lives, Brown picked up Lawson's gun and headed for the border.

The first community the ranchers galloped into was Fisherville, a brawling mining camp without a police force. That, as it turned out, was no drawback. The miners were used to settling their own scores. Four of them set out with shotguns to run down the killer. They had no trouble following Brown's trail. He had crossed the swift St. Mary's River on a raft but had lost most of his gear in the crossing. Short of food, he had begged a few supplies from a man named Joe Davis. Twelve miles from Davis's camp he had demanded ammunition from a group of Chinese, and rode off in anger when he realized they had none to give him. The posse questioned a blacksmith, who told them that only hours earlier Brown had boasted of killing a constable and had promised to kill the two Dutch ranchers. The outlaw's trail led south, and the posse followed it right across the American border. They lost track of him briefly but picked up the scent again when an excited Indian told them about a one-eared man who had tried to steal his guns and ammunition. Guessing at where the fugitive would appear next, they waited in ambush at a place on the Walla Walla Trail, about forty miles south of the Canadian border.

Reports have it that Brown rode into the trap with a gun in one hand and a knife in the other, but this doesn't seem likely. He doubtless thought his pursuers were behind him, not waiting ahead by the trail, and would hardly have been riding through the bush with his hands full of weapons. But ready for trouble or not, he didn't have a chance when the posse opened fire. The four avengers, all wielding shotguns, literally blew him out of the saddle. Then they buried his "dastardly carcass" by the Walla Walla Trail. No one was ever charged in this rare instance of Canadian vigilante "justice." For everyone concerned Brown's death was a case of good riddance.

Antoine Lucanage, a thirty-five-year-old French Canadian, had become well established as a West Coast bootlegger by 1865. Working out of Bella Coola, he ran up and down the shore of British Columbia in a black-hulled, thirty-foot sloop, trading booze for furs. The rotgut he sold the Indians was particularly nasty. The main ingredient was camphene, a distillate of turpentine. Equipped as he was with a fast boat and a good knowledge of the sounds and inlets of the rugged coast, Lucanage was a hard man to catch. However, in the spring of 1865 a determined official, John Ogilvie, customs officer and Indian agent at Bella Coola, caught the bootlegger with a boatload of spirits a few miles from town. He confiscated the booze and the sloop, arrested Lucanage, and placed him on the steamer *Nanaimo Packet* to be taken to jail in New Westminster. Lucanage had other plans. Near Salmon River, at the south end of Johnstone Strait, he slipped overboard during the night, swam to shore, and hid out for a week with friendly Indians. When the northbound schooner *Langley* sailed by, Lucanage hailed her and caught a ride to Bella Coola. He told the skipper, Captain Vanovick, that he was heading for the Cariboo, then disappeared into the woods.

Ogilvie was annoyed by his prisoner's escape, but he did not believe the outlaw had headed for the Cariboo. The Chilcotin Indians were hostile, and it was unlikely that Lucanage would risk travelling alone through their country. Ogilvie thought it more likely that the fugitive would stay hidden until the *Langley* started her trip south and then sneak aboard. One week later, on May 6, 1865, the *Langley* weighed anchor and sailed down the narrow Bentinck Arm, bound for Victoria. Ogilvie watched her for a while as she struggled against a strong headwind, then stepped into a canoe manned by four strong Indian paddlers. With him were a man named John Smith and Morris Moss, a Jewish merchant who had earned a reputation as an Indian fighter. Sometime after dark they caught up with the *Langley*, which was still fighting wind.

Ogilvie hailed the skipper and told him he was looking for the criminal Antoine Lucanage. Captain Vanovick replied that he had not seen Lucanage and that the man couldn't be on his ship. Then he invited Ogilvie's party aboard for supper. They accepted. Smith and Morris remained on deck with the Indians while Ogilvie went into the forecastle to help the captain fire up the stove and prepare some food and tea. How and when Lucanage got aboard the *Langley* is not known, nor is there any evidence that Vanovick knew he had a stowaway. Hiding in a locker in the forecastle, the outlaw took the skipper and customs officer completely by surprise. As Vanovick lit the stove,

Lucanage burst from his hiding place, his gun blazing. Pierced by two bullets, Ogilvie hauled himself up the ladder and collapsed on deck, groaning, "I have been shot! That coward Antoine has shot me."

Moss and Smith, who had gone into the main cabin, rushed out on deck. Then the panic-stricken captain appeared. Moss asked him for a lantern so he could go below and seize Lucanage, but Vanovick said there was none on board. The skipper was in such a state of shock that he didn't respond to Moss's demand that he turn the schooner about and head back to Bella Coola. Moss finally rushed to the wheel to do it himself.

As Smith tended to the wounded Ogilvie, Lucanage leaped up from an open hatch, brandishing a pistol and a knife. He caught Smith off guard and stabbed him twice, then attacked Ogilvie, screaming "I am mad! I am mad!" The Indians, terrified at the sight of the homicidal white man, piled into their canoe and paddled away. Ogilvie, though mortally wounded, still had fight in him. He struggled with Lucanage and managed to wrest the gun from his hand. He fired two shots but missed as the outlaw disappeared down the companionway. Minutes later Moss, who was aft at the wheel, spotted Lucanage moving in the bow, armed with the knife and an axe. He drew his gun and aimed, but as he released the wheel, a swinging boom struck him on the head and knocked him overboard. He was rescued by the Indians. Shouting that he would "split in two" any man who interfered with him, Lucanage launched the *Langley*'s boat and rowed for shore. Captain Vanovick, somewhat recovered from his fright, fired several shots at the murderer but missed. While the Indians took Moss ashore to get help, Vanovick put Ogilvie and Smith in his cabin. Ogilvie died there the next afternoon.

With Ogilvie dead, Moss was the senior official in Bella Coola, and he quickly began a search for the killer. The provincial government circulated a poster, offering a $1,000 reward for Lucanage's capture. For the next three months Canadian and American police searched up and down the coast, following rumours that Lucanage had been seen in places as far apart as Queen Charlotte Sound and San Francisco. They found nothing. Not until October did Moss learn what had happened.

After his escape from the ship Antoine Lucanage had hired Indian guides to take him across Queen Charlotte Strait to Vancouver Island. They landed him at Hardy Bay, where he headed into the bush, claiming he had a cache of whiskey hidden there. One of the guides, a man name Ahmete, suspected that Lucanage meant to run off without paying him and followed stealthily behind. When the outlaw realized he was being followed, he tried to shoot the Indian, but his gun misfired. Ahmete ran back to camp, borrowed an old musket, quickly caught up with the treacherous white man, and shot him in the back. Writhing on the ground, Lucanage begged for mercy, but Ahmete pressed his foot on the outlaw's throat and strangled him to death. He took the dead man's clothes and left the corpse to rot where it lay. The decomposed body was identified, months later, by the revolver, which Ahmete had not bothered to steal. No charge was laid against the Indian.

While the whiskey traders were busy debauching the natives, outlaws of a more traditional type were roaming the mountain trails. Most were on the run from American sheriffs or, worse, American lynch mobs, and most were petty criminals. But a few were big-time hijackers of gold dust, who left large caches of loot hidden in western Canada when they met their untimely if well-deserved ends.

Boone Helm was the first of this crew. A big Kentuckian, he was lethal with a six-gun or a Bowie knife. Working as a rustler, robber, gunslinger, and policeman, he cut a violent swath through California, Oregon, Utah, and Idaho, where he is credited with killing more people than Billy the Kid. He survived one brutal winter in the western mountains by shooting and eating his partner, a man named Elijah Burton. He was on the run from a murder in Idaho when he arrived in Victoria on October 12, 1862. His first evening in Canada Helm was tossed into jail for refusing to pay his tab after drinking his fill at a bar. A Victoria magistrate, well aware of Helm's reputation and of the Idaho murder charge, imposed a heavy fine and a month in jail, hoping that would be enough to hold him until extradition could be arranged. But as it turned out, the legal process was so slow that the killer was actually turned loose before the extradition trial could be arranged.

Helm disappeared into the wild Cariboo gold rush country, picked up a partner, and together they cornered, killed, and robbed three prospectors, who were carrying nuggets and gold dust valued at $32,000. They apparently hid the loot before escaping across the American border. A year later Helm was back in British Columbia, robbing travellers on mountain trails as he made his way toward the scene of the triple murder. Before he could reach the hidden treasure, he was captured and deported to Idaho in chains. Incredibly, the authorities there were unable to prove the charge against him, and he walked out of the courtroom a free man. He never got back to Canada.

After his release Helm joined forces with Henry Plummer, a Montana gunman who wore a sheriff's badge by day and a highwayman's mask by night. When the vigilantes of Virginia City, Montana, caught on to Plummer's game and went after his gang, Helm was snared in the roundup. On January 14, 1864, he and four other members of the Plummer gang were hanged from the rafters of a half-finished building while a crowd of about six thousand looked on. With a show of bravado at the end, Helm turned to a man already jerking at the end of a rope and quipped, "Kick away, old fellow. I'll be in hell with you in a minute."

In 1884 Edward "Bulldog" Kelly was just another American drifter knocking about the Kootenays, apparently looking for a job or a grubstake. But on November 27 he turned killer. Hiding in the bush near a roadhouse called the Hog Ranch, about twenty-four miles from the town of Golden, where the Kootenay Trail ran beside the Kicking Horse River, Kelly watched three riders urge their horses through the snow. A young blacksmith named Manuel Drainard broke trail. Behind him was Robert Baird, a Montana liquor salesman heading home from a profitable trip, with $4,500 in cash and gold. The third man was a Métis packer and guide called Harry. Without warning, a slug from

Kelly's Winchester struck Baird in the chest, killing him instantly. Drainard, unarmed and frightened, took flight at once. As he galloped off, Kelly fired again, striking Harry in the hip. Though wounded, the Métis rode straight for his attacker, firing his own rifle. This counter-attack surprised Kelly, who managed one more shot before Harry flung himself from the saddle, knocking the rifle from his assailant's hands. For perhaps fifteen minutes they slugged it out. Then, weakened from loss of blood, Harry slumped to the ground unconscious. The victorious Kelly delivered a few savage kicks to the head and left him for dead.

When Harry regained consciousness, he was stiff, sore, sick, and alone but lucky to be alive. Baird's naked body lay frozen in the snow. His horse stood nearby. The saddlebags with the $4,500 were gone. Harry managed to hoist himself to the back of the dead man's horse and head for the Canadian Pacific construction camp at Kicking Horse. Drainard, meanwhile, had recovered his nerve and returned to the scene of the shooting. Finding Baird dead and no sign of either Harry or the killer, he headed for Golden to inform the police. He had recognized the bushwacker as Bulldog Kelly.

The pursuit was prompt but unsuccessful. Police found spent cartridges at the murder scene and Kelly's rifle in the Kicking Horse River, where he had probably dropped it by accident. The provincial government joined Baird's employer in offering a reward of $1,250 for Kelly's capture. This drew dozens of volunteers into the manhunt, but after a week the search ground to a halt. Kelly had apparently vanished. He was next seen on a train near Winnipeg by officers of the North West Mounted Police, but he jumped from the moving train before it reached a station and disappeared across the border. After a lengthy investigation the police had proof that Kelly was the killer and had learned his real identity. He was Edward Loughlin of Illinois, and he had used the name McNaughton before switching to Kelly. Through good detective work, police chief Murray of Winnipeg traced Kelly to a small town in Dakota and captured him by breaking into his hotel room in the dead of night.

Canada applied for extradition, and an American commissioner ruled in its favour. But it was soon evident that Kelly was no ordinary highwayman. He was, it seemed, a Fenian activist with friends in high places. The Fenians, an Irish terrorist organization committed to destroying British rule in Canada, managed to delay the extradition and gathered funds for Kelly's defence. Kelly's lawyer, the able "Big Tom" Ryan, even enlisted the aid of Secretary of State Thomas Bayard and, finally, of President Grover Cleveland himself. Millions of Irish voters, Ryan warned, would be outraged if a good son of the Auld Sod was shipped off to the hated British in Canada. No "tight-pants dude" should be allowed to deliver an American to the "bloodhounds of the so-called British justice," the American press insisted. After months of legal jousting the Americans set Kelly free. Two years later he was reported hanged by a lynch mob in Colorado, but this turned out to be false. He lived to be killed by a train in 1890.

The money Kelly stole from Baird was never recovered, and he did not have it with him when he fled to the United States. Shortly before he was crushed under the wheels of the train, he told some friends that he had a large stash of money in Canada—enough to retire on—and that he was heading north to retrieve it. Presumably the loot still rests in its hiding place.

On July 19, 1892, coach driver Billy Parker was urging his six-horse team along a dusty Cariboo road. In the strong box under his feet was $15,000 in dust, nuggets, and gold bars. Highway robbery was almost unheard of in the Cariboo, so Parker was caught totally off guard when, near Bridge Creek Hill, a masked bandit stood in the middle of the road and ordered him at gunpoint, "throw down the box." The man appeared to be elderly, but there was nothing feeble about the tone of his voice or the way he wielded his Winchester. Parker surrendered the box of gold, then, at the bandit's command, whipped his team down the road.

Days later, while police and volunteers combed the hills and watched the trails for signs of the unknown outlaw, word spread through the Cariboo country of a big strike on Scottie Creek, about twenty miles from Ashcroft. Old Sam Rowlands, who had been panning the creeks for twelve years, had finally struck a bonanza. A supposedly played-out claim he had bought a few weeks earlier was producing gold almost every day. Eager prospectors rushed to stake claims, but a few old-timers were puzzled. Scottie Creek had long since been picked clean; how was it that Rowlands could find a rich deposit where others had found nothing?

After weeks of digging, sluicing, and panning, with little or nothing to show for their work, other miners began to wonder why only Rowlands was finding the yellow metal. They had never known a strike to be confined to the boundaries of one small camp. Activities within that camp were strange too. Rowlands's four hired men, two Chinese and two Indians, never found any gold in the mud and water they poured through the sluice box. The colour only showed when the helpers were eating lunch or supper and Rowlands was working alone. Just as puzzling was the sudden change in Rowlands's behaviour. Once a friendly chap who got along with miners wherever he went, Rowlands became increasingly hostile to his neighbours. He forbade his workers to speak with other miners and chased trespassers away with a gun. When the luckless and suspicious miners pressed him with questions about his unusual strike, old Sam grumpily explained that he had found a rare mother lode—the source of all the nuggets and dust that had been gleaned from Scottie Creek in earlier years.

The other prospectors didn't buy this. They understood enough about gold ore to know that Scottie Creek was not likely ground for a mother lode. They took their suspicions to the police in Ashcroft, who quickly made the connection between the stage robbery and old Sam's windfall. A constable disguised as a miner went to Scottie Creek and kept watch for several days on Rowlands's camp. When he was satisfied that Rowlands was laundering stolen gold through his claim, he arrested him on suspicion of robbery.

The grizzled old scoundrel did not resist arrest but argued that he had come by his treasure honestly. He was taken to Clinton for trial, and the police seized $3,000 in dust and nuggets he had deposited in the vault of a local store. The Crown's case was circumstantial: Billy Parker could not identify

Rowlands as the masked man on the road. But a close examination of the impounded gold sealed Rowlands's fate. If all of his dust and nuggets had come from one place, there would be consistencies in shape and texture. A seasoned prospector could tell which creek or river a sample of gold came from by looking at it through a magnifying glass. The gold Rowlands had "mined" on Scottie Creek came from all over the Cariboo. The court quickly concluded that such an assortment could only have come into his possession via the strongbox on Billy Parker's coach.

Old Sam turned out to be the American bandit Jack Rowlands, who had escaped to British Columbia in 1880. He was sentenced to seven years in the New Westminster penitentiary but escaped in 1894. In spite of an intense police search he slipped out of the country and was never seen or heard from again. As for the remaining $12,000 in gold the police did not recover, it is unlikely the old bandit would have had a chance to pick it up as he fled for the American border. It is probably still where he hid it, somewhere between Bridge Creek Hill and the mine on Scottie Creek.

One of the largest caches of outlaw gold—today worth perhaps a third of a million dollars—was left behind by Matthew Roderick, a sickly American miner with a bad back. On August 18, 1896, A.D. Keane, superintendent of the Cariboo Mine near Camp McKinney, British Columbia, was transporting a load of bullion to the railhead town of Midway. Though a police constable or a party of volunteer miners usually escorted gold shipments along this twenty-mile stretch of rough road, on this occasion Keane was alone on the wagon, the gold wrapped inconspicuously in a plain canvas sack. Three miles out of Camp McKinney he was waylaid by a masked gunman who made off with the sack of gold.

Evidence found at the scene of the robbery and in a garbage heap behind a cabin pointed to Matthew Roderick as the thief, but by the time the police had his name and description, the outlaw had fled to the United States. Police sent information to the American authories, posted a $3,500 reward, and hired a Pinkerton detective to track the man down. After weeks of investigation Roderick was located in Seattle, where he was living quietly with his wife and, from all appearances, getting by on a modest income. Certain that Roderick had hidden his loot in Canada before jumping the border, the authorities of both countries sat back and waited for him to make his move. An American policewoman, working undercover, made friends with Mrs. Roderick and kept the pair under surveillance.

Roderick didn't make the police wait for long. Maybe thinking the heat was off or perhaps worried that someone might stumble across his plunder, he made arrangements for a trip east, then saddled a horse and headed for Canada a scant two months after the robbery. American police and a Pinkerton agent shadowed him all the way to the border and informed the Canadians of his movements. After Roderick crossed into Canada, mine superintendent Keane and a party of policemen, miners, and Indian guides took over. Taking care not to alarm the bandit, they stuck close to him as he made his way towards the buried treasure. They had the evidence needed to convict him of the robbery but wanted to delay the arrest until he had led them to the gold.

Unfortunately Keane, the man he had robbed, stumbled across Roderick on a lonely trail on the night of October 26, 1896. Keane certainly didn't have his wits about him. "Is that you, Matt?" he asked nervously. The other man dismounted and cocked his rifle. Startled by the click of the cocked hammer, Keane whipped out his Colt and fired. The shot may have saved his life, but it ended all hope of recovering the gold. Matthew Roderick died instantly and took the secret of his hidden booty with him. It seems virtuallly certain that a third of a million dollars worth of nuggets and gold dust are still hidden somewhere near the Kettle River in southern British Columbia.

Chapter 15
Charcoal

THE INDIAN THEY CALLED CHARCOAL seemed an unlikely candidate for the status of legendary outlaw. Small, bow-legged, forty years old, meek under white oppression, he lived quietly on the Blood Indian reserve along the Belly River in south-western Alberta, kept a few horses, gambled with friends, and perhaps drank a little hootch when he could get it. He was described by Superintendent Sam Steele of the North West Mounted Police as "well behaved."

Among his own people, however, he had quite a different reputation. Si'k-okskitsis (Black Wood Ashes) was perhaps the most feared man of his tribe. Son of a renowned warrior, he had formerly been Bad Young Man, member of a small clan called the Shooting-Up Band. He had distinguished himself in raids against five neighbouring tribes, had killed their warriors, stolen their horses, and had spread his fame across the foothills of the Rockies and the adjoining prairie. Now in middle age he was respected as a shaman, a man on familiar terms with the world of spirits. He was a member of the top-secret Horn and Dog Society, an exclusive brotherhood of the most powerful magicians, and he carried the Bear Knife, the most coveted badge of courage. To win the Bear Knife, a candidate who already had great power and status among his people underwent a torture ceremony, then stood as the target for a knife-thrower and caught the blade in his bare hands. The Bear Knife symbolized the courage and power of the grizzly bear.

When the first police patrols reached southwestern Alberta in 1875 and 1876, they began to hear stories of a Blood warrior of supernatural courage and daring, feared by the Cree, the Shoshone, the Kootenay, the Crow, and the Assiniboine. They dismissed the stories as legendary, never connecting them to the meek little Indian whom they regarded as so harmless and well behaved. By 1896 they had forgotten the stories altogether.

Charcoal had fallen foul of the white man's law just once. Back in 1883 he had been caught cheating on his treaty ration. Actually he had been feeding not only himself, his two wives, and children but also three mooching brothers, and he had claimed the whole lot as dependants. Treaty food cut off, no game left to hunt, the buffalo exterminated by the whites, Charcoal had caught and slaughtered a steer to feed his family and had been sent to jail in Fort Macleod for a year. Barely surviving on the prison rations, he had returned home to find that one wife had left him and the other was dying of starvation. All but one of his children, his daughter Owl Woman, were dead.

According to the police, Charcoal had learned his lesson. He made no trouble for the white rulers between 1883 and 1896. He accepted their meagre dole and handful of treaty money, made no complaints, took part in the magical cere-monies that were all that was left of the Indian way of life, and looked to the outside world like the typical cowed survivor of genocide, subsisting on a pauper's pittance and waiting to die in a hovel.

Throughout his life Charcoal had watched the tragic decline of the Blood tribe. Epidemics of smallpox and tuber-culosis had swept across the Plains like killing winds, carrying off hundreds of his people. He had recovered from smallpox in his youth, but most Indians did not. Then the American whiskey traders had moved in, stripping the Indians of their possessions and their dignity, and the country of its buffalo. Thousands and thousands of buffalo, essential to the nomadic life of the Plains, were killed and left to rot, their hides traded for the white man's evil brew and sent off to make leather belts for the machines in eastern factories. Professional white hunters armed with buffalo guns joined in the slaughter until the great herds were virtually extinct. The red-coated police had come as saviours, driving out the white outlaws and closing down their forts, but they remained as servants of a white establishment determined that the remaining "wild" Indians must be pushed off their land and confined to reserves. The Bloods were invited to the great treaty meeting at Blackfoot Crossing in 1877, but many of their leaders, including Charcoal, did not attend. In that "treaty" the Bloods and other tribes were forced to give up their territory and move to reservations.

Charcoal had joined a band of non-treaty Bloods who went south into Montana in 1879, following one of the last of the buffalo herds. The Americans too were busy destroying the Plains Indians and penning the survivors on reserves. It had been three years since Sitting Bull, Crazy Horse, and other gifted chiefs had led the Sioux and their allies to victory over Colonel George Armstrong Custer's Seventh Cavalry at the Battle of the Little Bighorn, and the United States Army was still exacting bloody vengeance. As part of their campaign to subdue the remaining Indians, the Americans were systematically exterminating the buffalo, shooting them down as soldiers of a later day would destroy an enemy's supply depots. With nothing but starvation awaiting them south of the Medicine Line (as they called the international boundary), the hungry Bloods turned back to Canada, went to the reservations because they had no other choice, and accepted the North West Mounted Police as their masters.

After so many quiet years the police had no reason to expect trouble from Charcoal. If there were any rebellious Indians still around, they would likely be restless young men, like the Cree youth Almighty Voice, who had killed an officer in Saskatchewan and was even now giving the Mounties the run of their lives. But Charcoal, neither weak nor apathetic, was about to be roused by that classic prelude to violence, the love triangle—or in this case it might be more correctly called a love *rectangle*. Canadians who had never heard of Charcoal the legendary warrior were soon to read startling accounts of Charcoal the Indian outlaw.

In 1891, after his third wife had left him, Charcoal married Pretty Wolverine Woman, a widow nine years his junior with two small sons. Strong-minded and hard-working, she shared

Charcoal's interest in magic and ritual. Through his influence she became a leader of the Motokix, a sacred women's society. The couple got along well enough until the spring of 1896, when Charcoal took another wife, eighteen-year-old Sleeping Woman. Polygamy was accepted among the Bloods, but in this case there was a further complication: by summer Pretty Wolverine Woman had a lover. Medicine Pipestem was twenty-five-years old, handsome, vain, and a notorious woman-chaser. He was also Pretty Wolverine Woman's cousin, which made him an unwise choice for a lover. The Bloods strongly disapproved of relations between relatives, which brought shame not only to the lovers but to their families. The husband suffered the greatest dishonour of all for being unable to keep his wife faithful.

Charcoal was furious. As a proud warrior and tribal leader, he would have been justified in kicking the elder wife out of his house and killing her young lover. But the whites forbade killing, even if the victim thoroughly deserved it. The whites hanged killers, then buried them in boxes in the ground, where their spirits might remain trapped forever. Besides, even a revenge killing would not spare Charcoal the shame of having a wife who slept with her cousin. If the affair became known, he could lose status, perhaps even membership in the sacred societies. What he wanted more than anything was to keep the affair quiet. He confronted Pretty Wolverine Woman and Medicine Pipestem and warned them to end the affair and say nothing about it. Medicine Pipestem should have thanked his lucky stars that he was still alive. Instead, being a fool, he mistook Charcoal's discretion for cowardice. He not only continued the affair but bragged about it to his brother.

In September a rancher named Cochrane was hiring Indians to cut hay several miles up the Belly River from the Blood reserve. Charcoal and Medicine Pipestem joined the harvesters. Like most married workers Charcoal took his wife with him. By this time Charcoal was suffering from tuberculosis. Because he needed the pay, he tried to do his share of the work, but the pains in his chest sometimes left him too sick to go to the fields. One day near the end of the haying expedition he sent Pretty Wolverine Woman to gather willows and firewood so he could build a sweat lodge—a popular Indian cure. As he watched her leave camp, he saw her make a signal to Medicine Pipestem, who was sitting in front of his tepee. Suspicious, Charcoal picked up his rifle, mounted his horse, and followed his wife.

In an isolated clearing near an old shed Charcoal caught the pair in an embrace. Dismounting and aiming his gun, he ordered Medicine Pipestem to release his wife. The young man only laughed at the old man's jealousy. Charcoal begged them to end the affair and keep it quiet. "Only three of us know about this," he said. But Medicine Pipestem no longer feared or respected Charcoal. He mocked him until the once-great warrior ran away in anguish. Then, having humiliated a hero of the Blood tribe, he led Pretty Wolverine Woman into the shed. It did not take Charcoal long to recover himself. He was sick, he was growing old, his world was in ruins, but to run away was against his nature. He turned around and headed back to the shed, where Pretty Wolverine Woman and Medicine Pipestem were now locked in intercourse. The young Indian must have heard a sound or sensed a presence, because he looked up, and in that instant a bullet struck him in the eye and lodged in his brain. Pretty Wolverine Woman frantically pushed the body away.

"Kill me too!" she demanded.

"No. I'm not going to kill you," Charcoal said. "We'll wait until the redcoats find out, and then we'll die together."

Leaving the body sprawled on the floor, they returned to the Blood reserve.

The corpse was not discovered until October 12—often incorrectly reported as the date of the killing. Actually Medicine Pipestem had been dead for quite a while when his body was found—perhaps for as long as two weeks. Police were baffled because there were bloodstains on the floor but not a mark on the corpse. The eyes were closed as if in sleep, with no sign of a blow or a knife thrust. It was another three days before a doctor, performing an autopsy, pushed up an eyelid and discovered the bullet hole.

At first the police suspected another Indian who had threatened to get even with the young libertine for seducing his wife. But Charcoal was certain that sooner or later suspicion would fall upon him, and then the police would come after him to put a rope around his neck. He did not know that if he had given himself up, he would likely have escaped the death penalty. As far as Charcoal understood the white man's justice, he was as good as dead from the moment he pulled the trigger. But he was determined not to die alone. He had scores to settle, and he believed that a great warrior like himself must dispatch at least one important enemy to herald his entry into the land of the dead. Otherwise he would arrive without status.

His first choice for a victim was Red Crow, principal chief of the Bloods and brother-in-law of Medicine Pipestem, a man of high standing whom Charcoal hated. He approached Red Crow's house at night but was spotted by the chief's wife, who warned her husband to take cover. Then Red Crow's dogs sensed the intruder and raised the alarm. Charcoal silently withdrew. He went next to the home of Indian agent James Wilson, another important enemy, but the house was in darkness. Rather than wait in ambush until dawn, when he could have killed Wilson on his doorstep, Charcoal rode off impatiently to find other quarry. As he crossed the prairie between the Fort Standoff police station and the Blood reserve, he came within the sight of the home of Edward McNeil, a government instructor who was trying to turn former buffalo hunters into farmers. Charcoal saw a light and crept up to the house. Peering through the window, he saw McNeil working at his desk. When the instructor stood up and approached the window, Charcoal fired, then jumped on his horse and galloped for the reserve. This time his shooting had not been so accurate; McNeil was only wounded in the arm.

Next day, while police puzzled over the murder of Medicine Pipestem and the shooting of McNeil, Charcoal gathered his family, threatened them with death if they disobeyed, and told them to get ready for a journey. His two wives; his daughter Owl Woman; his stepson Bear's Head; his younger stepson known only as The Child; and his mother-in-law, Killed-On-Both-Sides, all did as they were told. He took the four women and two boys first to the home of Young Pine, an old friend who was a brother of Pretty Wolverine Woman. There he admitted the shootings: "I have done wrong. I have killed the boy upriver. I killed him because he was trying to take my wife away from me." When he learned from Young Pine that McNeil was not dead, Charcoal was despondent. He did not have his heavenly herald after all. He was in limbo, with no future in this world and no honour in the next. Nothing for it now but to run—and to look for another victim.

Young Pine, believing Charcoal had gone crazy, secretly sent his own wives and children for help, then tried to convince his brother-in-law that the police had no reason to suspect him of anything. For all the Mounties knew, another Indian had killed Medicine Pipestem. A white man might have shot McNeil. Young Pine, worried about the women and children, hoped to keep Charcoal in his house until the police arrived, but Charcoal grew suspicious. He trusted no one, not even an old friend. Levelling his gun, he ordered Young Pine away, then led his unwilling family across the prairie and foothills, heading southwest toward the mountains. At a place called Big Bend, not far from a police post, Charcoal robbed a woodcutter named Henderson of his overcoat, then continued his journey southwest.

Young Pine, meanwhile, was spreading the alarm through the Blood reserve. Charcoal, he told police, had gone beserk, had killed Medicine Pipestem, and was unhappy about his failure to kill Red Crow, Wilson, or McNeil. The police organized a manhunt, and Red Crow took to sleeping on the floor of his cabin, afraid that Charcoal might shoot him in his bed. The warrior–shaman was now a dangerous phantom who might strike anywhere. Indians and whites alike barred the doors of their houses and kept their rifles loaded.

Sam Steele, the famous roughrider, took personal charge of the hunt for Charcoal. He had more than one reason for wanting the renegade locked up as quickly as possible. In Saskatchewan Almighty Voice was still at large, and the failure of the North West Mounted Police to catch him had seriously damaged their image. It seemed ludicrous that the fabled scarlet riders, who "always got their man," could be fooled by a lone Cree who had not even achieved the warrior status of a man like Charcoal. Far-off in Ottawa a new government was being formed by Wilfrid Laurier's Liberals, a party which, in opposition, had recommended the disbandment of the North West Mounted Police. If the "Indian troubles" were not cleared up quickly, Laurier might well demolish Steele's beloved force, replacing it with militia units and local volunteer constabularies. Anticipating the lurid and inaccurate stories that would hit the newspapers, Steele quickly telegraphed Laurier, assuring him that the police were in control and would soon have the fugitive in custody. He also alerted American police in case Charcoal crossed the border.

Charcoal had no intention of running very far, least of all to the United States, which he could easily have reached, even with his family of six in tow. He butchered a steer, this time unconcerned about going to jail, then took his little band into the steep, heavily wooded hills near Chief Mountain. Deep in the pine forest he made camp in a hollow that was almost surrounded by high ground. He had covered his trail well and probably thought he could remain undisturbed for quite a while, but in the dawn of October 17 Indian scouts spotted his position and reported it to Steele. A posse of officers and Blood scouts, led by Inspector A.M. Jarvis, was soon moving into the hills.

After penetrating five miles of dense pine forest, the posse located Charcoal's camp at about 10 A.M. They decided to encircle the tepee and move in silently. The policemen even took off their boots and hats to lessen the chance of making a noise. But when someone stepped on a dry stick, Charcoal heard the crack and was instantly out of his tent, rifle in hand. The posse, lacking a sharpshooter, poured a rain of bullets into the camp without hitting anyone except Jarvis, whose scalp was grazed by a stray shot. Charcoal fled into the bush, followed by his wives and the boy Bear's Head. The posse rounded up Owl Woman, Killed-On-Both-Sides, and the little boy known as The Child. A hasty sweep of the area turned up no sign of the fugitives, who seemed to have vanished. The police had captured Charcoal's horses, his lodge, his food, even his sacred Bear Knife, and he had escaped with only his rifle, some ammunition, and three of his family, but this was small comfort to them. It was a miraculous escape.

Charcoal soon added to their embarrassment with a daring horse raid. After hiding in the woods for a day, he paid a sneak visit to a nearby ranch, where two policemen, Inspector H.J. Davidson and Constable Nettleship, had stabled their horses. While the redcoats were searching the bush on foot, Charcoal stole their horses, saddles, and a pair of government-issue field glasses. Riding double on the police horses, the four Indians headed straight for the American border, leaving an obvious trail. Just before crossing the line, Charcoal turned the party into heavily timbered hills, where tracking would be difficult, then turned north again. If the false trail convinced the police that he had fled to Montana, he would have time to rest and plan his next move.

Sam Steele was furious. He lectured Davidson about his "great error in judgment in leaving his horses without a guard." His men had not only allowed the Indian fugitive to slip right past them when they had him *surrounded*, but also came up looking like blithering idiots when Charcoal stole their horses and equipment. All this would look great in the newspapers, just great! And the Prime Minister! What could you expect him to do but fire the whole outfit, from the superintendent on down?

Steele decided he had to save face, even if it meant bending the truth. Charcoal, he reported, had fired the first shot, almost killing Jarvis. To admit that Jarvis had been hit by one of his own men would be the ultimate humiliation. In fact, Charcoal had not fired at all. And no matter how Steele tried to twist the story, he couldn't hide the basic fact: the little Indian had made the North West Mounted Police look like incompetent fools. It was not the sort of thing a man like Steele could tolerate. He offered a $200 reward (a lot of money in those days and that place). He recruited cowhands, ranchers, and more Indian scouts to join the manhunt. There was some alarm among the scattered white population over Steele's use of armed Indians. Could they be trusted not to ride off and cause more trouble? To ease such fears, the police watched the Indians closely and issued them only a few rounds of ammunition each. Far from plotting an uprising, the Indians were as anxious as anyone to catch Charcoal before he did more killing, and they were glad to collect their field pay of fifty cents a day.

By now Charcoal was moving north, away from the false trail he had left near the border. He wanted to reach the Porcupine Hills, where he had relatives who might be willing to help him. But the police horses he had stolen were now exhausted. He was forced to stop and make camp by the Oldman River, improvising a tent out of saddle blankets. Leaving his wives and stepson in camp, he raided a stagecoach rest station that was run by a Métis named Mose Legrandeur. The man was away, but his wife and children were home. When they saw a gun-toting Indian approach the house, they hid in a bedroom closet. But Charcoal had no time to waste on terrified women and children. Snatching a few loaves of bread, some meat, and a butcher knife, he fled back to the bush. A scant ten minutes later Constable Kerrigan rode into the station, where he found Madame Legrandeur trying to quiet her frightened children. When he learned that he had barely missed Charcoal, he sent an Indian known as Peigan Joe for help and set off alone, following the outlaw into the woods. Kerrigan found the missing police horses, but, perhaps fortunately for himself, he found no other trace of Charcoal, who was camped only three miles from the stage-coach stop.

Peigan Joe returned with Inspector A.R. Cuthbert, who quickly sent word to Steele for reinforcements. Within hours police and scouts had the area staked out. The police asked the local Peigans to help with the capture, but they would have no part of it. Charcoal did not know that the police were closing in. On October 18, after sharing Legrandeur's food with his family, he captured two horses from the Peigan herd and travelled to Tennessee Coulee, a high ridge with a commanding view of the surrounding country. There he could hide and keep watch for pursuers.

But a good hideout was not enough. He needed provisions and extra horses. Taking Bear's Head along to help with the horses, he rode back to the Peigan reserve, left the boy in the bush, and made two more efforts to rustle animals from the Peigan corrals. When a Peigan chief heard a suspicious noise outside his cabin and called out a challenge, Charcoal replied with a shot, then ran to the place where he had left the boy. Bear's Head was gone. Frightened by the gunfire, he had bolted, running until he reached another Peigan cabin, where he was given shelter. Certain that Bear's Head would soon be picked up by the police and forced to lead them to his hideout, Charcoal hurried to the home of his brother Running Crow. There he received food and extra clothing and boasted that he would kill a Peigan chief or a government agent. When he left, he almost ran straight into two policemen, but they were on their way to enjoy an evening with an Indian prostitute and Charcoal easily slipped past them in the darkness.

Next day, October 20, the Peigans turned Bear's Head over to the police. He was terrified and agreed to lead them to Charcoal's camp. Watching through the policemen's own field glasses from his vantage point on Tennessee Coulee, Charcoal saw his enemies approaching. By the time they reached his campsite, he was long gone, heading back to the Blood reserve with his two wives.

Steele was understandably unhappy with this renewed failure and angry about false reports that sent his men chasing down false trails. In the hills and on the prairie his army of manhunters were stumbling over each other. One posse chased a lone rider for miles, only to find that their quarry was a cowboy tracker, fleeing for his life because he thought he was being pursued by the bloodthirsty outlaw. While searchers scoured the countryside, Charcoal was visiting his brother Goose Chief on the Blood reserve. Practically under the noses of the police he stole three fresh horses and slaughtered a steer. Then, with his wives and as much meat as they could carry, he headed back into the hills.

By October 27 the police thought they had Charcoal trapped in the foothills near Dry Fork, but as they tightened their cordon, a light snow covered up the trail. Before the scouts could find new tracks, word came that he had stolen food and chickens from a ranch several miles outside the search area. While the posse moved to search this new ground, Charcoal used an old Indian trick and doubled back to Dry Fork.

On October 29 he tied up Sleeping Woman and Pretty Wolverine Woman so they couldn't escape and rode to the home of another of his brothers, Left Hand. There he received food, a .44-calibre Winchester rifle, and a supply of ammunition. Before he left the reserve, he boldly stole the tribe's champion racehorse. But when he rode his prize into camp, the place was deserted. Sleeping Woman had chewed through her ropes and cut Pretty Wolverine Woman loose. Then they had fled into the night, certain that Charcoal would kill them if he tracked them down. They knew he could follow a trail in the dark, so they ran for help at top speed.

He almost caught them just the same. They hadn't gone far before they heard him behind them, singing his war song and calling out their names. They were terrified. They fully believed he possessed supernatural powers, and he now sounded like some dreadful spirit seeking human blood in the darkness. They hid in the ruins of an old beaver lodge while he passed by. They lay breathless on top of a great rock while he walked below singing and calling to them. He said later that he only wanted to kill Pretty Wolverine Woman for her unfaithfulness; Sleeping Woman he would have allowed to go unharmed. They managed to keep out of sight, and in the morning they staggered, hungry and breathless, into the Blood reserve, where they were soon seized by the police. In her statement Sleeping Woman angrily denounced Pretty Wolverine Woman as the unfaithful wife who had caused all the trouble. The older woman, in her turn, gave the Mounties what information she could about the location of their camp. A posse searched the Dry Fork area, but by that time Charcoal had vanished.

Again, Steele was furious. The outlaw was now more dangerous than ever. Well-armed, mounted on the best horse in the region, unencumbered with women or children, he would be hard to find and harder to arrest. Steele already had some of Charcoal's relatives locked up. He now went after as many more as he could track down. He rounded up Goose Chief, Left Hand, and Bear's Backbone, with all their women and children. Without the slightest legal authority he jammed infants and adults alike into the Fort Macleod guardhouse, until he had more than twenty of Charcoal's relatives behind bars. He laid no charges because he could not prove that any of them had helped the fugitive. It was a straight case of tyranny, one of many such cases in the Canadian West. But Steele did not have to worry about complaints of unlawful arrest from Indians whose rights under the law were routinely ignored. So far as they were concerned he *was* the law.

When Charcoal learned of the arrests, he responded in the only way he could. On a cold night he hid behind a water trough at the Lee's Creek police station and fired a shot at Corporal William Armer as the man stepped out of his quarters to feed the horses. He aimed to kill, but in the dim lantern light the policeman was a shadowy target, and the bullet went through Armer's shirt-sleeve between his arm and his chest, missing his heart by about four inches. As Armer and the other man at the detachment ran to grab their rifles, the Indian quietly retreated. By dawn he was well away, helping himself to some food at a ranchhouse and stealing two more horses from the Peigan herd.

In desperation Steele turned to a plan suggested by the Indian agent Wilson: force Charcoal's own brothers to help bring him in. Left Hand was particularly vulnerable because one of the prisoners was his infant son, who was expected to die if kept in jail. Bear's Backbone was also under pressure. His teenage boy was facing a sentence of three years in jail for cattle rustling. Steele offered to let them all go if the brothers would agree to apprehend Charcoal. If they refused, he threatened to keep them all in jail until Charcoal was killed or arrested, then to have them punished for assisting the outlaw. Desperate, the two Indians agreed to help the chief of the redcoats catch their brother.

For the next few days Charcoal hid in the Porcupine Hills, venturing down just once to the Peigan reserve, where he raped a young Peigan woman. By November 9 heavy snow forced him to abandon the exposed hills for the more sheltered river valleys. He expected that Peigan scouts would be staying close to their fires in the severe weather, but by now he had done much to make the Peigans hate and fear him. In spite of the weather they sent out patrols. One of them picked up Charcoal's trail in the snow near Beaver Creek, and reported its findings to the police. On November 10, while one party followed the trail, another, led by Sergeant William Brock Wilde, set out from the Pincher Creek police post to head off the fugitive if he tried to reach the mountains.

Wilde was a man after Steele's own heart. The burly sergeant was a hard drinker, but fearless, tough, and a strict disciplinarian. Like Steele, he had little regard for native rights. In 1883, when the Cree chief Piapot tried to hold up construction of the Canadian Pacific Railway by planting his village across the railroad's right of way, Wilde boldly strode into the Indian camp and pulled down the lodges, defying the armèd Indians to stop him. Full of admiration for Wilde's bravery and fearful of the consequences if he killed one of the redcoats, Piapot moved his camp. Now this same Wilde was charging across the prairie toward the foothills to intercept the killer Charcoal. He made an excellent guess as to the fugitive's movements and caught up with him near Dry Fork. Charcoal had made camp and was cooking a meal as Wilde's party approached. Wilde advised his men to be cautious but to shoot if the outlaw didn't surrender instantly, adding, "If he's going to kill anybody it'll be me."

Despite all the caution, Charcoal spotted his pursuers. Sick and hungry as he was, he leaped onto his horse like an agile young warrior and galloped through the snow for the hills, leaving behind his second horse and all of his supplies. He easily outran most of the party on their tired ponies, while the shots they fired whistled overhead or ploughed into the snowbanks. But looking back he saw Wilde, mounted on a strong, fresh horse, gaining on him. Wilde was not carrying a rifle but brandished a revolver in his hand. Charcoal waited until the reckless sergeant was within easy gunshot, then wheeled around, propped the Winchester against his shoulder, and fired. The policeman spilled out of his saddle into the snow, shot through the left side of his body. Chanting his war song, Charcoal dismounted, fired another bullet into Wilde, then rode away on the officer's horse. He had finally killed an important enemy, a white chief who would herald his entry into the world of spirits, and despite cold, hunger, and sickness he was elated. Wilde's Peigan scouts fired a few shots at the outlaw and tried to keep up the pursuit, but none of their horses was fit for the job, and Charcoal once again escaped.

As Wilde was buried with full military honours, Steele mobilized still more men to join the hunt. Mounties,

Indians, and farm-hands set off in plummeting temperatures to track down the fugitive. On November 11 one group actually came within sight of him and opened fire, but Charcoal disappeared into the trees. But the Blood warrior's run was almost over. He had been a fugitive for a month and a half without ever going more than a day's ride from his home ground. He had eluded traps again and again, but now he was out of food, low on ammunition, reduced to one tired horse, and close to the point of physical collapse. Early in the morning of November 12, after a hard seventy-mile ride, he arrived at Left Hand's cabin looking for food and shelter. When Left Hand came to the door fully dressed, Charcoal suspected a trap and tried to run, but before he could reach his horse Left Hand grabbed him and called for help. Bear's Backbone rushed out and helped subdue his brother. Together they dragged him into the cabin, took his gun and knife, and tied him up while Left Hand's fat wife sat on him.

Sick, hungry, exhausted, betrayed, Charcoal was finally finished. "I give up," he told Left Hand. "Now you can be a chief for catching me." During the night, as he sat bound to a chair, Charcoal managed to pierce his arm several times with an awl hidden in his clothing. Blood dripping to the floor alerted his brothers to the suicide attempt, and they stopped the flow with flour and sackcloth. At daybreak the police came to take him away.

Charcoal was locked in the guardhouse at Fort Macleod under twenty-four-hour watch and not permitted anything that might be used for suicide or escape. He refused to eat, so they force-fed him. Though he had terminal tuberculosis, the doctors reported that he was faking illness. As he sank further and further into lethargy, they suggested that he was "putting on a crazy act." Steele visited his cell and was amazed at the little wisp of a man, all skin and bones, who had given the nation's finest so much trouble. He was tried for two murders, found guilty, and sentenced to hang. A few days before his execution he reluctantly sat for a photographer. The picture is a carnival piece, a studio fake. Charcoal's buckskin coat and leggings and feather head-dress are props, an Easterner's idea of the trappings of a wild Indian. A borrowed hat hides the manacles on the doomed man's wrists. Only the face, wasted and defiantly turned away from the camera, tells the real story.

Too weak to walk to the gallows, Charcoal was carried to his death in a chair. They hanged him shortly after 8 A.M. on March 16, 1897. Contrary to his wishes, his family was not allowed to take the body. Sam Steele, who had promised that Charcoal could be buried on the prairie according to Indian custom, committed one final piece of treachery by turning him over to the Catholic priest for burial in a wooden box in a Christian cemetery. The legendary warrior was "well behaved" at last.

Chapter 16
Red Ryan and the Gangsters of the Thirties

THE OLD-STYLE OUTLAW with his six-gun and trusty horse passed away with the nineteenth century. A new breed of armed criminal flourished in the Roaring Twenties and the Dirty Thirties. The picture we have of the American gangster has been made familiar by Hollywood: a nattily dressed hoodlum, one hand on a Thompson machine gun and the other on the steering wheel of a speedy black sedan. Though Hollywood glamourized the gangster, the picture isn't all that wrong. The gangster was—and remains today—ruthlessly violent, living in a subculture ruled by fear and brute force. In the twenties he battled the law and rival gangs for a piece of the lucrative booze trade. In the thirties he robbed banks and express companies, snatched the children of wealthy families to be held for ransom, and robbed gas stations or grocery stores.

With his moll, his rod, and his roll of hundred-dollar bills, the gangster is indelibly fixed in American lore. But in Canada? Well, yes, he was a familiar figure here too, though we have tended to push him out of mind. From the moment Prohibition, that ''noble experiment,'' became law in January 1920, Canadian bootleggers stood ready to supply the Great American Thirst. By land and sea Canadian liquor poured into the United States, earning huge fortunes for the manufacturers and smaller fortunes for those willing to risk their lives transporting it. When rumrunners, determined to deliver a cargo to American blind pigs and speakeasies, met police squads equally determined to stop them, they often shot it out like army patrols. On the roads running from Montreal into New York and Vermont, there were said to be shootings every night, and in a single year, 1928, American police killed 128 smugglers running booze from Canada. One American federal agent complained, "It is harder than trench warfare in France."

This warfare was not confined to lonely stretches of northern highway. Ships from the Maritimes and Newfoundland played cat and mouse with the American Coast Guard, landing huge cargoes of Canadian and European spirits on American shores. Much of it was raw proof, some of it shipped in fifty-thousand-gallon lots, to be diluted and flavoured in the marketplace. In March 1929 the Coast Guard cutter *Dexter* fired on the Canadian schooner *I'm Alone*, sinking her in the Gulf of Mexico, killing one of her crew, and carting off the others in chains to New Orleans. The attack had happened on the high seas, but the Americans claimed the vessel had been in American waters when the chase started. In any case the sinking was a clear violation of international law, and after a bitter exchange between Ottawa and Washington the Americans released Captain Randall and the surviving members of his crew.

The size of the operation is suggested by a dispatch from the American Secretary of State to the governor of Newfoundland, dated April 22, 1936, listing the names of 164 ships known to be smuggling liquor—twenty-seven of them registered in Newfoundland and thirty-four in the Maritime provinces. Because many states remained "dry" long after repeal of the prohibition amendment to the American Constitution in 1933, rum running and the hijacking of liquor cargoes continued right through the Dirty Thirties, though Al Capone, the most notorious American gangster, once explained his involvement in the Canadian liquor trade by remarking, "I don't even know what street Canada is on."

The thirties also saw the onset of the Great Depression. Millions of young men were on the streets, living by their wits—or, if they were bold and reckless enough, by their guns. Most of them led sordid lives and ended in verminous prisons. A few became media celebrities: John Dillinger, "Baby Face" Nelson, "Pretty Boy" Floyd, "Machine Gun" Kelly, and Clyde Barrow of Bonnie and Clyde fame. Some of them became folk heroes, partly from exaggerated press stories, partly from false reports circulated by glory-hungry policemen. In fact Kelly never shot anyone in his life; Nelson was a homicidal maniac; and Bonnie and Clyde's specialty was knocking off candy stores and gas bars for petty cash.

One of the most notorious Depression-era gangsters was Alvin Karpis, born Albin Karpowicz to Lithuanian immigrants in Montreal. Karpis spent his early years in Topeka, Kansas, where he ran errands for neighbourhood whorehouses and learned the art of looting. An eighteen-year-old friend showed him how to pull smash-and-grab jobs with a brick. Later he was a professional thief and bootlegger. By the early thirties he was a gunman for the infamous Ma Barker gang.

"Ma" Barker and her sons "Doc" and Freddie were anything but small-timers. They had connections in the underworld and with powerful, corrupt politicians. Their jobs were well planned and executed with military precision. In the course of their three-year crime spree they killed a number of people and picked up an estimated $3,000,000, much of which disappeared in payoffs. Though membership in the gang kept shifting, Karpis, whom Freddie had met in prison, was like one of the family. Known as "Old Creepy" in the underworld, Karpis was right-hand man to the Barkers in many spectacular bank robberies and two sensational kidnappings. "My profession was robbing banks, knocking off payrolls, and kidnapping rich men," he boasted in his autobiography. "I was good at it." He was so good, in fact, that top underworld bosses competed for his services as a gunman. But Karpis, who considered himself a working thief and "not a hoodlum," turned down their offers.

The Barkers' reign of terror ended in 1935, when Doc Barker was captured by the FBI in Chicago, and Ma and Freddie went down in a hail of bullets, shooting it out with the Feds in Florida. With the Barkers gone and Dillinger, Floyd, and Nelson all dead, Karpis rose to the status of Public Enemy Number One. He pulled off many robberies, including a Wild West-style train holdup, before the FBI caught him in New Orleans on May 1, 1936. According to J. Edgar Hoover, he, as number-one cop, had captured America's most wanted gangster almost single-handedly, but Karpis said this was a lie. He had been virtually surrounded by armed policemen, and Hoover did not appear until he and his companion were already covered by their guns. But Hoover squeezed a lot of publicity out of "his" capture of Public Enemy Number One and parleyed it into political power. Karpis later remarked, "I made that son of a bitch." Old Creepy got a life sentence and served twenty-six years in Alcatraz, much of it in solitary confinement. While he was there, his fellow inmate Doc Barker was shot dead trying to escape. Karpis was paroled in 1969 and deported to Canada. He died in 1979.

While Karpis and the Barkers were shooting up the Midwest in the early thirties, another Canadian gangster was licking his wounds in the Kingston pen in Ontario. Norman John "Red" Ryan had a record at least as long as Karpis's, but most of his depredations were in Canada, winning him the nickname "the Canadian Jesse James." Born in Toronto in 1895 to a working class Irish–American family, young Ryan grew up as a feisty street kid. He excelled in all the games his companions played and once saved two young friends from drowning when their boat overturned on Grenadier Pond. But he was even more adept at stealing, and shooting stray cats with a .22 calibre handgun he had won at a fair. His father had taken the revolver from him and hidden it, but Ryan found the hiding place and took the gun whenever he could sneak it out of the house. Once he used it to frighten an old lady who caught him and a friend stripping her cherry tree of fruit. On another occasion, when he and some friends had stolen a pair of motorbikes and gone joyriding along country roads, they had a collision with a

wagon driven by a Cooksville farmer named Bell. In an argument after the accident, Ryan pulled his gun and fired a few
haphazard shots, two of them striking Bell's horse. Bell
quickly retreated from the scene. That gun, Ryan said later,
gave him his first taste of "the power of a weapon." He was
seventeen at the time.

His troubles with the police had started five years earlier,
when he had been charged with stealing a bicycle and some
money. After that he had been in court on petty theft charges
and had spent some time in reform school. His youth, his
charming personality, and the minor nature of his crimes had
led the courts to be lenient with him. Ryan probably developed an attitude not uncommon in juvenile delinquents: he
could get away with anything.

That fantasy was brutally shattered in December 1912, a
few weeks after Ryan's confrontation with Farmer Bell.
Caught burglarizing a Queen Street cigar store in Toronto,
seventeen-year-old Ryan was sentenced to three years' hard
labour in the dismal Kingston penitentiary. An additional
three and a half years were added for the potshots he had
taken at Bell and his horse. Kingston was no place for a
teenage boy, whatever he had done. Indeed, if correction
and rehabilitation were the governing ideals of the penal
system, Kingston was no place for anyone. Punishment,
sometimes openly cruel, sometimes cruelly subtle, was its sole
reason for being. Hardened criminals, first offenders, tough
men, vulnerable boys, people convicted of everything from
nonviolent theft to armed robbery, murder, and rape were
dumped into the horrific world enclosed by the penitentiary's
high stone walls. One and all were subjected to the humil-
iations of the prison haircut and the checkered "jailbird"
uniform. The prisoner's day was a monotonous routine of
useless labour, bland food eaten alone in the cell, and
enforced silence. This, coupled with long hours of isolation
in a cell where not even pictures of loved ones were
permitted, was harder on a man's mind and soul than the
occasional strapping was on his body. If anything, it left him

less able to deal with society than he had been before incarceration. Educational facilities were practically nonexistent; the prisoner could not even learn a workable trade.

Of course, at every opportunity the convicts broke the rule of silence. It was during these stolen moments of hushed conversation with some of the hardest criminals in the country that young Ryan did get an education of a sort. All those men talked about was crime and how a smart man could make some easy money once he got out of the pen. "All we heard while in prison," he said later, "was boasting about the 'jobs' they had pulled and what they planned to do in all channels of crime when they got out."

On September 24, 1914, Ryan was paroled for good behaviour. The condition was that he go to work in his father's business as a tinsmith. When he left Kingston, he received $4.95, his pay for almost two years on the rock pile. Well versed by his prison tutors, Ryan had no intention of sweating away time in his father's metal shop. Early in 1915 he and another paroled convict obtained guns and robbed the Dominion Express Company and the payroll office of the Toronto Piano Factory. They then went to Owen Sound, where they planned to rob a bank. Before they could pull the job, they were spotted on a stolen motorcycle by Owen Sound police. After a high-speed chase, in which Ryan was wounded, the two were captured and shipped back to Kingston. Convicted on several charges, including two counts of armed robbery, Ryan now faced thirty-two years behind bars, and he was only twenty years old.

For two and a half years Ryan went through the old routine: work, eat, sleep—most of his time spent in lonely, silent isolation. As a parole-breaker he was kept under close watch, making prospects for escape very bleak. He might well have been on the verge of accepting Kingston as his residence for the better part of his life, when, in 1918, opportunity presented itself unexpectedly. The meat grinder of World War I had taxed the country's military manpower to the limit. There simply were not enough volunteers or conscripts to replace the tens of thousands who fell in the bloody fields and trenches of France. In desperation the recruiters began scraping the bottom of the barrel for cannon fodder. They offered convicts a ticket out of prison in return for service in the army overseas. Ryan grabbed at the chance and on March 26, 1918, left Kingston to be enlisted in the famed Princess Pats. He never shared in the regiment's military glory, however, because shortly after reaching England, Ryan deserted. Apparently "the power of a weapon" was not so thrilling when he pictured himself carrying his gun "over the top" in a mad charge across no-man's-land. Ryan lived by stealing from army supplies and robbing English shops until October 1918, when he was caught. He was thrown in the brig but soon escaped. He was recaptured and served a term in the stockade before being dishonourably discharged. Ryan then met an Australian sailor named Albert Slade, who subsequently disappeared. Using Slade's name and identification papers, Ryan joined the merchant marine and shipped out of England. His movements in the immediate post-war years are not certain, but it seems he worked as a ship's steward, visiting Brazil and Australia.

By early 1921 Ryan was back in Toronto, still going by the name Albert Slade. He married a girl named Elsie, tried unsuccessfully to "steady down to work," and finally went looking for a bank to rob. He spent several days in Hamilton, "sizing up the various branch banks for a lay that appealed to me." His first target, a branch of the Bank of Hamilton, proved to be an unlucky choice. The holdup was foiled by a scrappy bank manager, and Ryan escaped empty-handed. One day later, showing nerve worthy of a better cause, Ryan single-handedly held up the Union Bank on Hamilton's Main Street. He got away with $5,000.

For a while Ryan lived well. "I liked Hamilton, and was having a fine time around a little bungalow down in the Delta district where I can truthfully say that I met a fine bunch of fellows. There was a little good beer and we had some sociable times there."

Within weeks, however, the money was gone and Ryan was casing another branch of the Bank of Hamilton. This time he would use a partner and a getaway car. "Knocking them down," he said, "is the easy part of it, but it is the getaway that counts." A few hours before the robbery, Ryan and his partner, George McVittie, stole an old Ford. Ten minutes before closing time, while McVittie waited in the car, Ryan entered the bank. The tattered clothes he was wearing might have drawn a few disapproving stares, but the revolver he produced commanded immediate attention. Waving the gun in the face of Chester Gibson, the manager, Ryan barked, "Hands up and keep 'em up. No kidding. I mean business."

Gibson and an employee named Marshall reached for the sky, but a young clerk ran for a side door. Ryan bounded over the counter and stopped him. With the bank staff lined up against a wall, he rifled the teller's cage of $3,800. As he was grabbing the loot, a woman walked into the bank. Ryan told her to sit down and be quiet. He found the manager's gun in the teller's cage, and tapped Gibson with it as he asked whether there was any cash in the vault. Gibson said no, and Ryan didn't argue. He didn't have time. A bandit's secret to success was a quick job and a fast getaway. Ryan made a hasty exit through a side door and jumped into the Ford McVittie had kept running.

"There is a thrill when you have the swag," Ryan later said, "but you can never tell when they may get you in the back. I made my waiting limousine and returned downtown and parked the car in the centre of the city, and went and cut up the melon." The "melon," once divided, wasn't much for a high roller like Ryan, who liked to spend afternoons at the race-track. With money running through his fingers like water and the Hamilton police snooping dangerously close to his trail, he fled to Montreal with McVittie in tow. There, in October 1921, the pair tried to rob a branch of the Bank of Commerce. They were foiled by a gunslinging manager who exchanged shots with Ryan before the bandits fled in a stolen car. The only casualty was a teller, G.T. Drew, who fainted when Ryan opened fire with a pair of automatic pistols.

The robbers hid out in the YMCA on Drummond Street. Two days later, after yet another gunfight, they were captured and charged with robbery and shooting with intent to kill. Ryan was sentenced to forty lashes and seven years in jail. After taking his lashes, he was transported to Hamilton, where robbery convictions added another twenty-five years to his sentence. McVittie, convicted on only one count of robbery, got ten years.

This time there would be no early parole and no opportunity to sneak out via the army. Ryan was looking at a thirty-two-year stretch. "If I had got ten years, I would have tried for my good conduct time," he said later, "but when a man as young as I was . . . has such a long confinement ahead of him, it is a great temptation to make a break." Ryan spent months planning his escape and recruiting a band of like-minded convicts. One of them, Thomas "Runty" Bryans, was serving time for manslaughter. The others— Gordon Simpson, Arthur "Curly" Sullivan, and Edward "Wyoming" McMullen—were all professional robbers. Kingston's deputy warden, R.H. Tucker, described McMullen as one of the most dangerous men in Kingston. On the morning of September 10, 1923, the five made their break.

Near the east wall of the prison was a barn, tended by an elderly convict. A gang of prisoners grabbed the old man, bound him, and then set fire to a pile of straw. Under the smokescreen Ryan and company ran from the barn and used a makeshift ladder and a length of rope to scurry up one side of the wall and slide down the other. Ryan was the last to go. As he started up the ladder a guard, Matt Walsh, saw what was happening. He ran to the ladder and tried to shake Ryan off. Ryan dropped to the ground and seized a pitchfork, which had been left for just such an emergency. He stabbed Walsh in the leg, knocked him out cold with a single punch, then scrambled over the wall to join his companions.

The escapees made a mad dash for the home of millionaire H.W. Richardson, whose property adjoined that of the penitentiary. They had hoped to steal Richardson's fast car, but to their dismay the Richardsons, and their car, were gone. The only vehicle available was a run-down old Chevvy. They piled into it and roared away, hotly pursued by prison guards in a fleet of commandeered vehicles. Without guns to return the fire, they made their run under a barrage of bullets. The driver, McMullen, was hit in the hand but managed to keep control of the car in a wild chase through the streets of Kingston and out into the country. Three miles from the city, weak from loss of blood, he crashed into a gate. The fugitives leaped from the car and disappeared into a patch of swamp and brush known as Kemp's and McAdoo's Woods. McMullen could not keep going. He staggered a hundred yards or so, fell, tried to rise again, and collapsed. The guards found him and took him back to Kingston. For three days squads of police, guards, and soldiers scoured the woods looking for Ryan and his friends, but the convicts managed to evade them and live on food stolen from farms. Then they stole another car and drove to Toronto. "We were still in our prison uniforms," Ryan reported, "and went riding through the centre of the city avoiding accidents and crossings where we would be held up." Finally, they reached their destination and slipped quickly into the house, where they all slept soundly in the coal bin.

They changed their hideout, got new clothes, and picked a bank to rob. Ryan selected the Oakwod–St. Clair branch of the Bank of Nova Scotia because he had once worked as a tinsmith on the vault there. On the morning of September 27 they stole a car, switched its licence plates, drove around the neighbourhood, and checked out the streets. Ryan had to be sure of a clear getaway route. Meanwhile, Curly Sullivan cased the bank while changing a twenty-dollar bill. What followed could have been a blueprint for the exploits of Dillinger, Floyd, the Barkers, and other bank-robbing public enemies who would come along a decade later. About 1:15 P.M. Ryan and friends entered the bank and drew their guns. Only Ryan carried a real weapon. The others had dummies. Sullivan guarded the door and kept the few customers covered. Gordon Simpson told the manager, Leroy Oake, to open the vault. When Oake was slow to respond, Simpson knocked him senseless with the butt of his gun. Ryan swung over the counter and herded the bank employees into the manager's office. He pulled out the telephone wire, then filled a canvas bag with $3,000 from the teller's cage. Without wasting time on the vault, the gang hurried to their waiting car. A dazed Oakes fired a few shots after them, and a group of students from nearby Oakwood Collegiate tried to catch them, but the bandits made a clean getaway. Their car was found a day later in the parking lot of the Granite Club.

The bank robbers were quickly identified as the four escapees from Kingston. Indeed, in the next few days they were blamed for cracking a safe in Hamilton, robbing a post office in Queenston, and stealing a taxicab in St. Catharines. Actually, Sullivan and Ryan had parted company with Simpson and Bryans and were heading for the United States in a fast car. At the small town of Pottersburg, near London, Ryan later reported a close call with the law. It was night, and they had stopped to help themselves to some oil at a closed service station when a motorcycle cop pulled up. While Ryan waited in the car with a drawn gun, ready to blast the patrolman if trouble developed, Sullivan told the officer that they were from out of town, needed oil, and intended to leave $5 in payment. The policeman accepted the story and escorted them a few miles down the road.

The bandits dumped their car near Windsor, then crossed over to Detroit. According to one story, they were smuggled across the Detroit River in a bootlegger's boat, but Ryan later denied this. He said that he and Sullivan went through customs like regular citizens but were ready to shoot their way out if they ran into problems. They were well armed and had sewn hacksaw blades and other implements of escape into the seams of their clothing in case of capture. They bought a car in Detroit, where a current crime wave had police so touchy that they considered it unwise to steal one, and drove to Chicago.

Chicago was not to their liking either. Maybe the police there were a problem, but the Canadian outlaws might also have had word through the grapevine that such rising mobsters as "Scarface" Al Capone and his Irish rival, Dion "Deanie" O'Bannion, would not tolerate trouble-making interlopers. They moved on to Minneapolis, Minnesota, where Ryan dyed his hair black and Sullivan (using the name Brown) struck up a relationship with Irene Adams, a waitress at the Minneapolis Athletic Club. "I met Ryan and Brown early in November," Irene said. "They were well-dressed, pleasant, and certainly spent money like water. They told me they were automobile salesmen. Shortly after I met them, they went on a trip to New York, Philadelphia, Boston, and other eastern cities. They sent me postcards everywhere they went." The pair were actually on a robbing spree that took them from North Dakota to Massachusetts, in which they plundered at least six banks. Not forgetting their own backyard, they hit St. Paul, Minneapolis's twin city, and looted a bank of $5,000.

Throughout their lucrative swing through the United States, Ryan and Sullivan kept in touch with friends in Canada by inserting coded messages in the personal ads of *The Detective*, a popular American police magazine. The messages let certain people know where Ryan could be contacted through the mail. From one of these correspondents the Toronto police learned that Ryan was in Minneapolis and that he picked up his mail regularly at the general delivery window of the post office. Tucker, of the Kingston penitentiary, and Walter Duncan, chief of the criminal investigation branch of the federal Department of Justice, rushed to Minneapolis and conferred with local police.

On Friday, December 15, 1923, the police had the post office staked out when Ryan walked in to get his mail. As he stood at the counter, two detectives closed in on him.

Ryan, who didn't have to see a badge to smell a cop, drew his gun and fired. He missed, but one of the officers, Detective William Meehan, didn't. His bullet struck Ryan's right shoulder, knocking him off balance and sending the gun flying from his fist. He was quickly handcuffed and hauled out to the street, where other policemen joined the captors. Ryan shouted a warning across the road and Curly Sullivan, waiting in a car, opened fire, wounding a policeman and several bystanders. As Sullivan threw the car into gear and screeched away, a police bullet skinned his nose. That evening, when he had dinner with Irene Adams, he kept a handkerchief to his face, complaining of a nosebleed. Except for that, "he seemed real cool and collected," Irene said later.

The next day Detective Meehan and a colleague, William Forbes, visited Irene Adams's apartment, looking for Sullivan. He wasn't there so they decided to wait. "I will never forget that wait for him to rap at the door," Adams said. "When we heard him coming, the detectives told me to get out, but I saw him open the door. As he saw the detectives in the room, he started to pull his revolver. Detective Meehan shot over Detective Forbes's shoulder and Brown [Sullivan] fell across the doorway. It was horrible, but the detectives were cold as ice. Detective Forbes said, 'Nice work, Bill.' . . . I will select my friends more carefully in the future."

Sullivan had been shot through the heart. Ryan, recovering from his own minor wound, was taken to the morgue to identify the body. The experience shook him, and he wept, "I wish it had been me." But if he was grieved at the sight of his dead friend, he was even more angered by the press report that he had betrayed Sullivan by giving the police Irene Adams's address. Ryan bitterly denied the accusation, and the police confirmed that he had not sold out his partner, even under fierce third-degree interrogation.

Confined to a cold cell while lawyers and Canadian and American officials haggled over his case, Ryan complained about the lack of heat until the jailers gave him his overcoat. Tucked away in the lining was a file. Every night for almost three weeks Ryan worked on the bars and tore up clothing and bedding to construct a twenty-foot ladder. His plan was to get out of the cell, climb down the ladder to a floor below the maximum-security level, and escape down a staircase to a lightly guarded door, which opened to the street. If all went well, he would only have to deal with a single guard. He had cut through two bars and was almost ready to make his break, when he was told to get ready for transfer to another jail, pending extradition to Canada. His disappointment and frustration must have been obvious because guards immediately searched his cell and found the file and homemade ladder. His scheme thwarted, Ryan laughed and said, "It never hurts to try anything once."

While still in the Minneapolis jail Ryan began telling other prisoners and local reporters, "Crime doesn't pay. Brown [Sullivan] paid the price and I'm paying mine every day I spend in a cell. It is better to go straight and not have the police hounding you. Our experience should be a lesson to everyone." Chief Brunskill of the Minneapolis police, who received a silver trophy for the capture of the Canadian gangster, said "Ryan was by far the toughest and most desperate man ever held in our jail."

On January 14, 1924, accompanied by the Canadians Duncan and Tucker and two American detectives, including the sure-shooting Meehan, a shackled and handcuffed Ryan boarded a train for Canada. The homecoming was like that of a celebrity. At Blind River, Ontario, a *Toronto Star* reporter hopped onto the train and interviewed Canada's most famous bank robber. His articles made front-page copy. At the same time a *Star* editorial condemned the glorification of criminals and noted that a bandit's lot was "sordid and dreary . . . an unskilled labourer gets more real pleasure out of life." By the time Ryan's train reached Union Station in Toronto, his guard had swelled to fourteen detectives and uniformed policemen, making him seem all the more like a big-time international criminal, deserving top media coverage. Toronto church leaders, the board of directors of the Big Brothers organization, and representatives of the Women's Christian Temperance Union objected to the attention lavished on Ryan, especially to a proposed autobiography. Understandably, they did not see Ryan as a fit object of hero worship for the general public, particularly young people. The prosecuting attorney at Ryan's trial for bank robbery voiced their sentiments: "Certain newspapers have seen fit to picture him as a glorified hero, whereas the fact is, he is a vulgar criminal."

While he was in Toronto's Don Jail awaiting trial, Ryan shocked his keepers by presenting them with a seven-inch saw blade. He had brought it with him from Minneapolis and had stuck it to the sole of his foot with chewing gum while being searched. He explained that he now realized the game was up, and there was no point trying to escape. His lawyer, Austin Ross, entered a plea of guilty and asked for mercy, describing his client as "a broken man" whose career in crime was over. Judge Emerson Coatsworth was not moved. He sentenced Ryan to life imprisonment and thirty lashes. The government decided to cancel the flogging, in spite of protests from the police that it ought to be inflicted. Four months after his sensational escape, Ryan was back in Kingston, a "lifer" locked in solitary confinement. He stayed in the Hole for nine months, having contact with no one except the guards and the Roman Catholic chaplain, Father Wilfrid Kingsley.

He sought escape from the mind-destroying horror of solitary confinement by reading. He was never without books or magazines, but the Bible became his favourite. "I read the Bible purely as a narrative of history," he said later, "but subconsciously, I have no doubt, its splendid passages helped crystallize my purpose to reform." Father Kingsley encouraged the convict's determination to reform himself and began to speak on his behalf. He was taken from the Hole to a more comfortable cell, where he spent the next year and a half. In the last two months of this stretch he was allowed a solitary exercise period of twenty minutes a day.

Ryan was taken out of solitary in 1926 and put to work in the mail bag department, making new bags for the post office and repairing old ones. He also worked on a theft-proof lock, which he was unable to open himself after he had finished it, but the post office turned down his invention. Meanwhile, he was well on the road to rehabilitation. After two years in the bag room he moved to one of the choicest jobs in the prison: nurse in the hospital. By 1930 he was the head orderly-nurse.

A bank robber with a solid reputation as a "tough guy," Ryan already stood at the top of the inmate hierarchy. Now, through his work in the hospital, he won the esteem of the administration as well. He performed his nursing duties with surprising tenderness and dedication. He assisted the surgeon in the operating room. Among those he tended were his old breakout partner Edward McMullen and the most famous political prisoner in Canada, Tim Buck, leader of the Canadian communists. Buck would later write angrily of the special status of the prison "elite," all of whom had committed violent crimes: "Everything was upside down in the penitentiary. A boy who in a moment of deviltry had stolen a car . . . and another boy, only sixteen, who had stolen a pair of shoes . . . these were the lowest down the ladder. The fellows who were the elite were the men who used guns, stick-up men, especially those who had robbed, or attempted to rob a bank. Red Ryan was top in every respect because of his reputation. Even the administration treated him in a special way."

Ryan's special treatment included a comfortable room near the hospital, decent meals, and a nearly free run of the sick ward. "He used to go in and out any time he wanted; he had the keys," Buck said. But it was not his "elite" position that had won Ryan such privileges. It was his behaviour in prison. Besides working in the hospital, he assisted the priest at the altar and made small religious artefacts. Whenever the smouldering hatred and frustration of prison society erupted into violence, as happened in the riots of 1933, Ryan managed to keep out of trouble. He often lectured his fellow inmates on the need to go straight when they got out of prison.

This, clearly, was not the same Red Ryan who had started his life sentence a decade earlier. The Toronto press had been reporting on the famous bandit's progress as a model prisoner, and the stories had been reprinted across the country. The outlaw turned nurse was almost as much a media celebrity as the Canadian Jesse James. People began to sympathize with the one-time gangster who now wanted nothing more than "a little shop, cigar store, or haberdashery in Kingston . . . close enough to the prison so that all my friends, the guards and the officials of the warden's office, could come and visit me regularly."

Dr. O.J. Withrow, a former inmate who wrote a series of prison articles for the Toronto *Globe* in 1933, described Ryan as "kind-hearted, conscientious, loyal, innately honest and big-souled, whose only desire is to do the right thing in a big way if he is permitted." Ryan's friends and relatives, especially his brother Russell, wrote hundreds of letters to the papers and the government pleading his cause. Foremost of all the spokesmen in Ryan's camp was Father Kingsley. The hard-nosed priest, with his long-time knowledge of the toughest prisoners in Canada, was so struck by the change in Ryan that he wrote the parole board outlining the convict's "exemplary behaviour" and offering to take the repentant thief under his own supervision if parole could be arranged. Ryan's case, he argued, would stand as proof that the correctional system worked for those who obeyed the rules and made a genuine effort at reform. Among those who supported the priest's campaign for Ryan's liberation were Judge Coatsworth, who had sentenced him to imprisonment and the lash a decade earlier; Agnes McPhail MP, who brought his case before the House of Commons; Senator Harry A. Mullins, whose wife had seen the bandit in irons at Union Station in 1924; and the Honourable Ernest Lapointe, former Minister of Justice.

Ryan was getting used to receiving important visitors in the prison offices, but even he must have been stunned to learn that on Wednesday, July 24, 1934, he would have an interview with the Prime Minister of Canada, Richard Bedford Bennett. "Iron Heel" Bennett, who had been elected in the hope that his Conservative government might do something about the Depression and whose policies were making it steadily worse, was badly in need of something to improve his image. He spent almost an hour with the convict, accompanied by the Minister of Justice. Ryan reported that the Prime Minister "—questioned me about my progress, my outlook on life in general and plans I had formed for the future. He seemed genuinely and deeply interested and I found myself talking to him without restraint. He seemed pleased and impressed when I told him, as frankly as I knew how, just how I felt about the past and that I had made up my mind years ago to change my way of life." The Prime Minister promised he would discuss the case with "the Minister charged with responsibility in such matters," and for the next few months Ryan waited anxiously for news of his parole. The wheels of justice took a full year to make their turn.

In July 1935 Ryan's sister Isabella died. He was allowed to attend the funeral in Toronto unfettered and accompanied by just a single guard. He visited his family and was given a quick tour of the city, which had changed quite a bit in the twelve years he had been behind bars. On July 23 he got his ticket of leave. When the warden asked him if it wasn't "too wet to go out today," he replied "I'd go out in a bathing suit." Ryan said farewell to the guards and to his fellow inmates, whom he had so often exhorted to go straight, and they broke the rule of silence to cheer him. He collected his prison pay, $175, and a bundle of letters withheld for years by prison regulations. Some of them predated his 1923 escape, including one written fourteen years before by his wife, Elsie. Because he had never heard from her, he thought she had abandoned him, and he hadn't bothered to make contact with her in any way. She was now dead, and her fourteen-year-old message to her husband turned out to be a love letter.

Ryan's release was one of the few really popular things the Bennett government ever did. By coincidence it was just in time for the election, which would come in October. The newspapers made a great fuss over the paroled bandit, and some people began thinking that Bennett might be human after all. The ex-con wrote a letter of thanks to the Prime Minister, and Bennett graciously replied: "You have a host of friends who wish you well, and who have faith and confidence that you will succeed. No one is more sincere in that wish than I." Newspaper readers may have been influenced by all this, but western farmers, who had turned their broken-down, gasless motorcars into horse-drawn "Bennett buggies," remained unimpressed, as did the vast army of the unemployed, who turned out in droves to bury Bennett under a landslide of votes. It would be twenty-two years before his party managed to get back into power.

Ryan told his life story in a series of articles featured in the *Toronto Star*. Much editorial space was devoted to him. His opinions were widely quoted. He attacked the stupidities, cruelties, and gross inadequacies of the penal system. Reform groups everywhere lionized him. "I regard my release as a big experiment, the success or failure of which may affect the future of hundreds of fellows, in prison and out," he wrote. "If, in my way of life, I can justify the faith in human nature that has given me my freedom, I will have done something to atone for the terrible mistakes of the past and make the redemption of others, as unfortunate and reckless as I have been, easier and surer." Ex-cons who returned to crime were fools, he said. "If I ever go in for crime again I deserve to be shot."

Having "retired from the banking business for good," Ryan got a job as a car salesman in Toronto and moonlighted as a jack of all trades, including manager and bouncer at the Nealan House Hotel on King Street. He was in great demand to speak at picnics, bazaars, and sporting meets, always supporting the cause of prison reform. He collaborated with Dr. Withrow on a book about his life. Its closing line was "I am now a new man." Father Kingsley, Ryan's parole officer, could not have been more pleased. The lost sheep had not only returned to the fold but had become a sort of assistant shepherd, helping to rescue other lost sheep. Many ex-convicts came to Ryan for help. He not only tried to help them go straight but made them small loans when they were down and out. Ordinarily, a prisoner on parole is not allowed to associate with other ex-convicts. Ryan was a shining exception, a beacon showing others the way.

The priest, the press, the government—none of them suspected that Ryan was all this time the leader of a criminal ring, which he had been putting together, perhaps even before he left Kingston. His men included Harold Checkley, a professional burglar, and Edward McMullen, who had pulled off the prison break with Ryan back in 1923 and had been paroled in 1934. Ryan dyed his red hair an inconspicuous brown, but there was nothing especially suspicious in that. No one suspected that Ryan and McMullen were the gunmen who, in the course of a car theft, had killed Councillor Edward Stonehouse of Markham and seriously wounded his son on February 29, 1936. During that same winter there was a rash of bank robberies and burglaries in Quebec and Ontario, obviously the work of an organized crime ring.

Father Kingsley actually received an anonymous letter accusing Ryan of secretly "robbing banks and running around with women." He showed the letter to Ryan, who dismissed it as an example of the persecution suffered by ex-convicts who were trying to go straight. He thought he knew the author of the letter, a poisonous female: "a hateful witch who lived on suspicion." Ryan had been living high on his reputation as reformed bandit for just ten months when the shocked country learned the awful truth.

On May 25 Ryan and Checkley drove to Sarnia in a stolen maroon Oldsmobile they had used some weeks earlier in a Quebec bank holdup. The car's licence plates, also stolen, had been altered so that an E looked like an L. The bandits' target was the Sarnia liquor store, where they expected to make a good haul from the weekend sales. They parked their car on a side street a block away, and five minutes before the 6 P.M. closing time, they entered the building, dressed in railroad workclothes. Things went wrong from the start.

The sales counter was on the second floor, and the bandits had planned to wait at the bottom of the stairway until most of the crowd of last-minute customers had left through another exit. They locked the entrance door behind them and put on disguises—railway caps, bandannas, and goggles. They wanted the store practically empty before they struck, but a customer happened to look down the stairwell, forcing them to make their move a few minutes too early. The bandits, each armed with two guns, bounded up the stairs and took command of the sales floor, where about twenty people were still lined up making purchases. Checkley stood in the middle of the room, a menacing figure with his weapons drawn, and ordered the people to reach high and face the walls. Manager D.A. Macdonald, who had only been on the job two days, thought it was a prank until Checkley barked, "I mean business. This is a stickup!" Ryan, with his customary flair, leaped over the counter, waved his guns under the noses of the staff, and began to empty the till. He had probably expected a bit more time in which to force the manager to turn over the day's receipts, but had to settle for a paltry $394 in the cash box.

Meanwhile, a local resident, Geoffrey Garvey, had hurried to the liquor store to buy a bottle for the weekend and, frustrated at finding the entrance door locked, had gone around to the exit door, hoping to sneak up the stairs to the sales floor. As he reached the top steps, he saw the customers, their arms raised, covered by a gunman. Unseen by either of the bandits, Garvey hurried down to the street and ran to a cab stand across the road with news that the liquor store was being robbed. Moments later the phone rang in the Sarnia police station, only a block away. Detective Frank McGirr, Sergeant George Smith, and constables William Simpkins and John Lewis jumped into a car and rushed to the scene. Simpkins was stationed by the locked entrance door, while the others burst through the exit door and ran upstairs.

Ryan had scooped the last bills from the cash drawer and climbed back over the counter when he heard noise from the stairwell. He turned to the doorway and a moment later saw Lewis, the first policeman to reach the sales floor. Lewis had his gun drawn but hesitated to shoot, probably because a group of people were directly behind Ryan. If he missed the robber, the officer would surely hit one of the customers. The hesitation cost Lewis his life, because the "kind-hearted and big-souled" Ryan did not hesitate an instant. At point-blank range he fired four times at Lewis's chest. The policeman was almost lucky. One of the slugs bounced off a button on his uniform, and two more were deflected by a game and fisheries regulation book in his tunic pocket. But the fourth bullet was fatal, severing an artery near his heart.

As the constable fell, Ryan retreated across the floor. Then Smith and McGirr, neither of whom had ever drawn a gun in the course of duty, charged into the room. By this time all the customers had dived for the floor, and a wild gun battle between the two policemen and the two bandits was raging. Ryan was hit in the ankle. Both the robbers retreated to the entrance stairs, but a police bullet hit Checkley before he was half-way down, and he died whispering, "I give up." Ryan, whose .45 Colt automatic held eleven shots, fired them all up the stairs, trying to keep the policemen pinned down while he got the door open. Luckily for Simpkins and the curious crowd now collecting in front of the building, he couldn't work the lock. He still had bullets in his other revolver, a .38 Ivor Johnson, when he suddenly collapsed, shot through the neck. Two hours later he died in hospital.

The police found a bundle of dynamite in the bandits' car, and Ryan's brother discovered enough explosives to "blow up half Toronto" in a garage that the "reformed" gangster had been renting.

Red Ryan, dead at forty, left behind a stunned and angry public whom he had played for suckers. Six thousand of the curious filed through the Sarnia funeral home when Ryan and Checkley were laid out for exhibit, their ghastly bullet wounds in full view; but there were only two people at the graveside when the Canadian Jesse James was buried in Mount Hope Cemetery, Toronto: his brother and his sister-in-law. The Catholic clergy, angry at the way Ryan had made a fool of Father Kingsley, refused to give him the last rites or to have him buried in ground consecrated by the Church. Of the host of friends who had cheered his release ten months earlier, none felt more deeply betrayed than Kingsley, who had put his reputation on the line. He bitterly denounced the "treachery and hypocrisy" of the famous criminal.

A few days after Ryan's death, his pal Edward McMullen, who had fled to Vancouver after the murder of Councillor Stonehouse, was shot and killed while trying to crash the American border. Ryan, the fallen hero, had dealt a crippling blow to the good work of the prison reform movement. It would not begin to recover until after World War II. A Canadian judge, speaking shortly after Ryan's death, wryly commented that there would be "no more heroes among criminals in Canada for some time."

Afterword

It is with some relief that we "lay down the pen," having completed our two-volume survey of violence in Canada, an aspect of our history never before fully explored. We believe we have captured in these two books some of the colour, excitement, and pathos so often edited out of the three and a half centuries of Canadian history preceding World War II. We hope we have struck a blow at the myth of Canada's dull past: Canadian history is vibrant, exciting, and sometimes bloodstained. That Canadians do not exalt the bloodletting may well be a point in our favour. Pirates, privateers, bandits, lone outlaws were all common enough in our past, but Canadians have resisted the temptation to make heroes of them. A few have been newspaper celebrities for a brief time. None is now enshrined and glorified the way Jesse James, Billy the Kid, John Dillinger, or Bonnie and Clyde are celebrated in the United States. Canadians have a habit of glorifying not our criminals but our failed revolutionaries: Louis Riel, Gabriel Dumont, Louis-Joseph Papineau, William Lyon Mackenzie. We tend to romanticize such idealists— once they are safely out of the way.

As a people we are not in love with violence. The authors of this book are not in love with violence either. It is an interesting subject for study and speculation, an interesting problem for those concerned with humanity and our future. For that reason we wish to state our own conviction that violence is essentially a social problem, not one rooted in instinct or human nature. The compulsively violent criminal is a very rare bird, a freak on the border of insanity. The gangster, the terrorist, the vigilante is all too common but is almost invariably nurtured in a society or a subculture where violence is the accepted norm. We will begin to get rid of the problem once we begin to regard the killing of our own species as truly abnormal, like cannibalism.

Despite the violence so widespread in the world today, we believe humanity will eventually outgrow it, just as many cultures have outgrown the duel and the blood feud. The authors of this book are strongly opposed to capital punishment, which we view as a survival from the time when criminals were sacrificed on altars to appease the angry gods. We are deeply ashamed of the fact that in our own lifetime our courts of law sentenced people to be tied up and lashed with the cat-o'-nine-tails.

Perhaps we can learn a little from our past. Whitewashing the bloody, nasty bits will do us no good, but perhaps from our past we can learn to change our future. Perhaps, like Isaiah, we can look forward to a time when "the wolf shall dwell with the lamb."

Bibliography

Bates, Walter. *The Mysterious Stranger*. Woodstock, N.B.: Non Entity Press (reprint) 1979.

Beirne, Francis F. *The War of 1812*. New York: E.P. Dutton, 1949.

Calnek, W.A. *The History of the County of Annapolis*. Halifax: Mika Publishing Company 1897, (reprint) 1980.

Chapelle, Howard I. *The History of the American Sailing Navy: The Ships and their Development*. New York: Bonanza Books, 1949.

Clark, William B. *George Washington's Navy*. New Orleans: Louisiana University Press, 1960.

Cross, Michael S. *The Shiners' War: Social Violence in the Ottawa Valley in the 1830's*. Canadian Historical Review, Vol. LIV, No. 1.

Dawson, George H. *The Hogan Murder*. Unpublished ms. Metropolitan Toronto Police Museum (undated).

Dempsy, Hugh A. *Charcoal's World*. Saskatoon: Western Producer Prairie Books, 1978.

Finnegan, Joan. *Giants of the Ottawa Valley*. Burnstown Ont.: General Store Publishing House (undated).

Grantmyre, Barbara. *Lunar Rouge*. Fredericton: Brunswick Press, 1963.

Horan, James D. *The Outlaws*. New York: Crown Publishers, 1977.

Horwood, Harold. *Pirates in Newfoundland in the 17th, 18th and 19th Centuries*. St. John's: Newfoundland Historical Society, 1967.

Horwood, Harold & Butts, Ed. *Pirates and Outlaws of Canada 1610–1932*. Toronto: Doubleday Canada, 1984.

Jenkins, Brian. *Britain and the War for the Union*. Montreal: McGill-Queens U. Press, 1974.

Johnson, Dorothy M. *Western Badmen*. New York: Dodd Mead, 1970.

Karpis, Alvin & Trent, Bill. *Public Enemy #1*. Toronto, McClelland & Stewart, 1971.

Kelly, L.V. *The Range Men*. Toronto: Coles Publishing (reprint) 1980.

Kinchen, Oscar A. *Confederate Operations in Canada and the North*. N. Quincy, Mass.: Christopher Publishing House, 1970.

Leef, John. *The Atlantic Privateers*. Halifax: Petheric Press, 1978.

—— *A Bluenose Privateer of 1812*. Nova Scotia Historical Quarterly, Vol. III, No. 1.

—— *The Bounty Hunter*. Nova Scotia Historical Quarterly, Vol. III. No. 4.

Legget, Robert. *Ottawa Waterway, Gateway to a Continent*. Toronto: University of Toronto Press, 1975.

Macdonald, Helen G. *Canadian Public Opinion on the American Civil War*. New York: Columbia University Press, 1926.

McLennan, J.S. *Louisbourg from its Foundation to its Fall*. London: Macmillan, 1918.

MacMechan, Archibald. *Sagas of the Sea*. London: J.M. Dent & Sons, 1923.

—— *The Nova Scotia Privateers*. Toronto: Ryerson, 1930.

Nash, J. Robert. *Bloodletters and Badmen*. New York: Warner Books, 1973.

Paterson, T.W. *Outlaws of Western Canada*. Langly, B.C.: Stagecoach Publishing, 1977.

Prowse, D.W. *A History of Newfoundland*. London: Macmillan, 1895.

Robin, Martin. *The Bad and the Lonely*. Toronto: James Lorimer & Co., 1976.

—— *The Saga of Red Ryan*. Saskatoon: Western Producer Prairie Books, 1982.

Snider, Charles Henry. *Under the Red Jack: Privateers of the Maritime Provinces of Canada in the War of 1812*. London: Hopkinson, 1928.

Stafford, Ellen. (Ed.) *Flambouyant Canadians*. Toronto: Baxter Publishing, 1964.

Stewart, Robert. *Sam Steele: Lion of the Frontier*. Toronto: Doubleday Canada, 1979.

Trudel, Marcel. *Histoire de la Nouvelle-France—le comtoir, 1604–1627*. Montreal: Fides, 1963.

Trueman, Stewart. *Tall Tales and True from Down East*. Toronto: McClelland and Stewart, 1979.

Wallace, Clarke. *Wanted, Donald Morrison*. Toronto: Doubleday Canada, 1977.

Wallace, W. Stewart. *Murders and Mysteries*. Toronto: Macmillan, 1931.

Williams, Neville. *Contraband Cargoes*. London: Longmans, Green, 1959.

Winks, Robin W. *Canada and the United States: The Civil War Years*. Montreal: Harvest House, 1971.

Woods, Shirley E. Jr. *Ottawa, the Capital of Canada*. Toronto: Doubleday Canada, 1980.

Index

AGMV
MARQUIS
Québec, Canada
1998